Smithsonian

THE ULTIMATE QUESTION
AND ANSWER BOOK

PRESIDENTIAL FAMILIES

SMITHSONIAN Q & A: PRESIDENTIAL FAMILIES. Copyright © 2006 by
HarperCollins Publishers. All rights reserved. Printed in the United
States of America. No part of this book may be used or reproduced in any
manner whatsoever without written permission except in the case of brief
quotations embodied in critical articles and reviews. For information, address
HarperCollins Publishers, 10 East 53rd Street, New York, NY 10022.

HarperCollins books may be purchased for educational, business, or sales
promotional use. For information, please write: Special Markets Department,
HarperCollins Publishers, 10 East 53rd Street, New York, NY 10022.

Produced for HarperCollins by:

HYDRA PUBLISHING
129 MAIN STREET
IRVINGTON, NY 10533
WWW.HYLASPUBLISHING.COM

FIRST EDITION

The name of the "Smithsonian," "Smithsonian Institution," and the sunburst
logo are registered trademarks of the Smithsonian Institution.

Library of Congress Cataloging-in-Publication Data has been applied for.

ISBN-10: 0-06-089117-3
ISBN-13: 978-0-06-089117-6

06 07 08 09 10   QW   10 9 8 7 6 5 4 3 2 1

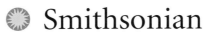

Smithsonian

Q&A

THE ULTIMATE QUESTION AND ANSWER BOOK

PRESIDENTIAL FAMILIES

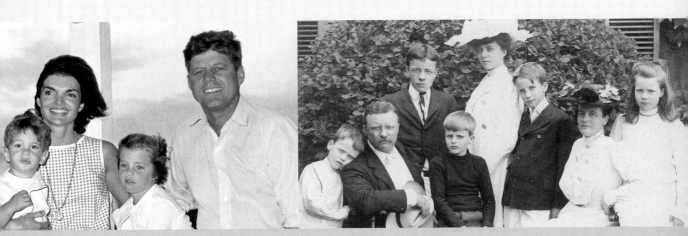

Edith P. Mayo

Collins

An Imprint of HarperCollinsPublishers

PRESIDENTIAL FAMILIES

Contents

Alice Roosevelt Longworth, Theodore Roosevelt's beautiful and spirited daughter.

Benjamin Harrison's grandchildren, Mary McKee, Marthena Harrison, and Baby McKee, have a party in the second-floor nursery of the White House.

Two presidential families were joined when Julie Nixon and David Eisenhower wed in 1968.

The Reagan White House china service, made by Lenox in 1981.

THE WHITE HOUSE: HOME AND SYMBOL

T he building we know today as the White House has been the home of every American president and his family since John and Abigail Adams arrived there in November of 1800, and from the beginning it has been a symbol of the authority of the executive branch. In the more than two hundred years since, the mansion has sheltered many kinds of families, withstood fire and war, housed a few great men, and a few scoundrels, been

"redecorated" numerous times and rebuilt twice, yet it remains a steadfast embodiment of the nation's collective memory. As the disgruntled Adams moved in, embittered by his recent loss to his former revolutionary friend turned foe, Thomas Jefferson, he mustered the courage to express his hope for the positive outcome of the nation's experiment in democracy by writing a benediction for the ages: "I pray Heaven to bestow the best of blessings on this house, and on all that shall hereafter inhabit it. May none but honest and wise men ever rule under this roof."

Above: The White House lit up at night. Since 1800, the mansion has been the home of the American presidents and their families.

Left: Currier and Ives's bird's-eye view of the capital circa 1880, showing the White House nestled in its parklike setting.

A view from the northeast of the fire-damaged President's House after the British attack on Washington, D.C., during the War of 1812.

Even when it was first built, the White House was an unusual building—almost as unusual as the new democracy itself. It was a single edifice that was at once the focus of governmental authority and the residence of the presidential family. This combination of functions brought together the actual power of the governing party with the ceremonial head of state—functions that were often separated in other political systems. It also combined the workplace and the home—an important coming together of two spheres of influence that were separate and distinct in other areas of American life, particularly for women. That these two distinct arenas were housed together had a profound impact on the conduct of both the social life and politics of the new nation. It provided a convenient vehicle, and the camouflage of a "domestic" setting by which women—the first ladies—could wield social and political power, if they chose to do so, without violating societal norms about "woman's proper place." More women than we realize chose to exercise that power, whether subtly or overtly.

The fledgling republic was a grand experiment. The new residence was thought too grand for a republic by some observers, not grand enough to compete with the residences of European heads of state by others. The new nation had no precedents or models. How would the chief executive exercise

authority, command respect, unify a diverse group of peoples without the trappings typically associated with royalty? Ceremonial forms are important to any ruler—even an elected one. George Washington and John Adams determined on a formal and dignified manner of conducting dinners and receptions and entertaining foreign dignitaries, seeking a middle ground between regal precedents and "mob" rule. Yet, they permitted ordinary people to come and meet with the president. Access to the chief executive by the people was a crucial distinction between American democracy and the royal courts of Europe.

Thomas Jefferson deemed the behavior of his predecessors too regal and emphasized the equality of citizens by eliminating rules of protocol among guests, both foreign and domestic, in a manner thought by many as almost too casual. It remained for the brilliant Dolley Madison to set a course that brought

Lyndon Johnson conducts a meeting in his bedroom in 1966. The White House has always served as both home and workplace for the president.

European (particularly French) style to receiving and entertaining while filtering it through the lens of American popular culture and the ideals of a republic. Her gowns, jewels, turbans, and elegant soirees were enough to delight even royalists, but she mingled with her guests freely, charming them all. She was the first to decorate the White House, consciously creating a stage for the conduct of politics and diplomacy—and for her own performance as first lady.

A series of younger, surrogate first ladies (daughters, nieces, daughters-in-law) from the 1820s through the 1850s often veered off into regal forms of receiving and entertaining but, by then, the experiment in democracy had taken hold and, besides, they were young and beautiful and could be indulged—and forgiven any excesses.

The name of the residence also underwent a series of transformations over the years as did the building itself. During the terms of office of those men who were the Founding Fathers of the nation, when it was clear that the presidency held supreme political power, the residence was known as the "President's House." After the first quarter of the nineteenth century, when a powerful congressional system was in political ascendancy and the president became more literally the "chief executive," the name of the residence reflected this not-so-subtle shift in power and was known as the "Executive Mansion." This title remained as the official name of the house throughout the remainder of the nineteenth century, although it was often referred to by its popular name, the "White House." Nonetheless, those asked to attend social events were issued invitations to the Executive Mansion. As Theodore Roosevelt took office at the beginning of the twentieth century, the United States had just won the Spanish-American War and was taking its place as a world power on the international stage. Roosevelt thought that the presidency and the residence needed a new image for a new century. The Roosevelts undertook a major renovation, revamped presidential style and image in entertaining, protocol, and diplomacy—and officially changed the name of the mansion to the White House.

Edith Roosevelt oversaw the 1902 renovation of the Executive Mansion. Theodore Roosevelt officially renamed the mansion the "White House."

Both Theodore and Edith Roosevelt used the White House to enhance presidential prestige and understood the mystique of the mansion as rich with the history of the nation. The White House was now not only a national but also an international symbol of political power. Roosevelt had refashioned the mansion for the new era as he redefined presidential power for the twentieth century.

Despite its burning by the British in 1814, the housing of army troops and the wounded during the Civil War, the excesses of the Gilded Age, the reforms of the Progressive Era, the Great Depression, and two world wars—and several attempts to tear down the edifice and rebuild anew—the White House has endured. The focus of press, photography, electronic media, and Internet coverage, in every age it has been both a backdrop for power and a residence for everyday living, housing lives of triumph and tragedy played out in the glare of a public spotlight—yet always a repository for the dramas of the historical past and the possibilities of the future.

CHAPTER 1

THE FOUNDERS AND THEIR FAMILIES

The fires of revolution, the hard-fought struggle for independence, and the creation of a new nation forged unbreakable bonds among the men and women of the Revolutionary War generation. Each of the first four presidents of the United States of America, George Washington, John Adams, Thomas Jefferson, and James Madison, shared an intimate connection to the revolutionary movement and to the birth of the new republic. And their wives and families fully shared in the risks, responsibilities, and sacrifices necessary to achieve the goal of independence.

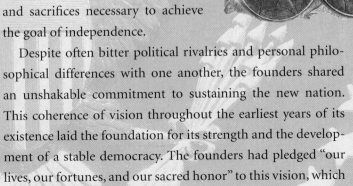

Despite often bitter political rivalries and personal philosophical differences with one another, the founders shared an unshakable commitment to sustaining the new nation. This coherence of vision throughout the earliest years of its existence laid the foundation for its strength and the development of a stable democracy. The founders had pledged "our lives, our fortunes, and our sacred honor" to this vision, which would guarantee the survival of the young nation.

Above: Portraits of George Washington and (from left to right) Thomas Jefferson, James Madison, and John Adams are framed against a curtain of drapery and furs surmounted by a star.

Left: Washington inspects the unfinished White House with architect James Hoban.

George and Martha Washington

Q: **What important benefits did Martha Dandridge Custis bring to her marriage to George Washington?**

A: When Martha met George in 1758, she was a wealthy widow, living on a large estate left by her first husband, Daniel Parke Custis. She brought to the marriage two valuable assets that George lacked: great wealth and superior social position. Both were invaluable in advancing her husband's career. George Washington, as did many presidents after him, "married up."

The wedding of George Washington and Martha Custis, painted by Junius Brutus Stearns. This was an advantageous marriage for Washington; Martha was of a higher status, wealthy, and socially gracious.

Q: **Where did George and Martha Washington live during his presidential administrations (1789–97)?**

A: The Washingtons never lived in Washington, or in the building now known as the White House. The new nation's capital in Washington, D.C., was under construction during Washington's presidential terms. The first capital of the United States of America was New York City, where George and Martha moved into a large rented house on Cherry Street in 1789. When the capital moved to

George Washington's first inauguration was held on the balcony of Federal Hall in New York City on April 30, 1789. New York was the nation's first capital.

Philadelphia in 1790, the Washingtons rented an elegant mansion on High Street until the end of the administration. Later, John and Abigail Adams lived in the High Street mansion for most of Adams's presidential term as well, and moved to Washington, D.C., in 1800.

Q: **Why was it important for George and Martha Washington to set a new style for the new nation of the United States of America?**

A: After the Americans had won the Revolution and thrown off royalty, most citizens did not want a chief executive who resembled a king. The Washingtons were keenly aware that they were setting precedents and realized that the style of the first president would profoundly shape the nation. They and their advisers debated how the president and his wife should comport themselves in public, how to convey dignity, command respect, project authority, and govern a nation without relying on the trappings of royalty. The Washingtons chose a dignified and formal style for entertaining and public events, yet welcomed ordinary citizens to mingle with them at the President's House. This public access to the chief executive marked a critical difference between American democracy and European royalty.

The Republican Court by Daniel Huntington. Although she spent many years as a military wife, Martha Washington was a practiced hostess. She knew that as the wife of the first president she was setting precedents for all future first ladies who entertained in the President's House.

Q: What was Martha Washington's role in her husband's presidential administration?

A: As were many privileged, upper-class women of the eighteenth century, Martha had been brought up to administer a large household, oversee its production, and entertain to advance her future husband's career. Hosting social events for the leaders of the new nation and for foreign diplomats was an essential part of politics and diplomacy. Martha's social skills, warmth, and graciousness softened the president's stiff formality at public events.

The Washingtons' decision to host public entertainments and state events jointly established the president's wife as his social and ceremonial partner and hostess for the nation. This role has been played by every first lady (a term not used until the mid-1800s) from Martha Washington's time to the present.

George Washington stood for this oil painting by Gilbert Stuart in 1796, his last complete year in office. It has since become one of the most famous depictions of him.

> **It is of great Importance to fix the Taste of our Country properly . . . everything about you should be substantially good and majestically plain.**
>
> —*Gouverneur Morris, American statesman*

George and Martha pose with Martha's grandchildren, "Little Wash" and Nelly Custis for artist Edward Savage. Standing in the corner is William Lee, their servant. Nelly and Wash lived with the Washingtons at Mount Vernon and, later, at the executive mansions.

Martha Parke Custis, also called "Patsy," Martha Washington's daughter by her first marriage.

Q: **How did the Washingtons entertain during the president's term of office?**

A: In the early days of the republic, entertaining was an essential part of politics and diplomacy. Anyone wishing to pay respects to the president had to call at a specified time on designated days of the week. The president held events each week for men only; Martha held afternoon receptions for women on Tuesdays and Fridays, while official dinners were held on Tuesdays and Thursdays at four o'clock. Martha hosted a formal reception, known as a drawing room, each Friday evening that both men and women attended. She received her guests while seated.

Q: **What was the practice of "fostering"?**

A: Fostering was the common practice, in the colonial and early republican era, of taking in children of relatives who could not care for their offspring, or children who had been left orphans. Because of the unusually high birth and death rates of the period, many children were left with a single parent—or no parents at all. In such cases, relatives took in some of the children and raised them as their own, but without a formal adoption process. This custom can be seen in both the Washington and Adams families.

Q: **Who were the children who lived with President and Mrs. Washington in the executive mansions?**

A: George and Martha Washington had no children together, but Martha's two grandchildren, Eleanor Parke Custis, called "Nelly," and George Washington Parke Custis, known as "Little Wash" or "Tub," lived with their grandparents.

Martha Washington had four children by her first marriage to Daniel Parke Custis: Daniel and Francis, who both died in childhood; Martha, nicknamed "Patsy"; and John, called "Jacky." Patsy died of epilepsy at the age of seventeen. Jacky, Martha's only surviving child, married Eleanor Calvert of Maryland, with whom he had four children. He had been assigned as an aide to General Washington during the Revolutionary War but, soon

> "One of those unassuming characters which create Love and Esteem."
> —ABIGAIL ADAMS, ON MARTHA WASHINGTON

Martha Washington at Mount Vernon. Martha spent her last years at the spacious Virginia farm. The main house, now a national historic site, can be seen in the background.

after the battle of Yorktown, was struck ill. Jacky Custis died of "camp fever" (probably typhus) at the age of twenty-seven. He left his wife, Eleanor, with four young children.

Martha was bereft at the loss of Jacky, and Eleanor Calvert Custis, as a widow, found it difficult to bring up her family. The Washingtons reached an agreement with her to take in and rear as their own Eleanor's two youngest children, Nelly and Wash. At Mount Vernon, Nelly and Wash enjoyed privileged lives. Both children received extensive educations from tutors. When the family moved to Philadelphia, Nelly, a teenager during Washington's presidency, eagerly participated in the elegant social whirl in the capital.

Although treated as a republican "princess," Nelly reserved her deepest feelings for her grandparents, especially her grandmother. She wrote of Martha, "she has been more than a Mother to me. It is impossible to love any one more than I love her."

This brass candle stand served an interesting function in American history. According to family legend, Washington wrote his farewell address by its reflected light.

John and Abigail Adams

Q: **Who was the first president to live in what is now called the White House?**

A: When the American government moved from Philadelphia to Washington, D.C., in late 1800, the new nation's capital was still a muddy village under construction. John Adams entered the partially completed President's House on November 1, 1800. On his second day there, he wrote his wife, Abigail, what has become a blessing for the future: "I pray Heaven to bestow the best of blessings on this house, and on all that shall hereafter inhabit it. May none but honest and wise men ever rule under this roof."

John Trumbull painted this portrait of John Adams in 1793, seven years before Adams moved into the President's House in the new city of Washington. Adams was at that time vice president under George Washington.

Q: **In what condition did Abigail find the President's House when she arrived?**

A: When Abigail Adams arrived on November 16, 1800, she found only six of thirty-six rooms on the west side of the first and second floors in usable condition. The house was still damp from drying plaster walls, and fireplaces had to be kept burning to warm and dry the house. Abigail complained that there was not enough wood for the fires, and that the house was surrounded by builders' huts. The east end of the house was unusable. "We have not the least fence, yard, or other convenience, without [outside] and the great unfinished audience-room I make a drying room of, to hang up the clothes in." What Abigail once used as a laundry room is now the East Room, site of elegant entertaining.

Her prediction for the city's future was as gloomy as her assessment of the house was bleak. In a letter to a friend, Abigail bemoaned the state of the capital, "What pleasures the federal city shall afford I know not. . . . The roads are . . . so bad, the buildings so remote from each other that I fancy, it will not be a residence much sought for many years to come."

Q: **What Adams family members lived in the President's House?**

A: The Adams's youngest son, Thomas, then in his late twenties, lived with his parents in the White House. Their eldest son, John Quincy, had already embarked on his diplomatic career abroad. Sadly, when Abigail arrived in the capital, she had just visited their middle son, Charles, in New York, who was dying from the effects of alcoholism. Charles, who had nowhere else to turn, was living with his sister Abigail. Nabby, as she was called, provided a place for him in her New York home. It was the last time Abigail saw Charles alive.

Alcoholism scarred Abigail's extended family as well as her immediate family. She and John took in as their own several

of the children of her relatives whose lives had been blighted by an alcoholic parent. John Adams brought with him to Washington William Shaw. Billy, as he was called, was Abigail's brilliant but eccentric nephew, who served as the president's private secretary, a position akin to today's chief of staff. The son of Abigail's sister Elizabeth, Billy was a vital aide in the Adams administration but was emotionally scarred by his father's chronic inability to support the family and his subsequent death from chronic alcoholism.

Abigail arrived at the Executive Mansion with her twelve-year-old niece,

Louisa Smith, the daughter of Abigail's alcoholic brother, William Smith. Louisa was a bright but willful child, and Abigail wrestled with how best to guide and discipline her. She also brought along her three-year-old granddaughter, Susannah Adams, the daughter of son Charles.

Above: The President's House was unfinished when the Adams family moved in. The future East Room, then without plaster on the walls or flooring, was where Abigail, shown here with granddaughter Susannah, often directed servants to hang the wash.

Left: John Quincy Adams held the post of United States minister to Russia while his father served as president. John Quincy would himself be inaugurated president of the United States in 1825.

> My children give me more pain than all my enemies.
> —JOHN ADAMS

Q: What other political wife was a good friend to Abigail Adams?

A: As wife of the first vice president of the United States, Abigail became a close friend to Martha Washington, wife of its first president. Abigail was often called upon to aid Martha in official entertaining, drawing on her experience of the British and French courts and society abroad from the years her husband had served as a foreign diplomat.

Q: How did the Adamses entertain in Philadelphia and, later, in Washington?

A: In Philadelphia, the couple hosted a formal dinner once a week and held a drawing room, a more casual affair, on Tuesdays and Thursdays. When the Adamses moved to Washington in late 1800, their entertaining was restricted by the unfinished condition of the house and the president's defeat for a second term. Nonetheless, by the end of November 1800, Abigail had hosted all 138 members of Congress for a formal visit to

the President's House. John and Abigail held their first public reception in the President's House on New Year's Day 1801. As had Martha Washington, Abigail remained seated to receive guests. No hands were shaken, a custom practiced by Washington. After paying their respects to President and Mrs. Adams, the guests were served refreshments by a waiter; they included cakes and tarts, curds and cream, tea, coffee, punch, floating island, trifle, syllabub, and other sweets of the period.

Abigail entertained with flair but was concerned about the expense of overly lavish receptions and gatherings. She complained that when Washington was setting precedents, he should have been more considerate of those who would follow him who might not be so wealthy.

Abigail Adams clearly grasped the importance of entertaining to politics, commenting, "More is to be performed by way of negotiations many times at one of these entertainments, than at twenty serious conversations."

Q: How did Abigail react to her role as first lady?

A: By the time John Adams became president, the partisan press had grown vitriolic. Before her husband was inaugurated in 1797, she wrote to a friend, lamenting, "I expect to be vilified and abused with my whole family when I come into this situation." She feared she would have "to look at every word before I utter it, and to impose a silence upon my self, when I long to talk." Still, Abigail's marriage had always been a political partnership as well as a love match. Immersed in the political battles of her day, she could not "impose

John and Abigail hosted a dinner on New Year's Day 1801, despite the unfinished state of the President's House. This invitation was addressed to member of Congress General Theodorus Bailey and his wife.

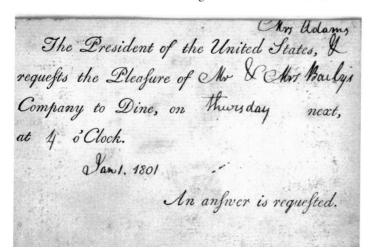

The President of the United States, & requests the Pleasure of Mr & Mrs Bailys Company to Dine, on thursday next, at 4 o'Clock.

Jan 1. 1801

An answer is requested.

Abigail exerted political influence over John, although eighteenth-century women were encouraged to "keep within compass" and follow prescribed rules of behavior.

Abigail Adams. The wife of the second president of the United States, Abigail set precedent as political partner to the president.

a silence" upon herself. After all, when the men were setting up the government she had written John that, "I can not say that I think you very generous to the Ladies, for whilst you are proclaiming peace and good will to Men, Emancipating all Nations, you insist upon retaining absolute power over Wives."

During his presidency, she continued to be politically outspoken. Her husband's enemies called her "Mrs. President"—not a term of endearment. It reflected public suspicion about her influence over the president. Risking criticism as a wife who stepped beyond the bounds of what was considered a proper role for a woman, she established the role of political partner to the president, a precedent that some of the women who followed in her footsteps would choose to embrace.

> "Do not put such unlimited power into the hands of the husbands. Remember all men would be tyrants if they could."
>
> —*Abigail Adams*

Thomas Jefferson

Q: **What changes in presidential style did Thomas Jefferson make?**

A: Jefferson, a passionate advocate of equality and the common man, deemed the social conduct of his predecessors far too regal. He ended the drawing rooms and weekly levees, or formal receptions, of Washington and Adams. In a dramatic and deliberate reversal of style, he dispensed with traditional formality and protocol at dinners and designated no distinction of rank among his guests. Jefferson's emphasis on equality shocked some, offended others, and caused consternation among foreign diplomats, who were used to having their "ranks" recognized. Yet Jefferson's informal, almost casual, style had a profound impact on establishing equality among all citizens.

Rembrandt Peale painted this portrait of Thomas Jefferson. A primary concern of Jefferson was to establish equality among all citizens.

Q: **What was unusual about Jefferson's dinners?**

A: Despite his belief in equality, Jefferson's entertaining was lavish and always in the French mode, a habit adopted during his diplomatic service in France. Jefferson employed a French chef, Honoré Julien, and his presidential dinners were renowned for their imported French wines and distinctive cuisine, served on exquisite china or silver serving dishes. Jefferson is credited with introducing ice cream to the President's House. The regular use of French cuisine, and the custom of serving oneself, marked a decisive departure from the dining styles of Washington and Adams.

Jefferson hosted small, informal dinner parties for twelve to fourteen guests several evenings a week, and used these social occasions to political advantage. To insure the privacy of political conversations, he dispensed with the usual dinner servants. He instead installed a set of revolving circular shelves in the walls so that waiters did not have to enter the room and dishes could be removed without opening and shutting doors. He also installed "dumb waiters" in the dining room, tiers of shelves on wheels that held the various courses of the meal, enabling his guests to serve themselves throughout the meal.

Capital commentator Margaret Bayard Smith, who reported on many of the early presidential administrations, confided to her readers: "When he had any persons dining with him, with whom he wished to enjoy a free and unrestricted flow of conversation . . . by each individual was placed a dumb-waiter, containing everything for the progress of dinner from beginning to end." Jefferson developed other innovations to further facilitate the flow of conversation among his guests. Smith again provides us with a description. "One circumstance though minute . . .

has a great influence on the conversational powers of Mr. Jefferson's guests. Instead of [tables] being arranged in straight parallel lines [he uses] the circle or round oval table where all could see the others faces and feel the animating influence of looks as well as words. . . . The small, well assorted company seated around a circular table will insure more social enjoyment."

Q: What public receptions did Jefferson hold?

A: Instead of the weekly levees and drawing rooms held by his predecessors, Jefferson decided to hold only two public receptions a year: one on New Year's Day and another on the Fourth of July. He held his first reception at the President's House on July 4, 1801. The public was invited to attend, and Jefferson received his guests in what is now the Blue Room. Instead of bowing to his guests, which he thought an aristocratic formality, he shook hands with them—a far more democratic gesture. Many who came were astonished to find in attendance five silent Cherokee Indian chiefs, who were then in Washington to celebrate the new treaty of friendship with the government.

The Fourth of July reception in 1803 was particularly notable because it was a double celebration. Jefferson announced the acquisition of the Louisiana Territory, with bands, banners, and cheers for the United States, which had virtually doubled in size with the stroke of a pen.

Left: A handwritten recipe for vanilla ice cream, with Savoy cookies on the back, is one of many in Jefferson's large collection of French recipes.

Below: Jefferson used the Green Room, today an elegant sitting room, as a dining room and covered the floor with canvas painted green.

> **When brought together in society all are perfectly equal, whether foreign or domestic, titled or untitled, in or out of office.**
>
> —THOMAS JEFFERSON

Q: Who was Jefferson's first lady?

A: Jefferson had two first ladies. He had been a widower for nineteen years when he was elected president, and in that day, it was thought improper to have a gathering of mixed company without a hostess. He therefore asked his eldest daughter, Martha Jefferson Randolph, to act as his hostess when she visited the President's House from their home in Monticello. He also requested Dolley Madison, the wife of his close friend and ranking cabinet officer, James Madison, to be his hostess. Thus began Dolley Madison's reign as "queen" of Washington society—a somewhat ironic term in a republic.

Martha Jefferson Randolph assisted her father as hostess. Dolley Madison, future first lady, also served in the position.

Q: Who was the first child born in the President's House?

A: James Madison Randolph, son of Martha Jefferson and Thomas Mann Randolph Jr., was the first child born in the President's House, on January 17, 1806. He was born during one of his mother's lengthy stays in the capital. Jefferson insisted on choosing the names of all his grandchildren himself, naming this grandson after his good friend James Madison.

Q: What family members resided with the president?

A: Jefferson's daughter Martha gave birth to a total of twelve children. One died in infancy, and several were born after Jefferson's presidency. During Jefferson's presidential years, Martha

Thomas Jefferson Randolph, known as "Jeff." The president's grandson was a frequent White House visitor and held an important position there: passing the decanters of French wine to guests at the dinner table.

made two lengthy visits to Washington and brought her son Thomas Jefferson, called "Jeff," and five daughters: Anne, Ellen, Cornelia, Virginia, and Mary. Jefferson affectionately called his granddaughters "the sisterhood." He relished the time with his grandchildren; he played with them, read to them, and showered them with gifts.

He took a special interest in Jeff's preparations for boarding school in Philadelphia, building his wardrobe and dispensing advice on his studies and the kind of company he should keep at school. Jefferson was, however, ultimately disappointed with his grandson's lack of scholarly accomplishment.

Jefferson also especially encouraged granddaughter Ellen, in whom he recognized great intellectual ability. Jefferson told her he hoped that when she grew up, "you will become a learned lady."

Q: What special holiday did the family enjoy together?

A: One year while in the President's House, Jefferson had the pleasure of celebrating Christmas with his daughter and six of his grandchildren. He hosted a large children's party, with Dolley Madison acting as hostess. About one hundred children were invited to share in the fun, play games, and enjoy the food that Mrs. Madison had carefully selected for the event. The president showed them his pet bird, which perched on his shoulder and took food from his lips. Jefferson even took out his violin and played music while the children danced.

Q: What family member died during Jefferson's presidency?

A: Jefferson's second surviving daughter, Maria, was the beauty of the family, but very frail. Polly, as she was called, married John Wayles Eppes in 1797. On April 17, 1804, shortly after childbirth, she died at her home in Virginia. Polly most likely succumbed to childbed fever, a common infection in that period, for which there was no cure, and which often took the lives of women who had just given birth. Jefferson's own wife, Martha Wayles Skelton Jefferson, had died after childbirth many years before. The president arrived at Polly's home just before she died, and was grief-stricken at her death. She was only twenty-five years old.

Thomas Jefferson kept few of his wife's possessions after her death in 1782. This thread case, with some of its original pins and needles intact, is one of the items surviving.

An only daughter and numerous family of grandchildren, will furnish me great resources of happiness.
—THOMAS JEFFERSON, IN A LETTER TO CHARLES THOMSON

James and Dolley Madison

Q: Why did Dolley call James "the great little Madison"?

A: As a vivacious young widow in Philadelphia, then the capital city, Dolley Payne Todd attracted many suitors, including James Madison, a brilliant congressman from Virginia. Dolley was a tall, blue-eyed charmer with fair skin and black curls. James was known both for his towering intellect and his small stature (he stood five feet, four inches tall). Dolley confided her excitement to her friend Eliza Collins when she learned that James had asked to meet her. "Aaron Burr says that the great little Madison has asked to be brought to see me this evening," she wrote. Four months later Dolley and James were married.

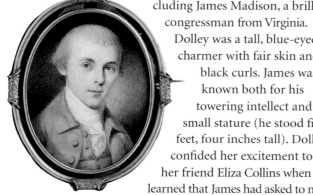

Above: James Madison exchanged this miniature, painted by Charles Wilson Peale, for one of his fiancée, Kitty Floyd. It contains a lock of his hair. Kitty returned it to him when she broke their engagement.

Right: Dolley Madison, the first to decorate the White House, continued the tradition of entertaining and socializing, as well as providing an elegant backdrop for politics. This view of the South Portico was proposed by architect Benjamin Henry Latrobe.

Q: How did Dolley Madison decorate the President's House in Washington?

A: An experienced hostess after eight years as wife of the secretary of state and frequent hostess for President Jefferson, Dolley was the first to decorate the President's House. She defined the public space of the chief executive by creating the President's House as an elegant stage on which her husband could conduct politics and diplomacy and as a backdrop for her performance as first lady. The distinguished architect Benjamin Latrobe, who directed the construction of many government buildings in the capital, assisted her. He purchased elaborate drapery fabric and furniture from stores in Philadelphia and New York and also designed furniture for the mansion, made by craftsmen in Baltimore. The furniture was a mixture of French, which Dolley favored, English Sheraton, and an elegant classical Greek-influenced style designed by Latrobe. When Dolley held her drawing rooms, the guests unanimously agreed that she had created a stunning effect.

Q: Did the Madisons' entertaining style differ from that of previous presidents?

A: James was ill at ease at social events, but Dolley was a sparkling hostess. Socially adept and politically savvy, she camouflaged politics under the guise of entertaining to advance her husband's political agenda. As hostess for Jefferson and then for her husband, she was the social leader and most important woman in the

> **Our hearts understand each other.**
> —*Dolley to James Madison*

Dolley Madison serves wine as others enjoy society. A poem published with the drawing by L. M. Glackens reads, of Madison's time as president: ". . . that laughter bubbled, overrun."

nation's capital for sixteen years. She established an American style in entertaining, creating public ceremonies appropriate for a new republic by filtering European customs through American popular culture and democratic ideals. Her style was more structured than Jefferson's but less formal than Washington's and Adams's. She did not "receive" formally, but mingled freely with her guests in a warm and gracious manner. Her weekly parties, called "Wednesday drawing rooms," attracted so many guests that they were also known as "Mrs. Madison's Crush." Her "dove parties" for wives of politicians helped establish the social and political networks crucial to Washington politics.

She employed Jean Pierre Sioussat, whom she had hired away from the British minister Anthony Merry, as her master of ceremonies for social events. Sioussat's knowledge of French customs and food (then the diplomatic standard of the Western world) made this "French John" particularly valuable at official

functions. The American food, prepared by a French chef, at both ceremonial and private dinner parties, was sumptuous.

Q: Why were female social networks so critical to the new nation?

A: In the days before formal political parties, the social networks of Washington were the same networks through which politics and diplomacy were conducted. Dolley defined a sphere of influence for women as hostesses of social events that stood at the juncture of public and private life—that of society—where women wielded enormous power through the ceremonial forms of dinners, receptions, and entertainments. As first lady (a term not then in use), she presided over this sphere and set precedents for her successors. The dove parties she held were enjoyable ways to educate the wives of government officials about the political issues of the day so that they could take a knowledgeable part in the social and political life of the city.

Q: How did Dolley Madison dress for her social events?

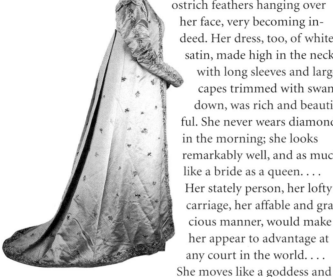

A: Fortunately, an eyewitness has left us with a description of Dolley Madison's finery, consisting of "a turban of white satin with three large white ostrich feathers hanging over her face, very becoming indeed. Her dress, too, of white satin, made high in the neck with long sleeves and large capes trimmed with swan's down, was rich and beautiful. She never wears diamonds in the morning; she looks remarkably well, and as much like a bride as a queen. . . . Her stately person, her lofty carriage, her affable and gracious manner, would make her appear to advantage at any court in the world. . . . She moves like a goddess and she looks like a queen." The lavishness of her gowns, jewels, trademark turbans, and evening shoes, purchased mostly from Paris, were the talk of Washington society, where contemporary accounts often describe Dolley, who was quite tall for a woman in that era, as "queenly."

Above: Dolley Madison's ivory satin robe, in the fashion of the years just before 1820. It had a raised waist, narrow, diamond-shaped back, long narrow sleeves, and an open-front skirt.

Right: R. G. Thompson created this print of the view from the Potomac of the British attack on Washington under Major General Ross, August 24, 1814.

Q: What catastrophe befell the President's House in 1814?

A: The British, still angry about losing their colonies and threatened by American plans for expansion, attacked the United States again in the War of 1812. In 1814, British troops advanced into Washington. While the president was in Maryland directing the troops, Dolley received word that the British were advancing toward the President's House. She bravely saved state papers, costly silver, the famous Gilbert Stuart portrait of George Washington, and other valuables, and fled to Virginia in a wagon just before the British burned the White House. Many in Washington talked of moving the capital back to Philadelphia. But Dolley immediately began to entertain on a grand scale in her temporary residences at the Octagon House and on Pennsylvania Avenue—a public statement that the Madisons and the government would carry on as usual, undeterred by the British destruction.

Q: Did the Madisons have family in the President's House?

A: The Madisons had no children of their own, but Dolley's son from her first marriage, John Payne Todd, lived with them in the early years of Madison's presidency. Payne, as he was called, was an arrogant, troubled child who became a troublesome and alcoholic adult. He attended Saint Mary's Catholic College in Baltimore, Maryland, but when he began appearing in public with an older woman friend of his mother's, the Madisons sent him to Saint Petersburg, Russia, as an unofficial attaché to the peace negotiations after the War of 1812. They hoped to interest him in the diplomatic mission and find him some useful occupation. Payne, however, took up with a Russian princess, who was mysteriously abducted and never seen again. He traveled through Europe, gambling and drinking, while the Madisons struggled to pay off his mounting debts. From the time he left the President's House until James Madison's death in 1836, Payne's profligate lifestyle cost his parents over $40,000—an enormous sum at that time. After returning home, he mismanaged the Madisons' Montpelier plantation, further plunging his mother into debt. Payne was sent to debtor's prison twice and remained a constant source of worry, embarrassment, and financial distress to Dolley.

Gilbert Stuart, a popular artist of American dignitaries, painted Dolley and a companion portrait of James to hang in their Virginia home, Montpelier.

Q: Who called Dolley Madison "truly our First Lady for a half-century"?

A: After James Madison died, Dolley Madison left Montpelier plantation and moved back to Washington, where she lived in a residence on Lafayette Square. Although now impoverished from the debts accumulated by Payne, as well as his mismanagement of the plantation, Dolley again became a favorite in the capital's society. She was often invited to dine at the President's House by succeeding chief executives and their wives.

When Dolley died in 1849, she was remembered at a large funeral in Washington attended by Congress, President Zachary Taylor, and other notable Washington figures. Taylor, in his eulogy, said, "She will never be forgotten, because she was truly our First Lady for a half-century," acknowledging Dolley as the social leader and most important woman in Washington during the formative years of the young republic.

> "My dearest Payne, had I known where to direct should have written to you before this—not that I had any thing new to communicate, but for the pleasure of repeating how much I love you, & how much I wish to see you, & to hear of your happiness."
>
> —*DOLLEY MADISON IN A LETTER TO HER SON, PAYNE*

CHAPTER 2

CONSOLIDATING NATIONHOOD

When James Monroe took office in 1817, the United States had already defended itself in a second war with Britain. The Louisiana Purchase had doubled the size of the country and opened the gateway to the West, but provoked bitter debate over the extension of slavery into new territories. These debates would be resolved through a series of compromises, and papered over with the rhetoric and reality of territorial expansion. The eastern coast was consolidated in 1821 when Spain ceded the Floridas, while the Monroe Doctrine warned European powers to keep out of the Americas. John Q. Adams instituted a bold program to bind the nation together through construction of new highways and canals. Andrew Jackson decisively defended the Union against the first direct sectional threat by South Carolina's nullification of protective tariffs and signed the Indian Removal Act in 1830. By extending its territory along the Atlantic coast, forming states on its midwestern borders with Canada, and laying claim to Oregon, the new nation asserted its claims across the continent.

Above: Chief Justice John Marshall administering the oath of office to Andrew Jackson on the east portico of the U.S. Capitol, March 4, 1829.

Left: The United States circa 1816. By the early nineteenth century, the nation no longer consisted of thirteen Atlantic colonies but instead included the vast wilderness west of the Mississippi River.

James and Elizabeth Monroe

James Monroe was a tall, slender man with a quiet, dignified manner. He lacked personal charisma but distinguished himself through his energy and ambition. He was both a successful diplomat and prudent administrator who worked to carve out a national identity for the fledgling republic.

British. They reopened the mansion to the public at a gala New Year's Day reception in 1818. Washington's newspaper, the *National Intelligencer,* reported, "The President's House, for the first time [since the fire] was thrown open for the general reception of visitors. It was thronged from twelve to three o'clock by an unusually large concourse of ladies and gentlemen. . . . It was gratifying once more to salute the President of the United States with the compliments of the season in his appropriate residence." The women of Washington, anticipating the return of the social season at the Executive Mansion, were to be bitterly disappointed.

Q: Why was Monroe's administration known as the "Era of Good Feelings"?

A: The term was coined when Monroe, a Democratic-Republican, toured New England, formerly a stronghold of the Federalist Party, and was received with acclaim. His warm reception there signaled an end to the bitter party conflict of earlier years and the coming together of the new nation. It was, however, a lull before the growing sectional storm that foreshadowed the Civil War.

Q: When did the Monroes reopen the Executive Mansion after the disastrous fire that had destroyed it?

A: The Monroes moved back into the Executive Mansion in the fall of 1817, three years after its burning by the

Q: Why did the president's daughter act as official hostess?

A: The president's wife, Elizabeth Kortright Monroe, was not in good

Elizabeth Kortright Monroe, James's lovely but sickly wife.

health (evidence suggests she may have had epilepsy). Because she was frequently ill, Elizabeth called upon her elder daughter, Eliza, to act as surrogate hostess and manager of Executive Mansion social events. Thirty-one-year-old Eliza was married to a distinguished Virginia lawyer, George Hay, who served as the president's private secretary and political confidant. Eliza, however, was arrogant and abrasive, and her imperious manner angered official Washington.

Q: What caused the "not so good feelings" during the Monroe administration?

A: Elizabeth had lived in France with her husband for many years as a diplomatic wife. Known as *"la belle Americaine"* by the French, she admired the pomp and lavish entertaining style of European courts. As first lady, she introduced a version of that pomp and protocol to the Executive Mansion, seating herself on a raised platform to receive guests. Her return to extreme formality was not appreciated in Washington circles; her reserve was thought "haughty," and her entertaining was disdained as too "regal." It must have been difficult to follow the beloved Dolley Madison.

Opinions of Elizabeth did not improve even after she began to share many of the first lady's social duties with her daughter. Her worst offense was the announcement that neither she nor Eliza would pay or return calls, as was the custom, refusing even visits of congressional and diplomatic wives. She cited poor health as the reason. This refusal to "call," or visit, set off a firestorm in Washington's official circles and disrupted the social

Eliza Monroe Hay. Elizabeth's choice of her elder daughter as surrogate hostess proved problematic. Eliza proceeded to alienate many through her lack of experience and patience with the social niceties demanded of her role.

and political networks of the capital. The Washington wives retaliated with a boycott of the Monroes' social events. The situation provoked cabinet-level debates, but the Monroe women refused to change their decision. President Monroe called on Secretary of State John Quincy Adams to help solve what was generally referred to in the capital as the "etiquette wars." Adams grumbled in his letters about "the senseless war of etiquette visiting" but drew up a code of social etiquette for the president and his family that, with few exceptions, has continued to govern the social life of the nation's capital from that day to the present. Finally, in Monroe's second term, the boycott lost its steam, Elizabeth's policy was accepted, and official Washington, and their wives, returned to Executive Mansion social events.

> " This woman is so proud and so mean. . . . I never from the first moment of my acquaintance with her heard her speak well of any human being. "
>
> —Louisa Catherine Adams,
> *wife of then Secretary of State John Quincy Adams, on Eliza Monroe Hay*

Q: Who was married in the Executive Mansion during Monroe's term of office?

A: Maria Hester Monroe, James and Elizabeth's younger daughter, married her cousin, Samuel Gouverneur, in the Executive Mansion on March 9, 1820. It was the first wedding of a presidential child to take place in the Executive Mansion. At seventeen, Maria had fallen in love with Samuel, who had come to live in the mansion with his mother, Hester, the first lady's sister, and work as a presidential aide.

Eliza Monroe took charge of her sister's wedding plans and announced that the marriage would be held "New York style." This meant that the guest list would be limited to family and a small number of close friends—thus insulting cabinet members and foreign diplomats, prohibiting their attendance and their gifts, and alienating the groom.

Q: Who were the grandchildren in the Executive Mansion?

A: Hortensia Hay, daughter of Eliza and George Hay, was seven when she came with her parents to the President's House. She blossomed into a beautiful teenager while living there. James Gouverneur, son of Maria and Samuel Gouverneur, was born there, but the family was later devastated when it became apparent that he could neither hear nor speak. Little is known of his life.

Q: How did the Monroes leave an indelible mark on the Executive Mansion?

A: In addition to changing the protocol and calling customs, the Monroes purchased elegant furniture. Monroe sold to the government much of the furniture that he and his wife had purchased in France during his diplomatic service— and bought it back for his personal use after his presidential term. Also, in order to outfit the rebuilt President's House, additional furnishings were needed. Monroe ordered a suite of French mahogany furniture. His agents instead substituted a suite of gilded beechwood from the celebrated French craftsman Pierre Bellangé. The president also purchased the famous mirrored *plateau* for the dining room, with its figures of dancing nymphs (he had specified no naked women). He rounded out his purchases with French bronze clocks. These stunning pieces, still used in the White House, remain some of the most admired in presidential history.

As part of the refurnishing of the White House after the fire of 1814, Monroe ordered for "the large oval room" (Blue Room) a suite of French mahogany furniture. The agents, Russell & LaFarge, sent gilded beechwood instead, asserting that "mahogany is not generally admitted in the furniture of a saloon, even at private gentlemen's houses."

In 1817, the Monroes ordered a large gilded bronze *plateau* for the dining room. Made in the Parisian shop of Jean-François Denière and François Matelin, it was described as "mat gilt with garlands of fruit and vines with figures of Bacchus and Bacchantes and pedestals on which are 16 Figures presenting wreathes for receiving lights [candles] and 16 cups for changing at will, composed of 7 pieces altogether 13 [sic 14] feet 6 inches long, over 2 feet wide, set with its mirrors." Three baskets, a pair of urns, and a pair of stands accompanied it.

Q: **What special china service did the Monroes order?**

A: The Monroes also ordered the first state service of presidential china, a model for future state services. It was a large dessert service of French porcelain, made by the Paris firm of Dagoty and Honoré. The border rim was a reddish purple, known as amaranthe, decorated with five cartouches representing Strength, Agriculture, Commerce, Art, and Science. In the center of each plate was an American eagle with wings outstretched, backed by rays of sunlight. The eagle held the red, white, and blue shield of the United States of America. This eagle, known as the "Monroe Eagle," has since been used in various forms on several services of presidential state china, including the Lyndon B. Johnson service, at the request of Lady Bird Johnson.

James Monroe china. When Elizabeth and James Monroe ordered the first state china service, they again turned to France for this elegant porcelain dessert set.

> " A little flattery will support a man through great fatigue. "
>
> —JAMES MONROE

John Quincy and Louisa Adams

Q: How did John Quincy Adams's wife, Louisa Catherine, help him win the presidency?

A: As the son of John and Abigail Adams, John Quincy aspired to follow in his father's footsteps to the presidency of the United States. Having served as an American diplomat in Europe for many years, in Holland, Portugal, Prussia, Russia, and England, he was unfamiliar with the politics of Washington when he returned to the city to become Madison's secretary of state in 1817. His admittedly dour personality and lack of social skills were drawbacks to his advancement. Louisa's style, sophistication, and hostessing skills therefore proved crucial to her husband's career.

Louisa then launched what she called "my campaign" to help her husband win the presidency. By taking advantage of Washington's disrupted social networks in the "etiquette wars" during the Monroe administration, Louisa, as the wife of the secretary of state, asserted herself as Washington's most prominent hostess. By courting congressional wives and inviting cabinet members to dinners, she and her husband became the center of the capital's social scene. She used "party politics" to promote her husband's candidacy, literally entertaining their way to the Executive Mansion.

Although he had been reared for public service, John Quincy Adams proved to be the wrong man for the presidency. Known as aloof, stubborn, and fiercely independent, he failed to garner the support he needed in Washington, even among his own party. Historically, Adams has won more acclaim for his long congressional career than for his earlier presidency.

Caricature of the hotly contested presidential race of 1824. John Quincy Adams won it by a mere one-vote margin in the House of Representatives.

Q: How did Louisa's "party politics" further her husband's political ambitions?

A: In an era before political parties held conventions to select candidates, the power to nominate presidential hopefuls resided with congressional caucuses. But overt campaigning was seen as naked ambition and self-promotion, unseemly attributes in a candidate for public office. One had to cultivate influence and favor with Congress through another form of "party"—social entertaining. Acclaimed hostess Louisa focused the political spotlight on the candidate John Quincy, asserted social position, forged political alliances, and cemented friendships.

Q: Why was the custom of "calling" an important part of Washington politics?

A: Calling was a women's social ritual that had powerful political implications. It courted friendship, favor, and political power, and for political wives was an important part of their duties to advance their husbands' influence. A wife who was socially adept and politically savvy could be an immense asset to her husband's career. During the years when Louisa was promoting her husband, he would draw up lists of wives of congressmen and cabinet members whom she should visit to consolidate influence and cultivate favor.

In her promotional efforts, Louisa had called upon all the congressional wives, traveling around Washington's unpaved roads, visiting as many as twenty-five women in one day. She hosted sixty-eight congressional dinners between December 1823 and May 1824. It was a crucial but exhausting political task.

Q: Was John Quincy aware of his lack of sociability?

A: When President Monroe assigned him the task of drawing up a code of etiquette and protocol during the Monroe administration, John Quincy found the duty irksome and not a little ironic. He was a self-described misanthrope, who was as well known for his lack of social skills and his dour disposition as he was for his brilliant mind and devotion to duty.

The daughter of an American merchant and an English mother, Louisa Catherine Adams was the only first lady to be born outside of the United States. John Quincy first met her in France. Although for months he visited her family nightly, he always left when the daughters sat down at the piano to play and sing—he hated the sound of the female voice in song. Others appreciated Louisa's musical talent, however. Good music enhanced her Tuesday evenings at home and contributed to her reputation as an outstanding hostess.

> " Oh these visits have made me sick many times . . . and I really sometimes think they will make me crazy. "
>
> —LOUISA CATHERINE ADAMS

Q: What was Louisa's most brilliant social success before the presidency?

A: Louisa's most notable entertainment was a lavish ball to honor General Andrew Jackson, then a senator from Tennessee, on the anniversary of his 1815 victory over the British in the War of 1812. Jackson, the national hero of the Battle of New Orleans, was also a promising candidate for president in the upcoming election of 1824. The Jackson ball gave Louisa the opportunity to host a social occasion whose patriotism and power reflected on her husband. It was part of her months of "campaigning" for John Quincy's presidential bid and was a brilliant political move, amounting to a grand public relations coup that would involve the whole of Washington's political community.

Louisa recalled that she devised "a beautiful plan in my head" for this important event. She organized the ball as a grand theatrical event, with setting, music, actors, and stage (their F Street home had been enlarged specifically to accommodate entertaining on a grand scale). Louisa employed her entire family in creating the decorations of laurel, wintergreen, evergreens, and roses woven into garlands and wreaths. A large company was expected, so Louisa cleared the furniture from two floors of the house and installed large pillars to prop up the upper story so that it would not sag from the weight of the crowd and the dancing. At a ball given by the British minister the year before, Louisa had seen a "chalked" dance floor, with beautiful designs created by a man from Baltimore. She hired him to chalk her dance floor with slogans and pictures—eagles, flags, and "Welcome to the Hero of New Orleans." She carefully prepared for her moment in the spotlight, and received her guests in a "suit of steel," a glittering gown of steel-colored lamé with cut-steel ornaments for her head, throat, and arms, thus creating a dazzling impact. All eyes were on the Adamses, as Louisa had intended. The event was a brilliant success.

Q: What tragedies occurred in the Adams family?

A: Alcoholism continued to be a scourge of the Adams family and took as terrible a toll in the second generation as it had in the first. John Quincy and Louisa had three sons—George, John Adams II, and Charles Francis—whom they held to extremely high standards. All three attended Harvard. The eldest son, George, initially served his father as private secretary but then moved to Boston, where he went on drinking binges and fathered a child out of wedlock by a servant girl. He also mismanaged his parents' business affairs. At the end of John Quincy Adams's administration, George was called to

Although Andrew Jackson was a fierce political opponent of Adams, Louisa's brilliant ball feting the "Hero of New Orleans" was a social and political success.

Washington to direct the family's move back to Massachusetts. While returning on a steamship, George jumped overboard and drowned in an apparent suicide. He was only twenty-eight years old.

Q: Who was the only presidential son to be married in the Executive Mansion?

A: The Adams's second son, John, who was expelled from Harvard for participating in a student riot, married his mother's orphaned niece, who had come to live with the family. The wedding of Mary Catherine Hellen to John Adams II took place in a Blue Room ceremony on February 25, 1828. Mary Catherine had toyed with the affections of the Adams's other sons, George (to whom she had even become engaged at one point) and Charles, before marrying John, a situation that caused family consternation. George, Charles, and Louisa refused to attend the wedding. John also became an alcoholic and died at age thirty-one.

Q: How did Charles Francis Adams become a success?

A: Charles Francis Adams served as a congressman from Massachusetts and as a distinguished foreign diplomat— ambassador to Great Britain—in the mid-nineteenth century, continuing the legacy of his father and grandfather.

Charles Francis Adams, the Adams's youngest son.

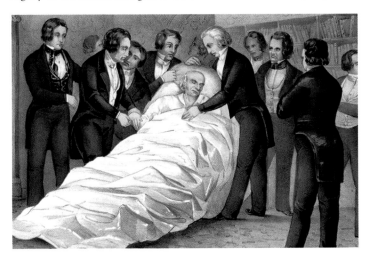

Q: What did John Quincy Adams do after his presidency?

A: Adams could not contemplate the idea of "retirement" or resist the call of politics and public duty. He was elected to Congress from Massachusetts as a member of the Whig Party, serving from 1831 until 1848, when he died shortly after collapsing on the floor of the House from a stroke. Known as "Old Man Eloquent" in his later years, he was a staunch and outspoken antislavery advocate.

Above: A tireless public servant until the very end of his life, John Quincy suffered a stroke on the floor of the House on February 21, 1848, and died two days later.

Left: Mary Louisa Adams, daughter of John Adams II. At the death of her father, Mary Louisa, along with her mother and brother, went to live with her grandparents.

> " No one knows the agonies I suffer. "
> —*JOHN QUINCY ADAMS*
> *about his son George*

Andrew Jackson

Q: Why was Andrew Jackson known as a "man of the people"?

A: Jackson represented the democratic, self-reliant "common man" image of the

American frontier, a contrast to the highly educated, Eastern elites who had previously served as presidents. He was also the first president elected from the West, chosen after many states had abandoned religious and property-owner-ship requirements as qualifications for voting. His victory represented the triumph of a broadly based, more democratic electorate. Jackson, a planter, soldier, and senator from Tennessee before becoming president, was hailed as the "Hero of New Orleans" and became a national icon when he defeated the British there in 1815, thus ending the War of 1812.

Above: The first president to be born in a log cabin, Andrew Jackson cultivated his frontiersman image. He was a dynamic military leader and his role in the defeat of the British at the Battle of New Orleans elevated him to a national hero. In 1824 he seemed destined to ride into the White House on his popularity. He did, indeed, receive the most popular and electoral votes, but did not receive a majority. The House of Representatives decided the race in favor of John Quincy Adams, outraging Jackson's supporters.

Right: Rachel Jackson, who died shortly before her husband took office.

Q: What rumors plagued the Jackson marriage, his political career, and possibly hastened Rachel Jackson's death?

A: As a young woman, Rachel Donelson, Jackson's future wife, married Lewis Robards, who proved to be a jealous and abusive husband. After the couple separated, Robards announced his intention to obtain a divorce, which required a petition to the state legislature. When Jackson and Rachel married in 1791, they assumed that Robards had obtained the divorce. It had not, however, come through, making Rachel, on a legal technicality, a bigamist. In 1794 the couple hastily remarried after the official divorce. Although the matter had perhaps more to do with the difficulties of frontier com-munication than with morals, Jackson's political enemies accused Rachel of bigamy and adultery—which was vicious slander. The political opposition press kept the "scandal" alive during Jackson's presidential campaign. Rachel died from a heart attack two months before her husband was to take office. She was buried in the white gown she had chosen to wear to the inaugural ball.

President's Levee, or all Creation going to the White House by Robert Cruikshank. View of crowd in front of the White House during President Jackson's first inaugural reception on March 4, 1829. The rowdy crowd destroyed the White House furnishings during the inaugural festivities.

Q: Why was Jackson's inauguration celebration a rowdy affair?

A: Jackson's image as a man of the people attracted an unruly crowd of twenty thousand to the Executive Mansion for the inaugural celebration. The crowd, labeled a "rabble" by contemporaries, invaded the mansion, damaging much of the furniture and china. Women screamed and fainted as men in muddy boots climbed on the elegant silk-upholstered sofas in an attempt to gain a glimpse of the hero. Jackson, pinned against a wall by the crush, had to be rescued and helped out a window to escape his "supporters."

Q: Which two women served as Jackson's first ladies?

A: Andrew Jackson had two young and beautiful first ladies during his two presidential administrations: Emily Donelson, his wife's niece, who was married to Andrew Jackson "Jack" Donelson, his wife's nephew and a presidential confidant; and Sarah Yorke Jackson, the president's daughter-in-law, who was the wife of Jackson's adopted son, Andrew Jackson II. This "all in the family" administration was a tightly knit clan that shared both strong kinship ties and a political philosophy.

> "The enemys of the Gen'ls. have dipt their arrows in wormwood and gall and sped them at me."
>
> —*RACHEL JACKSON,*
> *shortly before her death*

Political cartoon satirizing the dissension and political intrigue within Andrew Jackson's administration, surrounding the 1831 resignations of several members of his cabinet.

Q: What was the "Peggy Eaton Affair" and why did it disrupt the Executive Mansion and Washington society?

A: Margaret O'Neale grew up in Washington, the daughter of one of the best-known tavernkeepers in the city. The O'Neale tavern catered to Jackson supporters. Peggy, as she was known, married a ship's purser, John Bowie Timberlake, by whom she had two children. Timberlake died at sea, leaving Peggy a young widow whose beauty attracted many suitors. Local rumormongers reported that she had had an affair prior to her husband's death with one of the boarders at the tavern, widower John Eaton, Jackson's campaign manager. Eaton loved Peggy, and he married her, assuming that a wedding would quiet the rumors.

When Jackson appointed Eaton secretary of war, this elevated Peggy to the socially prominent status of cabinet wife. The women of Washington, led by the wife of Vice President John C. Calhoun, were horrified and refused to call on a woman with a "past"—thus freezing her out of the capital's social and political networks. Jackson believed that the gossip about her smacked of the slander against his wife, Rachel, and became Peggy's staunch defender. The furor over the refusal to socialize with her rose to a fever pitch; Jackson called a cabinet meeting to discuss the matter, declaring Peggy "is as chaste as a virgin." The women refused to relent. The affair culminated with the resignations of most of Jackson's cabinet.

The president's then first lady, Emily Donelson, was caught in an impossible situation: side with her uncle, the president, or offend all of Washington's wives. She left the Executive Mansion and returned to Tennessee with Jackson's beloved grandchildren, not to return until two years later, after the Peggy Eaton Affair, also known as the "Petticoat Affair," was over, proving once again the power of female social networks.

Q: How did the "man of the people" decorate and entertain in the Executive Mansion?

A: Jackson's friend and supporter Major William B. Lewis carried out the president's wish to finally finish the East Room. Although Jackson had made "presidential extravagance" a campaign issue, the East

> "I have the beautiful recollection of the whole stately house adorned and ready for the Company . . . the gorgeous supper table shaped like a horseshoe, covered with every good and glittering thing French skill could devise."
>
> —JESSIE BENTON FRÉMONT

Room was elaborately and elegantly decorated with four marble fireplaces and three great chandeliers of gilded brass and cut glass. Similarly, Jackson's style in entertaining was lavish and formal. His dinners were memorable events, and his Belgian chef, Antoine Michel Giusta, concocted sumptuous delights for his guests. Moreover, Jackson purchased numerous pieces of exquisite French silver from the departing Russian minister to add to those purchased by Monroe. Jackson ordered formal dining and dessert services of French porcelain that could serve state dinners of fifty guests.

Q: Who resided in the Executive Mansion with Jackson?

A: A large family and assorted friends lived with the president, including

Emily Donelson, Jackson's niece and White House hostess.

Jack and Emily Donelson and their children and, later, his adopted son, Andrew Jackson II and his wife, Sarah Yorke Jackson, and their children. The extended family included Jackson's aide, Major Lewis, and Mary Eastin, his wife's great-niece. Painter R. E. W. Earl enjoyed frequent and lengthy visits to the house.

Earl had painted the portrait of Rachel Jackson that hung in the president's bedroom, as well as portraits of Emily Donelson and Sarah Yorke Jackson.

Jackson dearly loved his grandchildren and lavished affection on them. Emily Donelson gave birth to three

children in the mansion: Mary (1829), John Samuel (1832), and Rachel (1834). The Donelsons' oldest son, Andrew, who was known as A. J., was a particular favorite. When A. J. attended boarding school in Virginia, he made the Executive Mansion his home. Jackson's adopted son, Andrew Jackson II, and his wife, Sarah, came to live in the mansion in 1834 with their children Rachel and Andrew III. The president called Mary Donelson his "Sunshine of the White House" and Rachel Jackson "my sweet little babe."

Q: What important changes to the Executive Mansion were made in the Jackson presidency?

A: The great East Room was completed and furnished, and the North Portico, begun a few weeks after Jackson moved in, was finished in September 1829. Running water was installed in 1833. Most people today, accustomed to modern conveniences, cannot imagine the vast improvement in daily life this brought to the venerable house.

The East Room today. In its earliest days, this now elegant room was used as a makeshift laundry. It was finally finished during Jackson's term of office.

CHAPTER 3

MANIFEST DESTINY: EXPANDING WESTWARD

Westward expansion was marked by rising bitterness between North and South over whether slavery should be extended into newly acquired territories. Instead of reducing sectional conflict as expansionist proponents had claimed, acquisition of new lands inflamed debates over slavery. Martin Van Buren continued the policy of Indian removal: The Seminoles were defeated in Florida, and the Cherokees were forcibly removed from Georgia on the Trail of Tears. Texas and Florida were admitted as slave states in 1845. The United States signed a treaty with Great Britain in 1846, extending the boundary between the Oregon Territory and Canada at the forty-ninth parallel, thus avoiding war. Victory in the Mexican War, and payment of $15 million, brought into the U.S. domain the former Mexican territories comprising the present-day states of California, Nevada, and Utah, and parts of Arizona, New Mexico, Colorado, and Wyoming. The Treaty of Guadalupe Hidalgo sealed this land acquisition. The Oregon Territory was organized and Wisconsin was admitted to the Union in 1848. Although the nation had successfully extended its dominion across the continent, it was about to tear itself apart over the burning issue of slavery.

Above: Inauguration of William Henry Harrison. Harrison delivered the longest inaugural address in presidential history outdoors, on a wet winter's day. One month later, Harrison became the first president to die in office.

Left: *American Progress*. "America" guides railroads, pioneers, and the telegraph westward, as Indians, buffalo, and wild animals run, leaving the way clear for settlement.

Martin Van Buren

Q: Why was Martin Van Buren often referred to as "Martin Van Ruin"?

A: Van Buren, who served as secretary of state and vice president under Andrew Jackson, was Jackson's handpicked successor. Van Buren, however, had the misfortune to be in office at the onset of the Panic of 1837, the worst economic disaster in the nation's history to that date. Although the panic was brought on by Jackson's economic policies—the abolition of the central Bank of the United States, the upsurge of local banks and associated profiteering, and the removal of fiscal controls—Van Buren was burdened with the blame.

Martin Van Buren was the first president born as a United States citizen. Often described as a "dandy," Van Buren was an exquisite dresser who enjoyed expensive wine and gourmet food.

Q: What policies did Van Buren pursue that further hurt his popularity?

A: Elected as Jackson's anointed successor, Van Buren was expected to continue access of the "common man" to the president. But Van Buren, an Eastern aristocrat, disliked large crowds and preferred elegant, intimate dinners with friends and political colleagues. He severely curtailed the public's access to the Executive Mansion by abolishing morning receptions and the weekly levees, which in the Jackson years the public had been encouraged to attend. In addition, he stationed police at the doors to the mansion to prevent intruders of questionable "class." Although Van Buren considered the protection of the president necessary, this move heightened his image as an elitist and contributed to his unpopularity.

Q: Who was Martin Van Buren's wife?

A: Van Buren had wed his cousin Hannah Hoes in 1807. The couple had grown up together in the close-knit Dutch community of Kinderhook, New York. Hannah bore five sons, one of whom died in infancy. The winter after bearing her fifth child, Hannah fell ill, apparently from tuberculosis. She died at age thirty-five, eighteen years before Van Buren became president. After he took office, there was, however, no shortage of Washington women who offered to relieve him of his widower's status. Nevertheless, Van Buren never remarried.

Q: What family members did Van Buren bring with him to the Executive Mansion?

A: The president's four surviving sons lived with him in the Executive Mansion: Abraham (b. 1807), John (b. 1810), Martin (b. 1812), and Smith (b. 1817). His sons were his closest friends and trusted advisers and were the first presidential children to attend their father's inaugural balls. Abraham worked as his father's private secretary and military aide. Martin organized his father's papers, with the hope of one day helping him write a book. Smith was a law student, and Van Buren instructed him on how to study, advising him that "the only way to acquire a fondness for the law is to read constantly."

John, sometimes called "Prince John" because of his travels abroad to European courts and his fondness for dapper dress, had problems with alcohol. Initially employed as an aide to his father, John drank to excess, provoking the president to dismiss him. Van Buren admonished him that "Washington is full of reports . . . that you had twice been carried drunk from the race course." Yet in later years John emerged as an able lawyer who served in the New York State congress from 1841 to 1843 and was appointed as New York state attorney general in 1845.

Van Buren's wife, Hannah Hoes Van Buren. The cousins married in 1807 and had five children. Hannah died eighteen years before Van Buren was elected president.

Political cartoon attacking the Van Buren administration as too "regal." Van Buren's Loco Foco, or Radical Democratic supporters, ride with him.

A true man with no guile.
—*ANDREW JACKSON, ABOUT MARTIN VAN BUREN*

Angela Singleton Van Buren, the president's daughter-in-law, began her service as White House hostess when she married Abraham Van Buren. Impressed with the elaborate displays she witnessed at European courts, she tried to adopt similar customs in the United States. After the Whigs relentlessly criticized her pretensions, she dropped her studied royal impressions.

Q: Which of Van Buren's sons married during his father's term in office?

A: Van Buren's eldest son, Abraham, married South Carolina belle Angelica Singleton in November 1838.

Dolley Madison, who had recently moved back to the nation's capital after the death of her husband, had taken up residence in Lafayette Square, directly across the street from the Executive Mansion. She, of course, noticed the all-male atmosphere pervading the residence and noted that the Van Buren presidency lacked a social hostess. When Angelica Singleton, Dolley's young relative by marriage, arrived to spend the 1837–38 social season in Washington, Dolley introduced her to the capital's society. Playing matchmaker suited Dolley, and with her encouragement Angelica and Abraham began a courtship. After their wedding, Angelica assumed the duties of Van Buren's first lady. She made her first appearance in that role at the New Year's Day reception of 1839.

Q: How did Angelica Van Buren carry out her role as first lady?

A: In the spring of 1839, Angelica and Abraham took a belated honeymoon abroad to visit Angelica's uncle, who was then the American minister to Great Britain. The couple was received with great fanfare at both the British and French courts. Angelica was greatly impressed with the elaborate ceremonies of royalty.

Upon her return, she tried to institute these court ceremonies at Executive Mansion receptions. In an elegant white

gown with a long train, and with ostrich plumes in her hair, Angelica received guests while seated on a raised platform, a sort of improvised throne. She would pose in a "tableau," with honored female guests, also dressed in white, in attendance. The tableau was a ceremony commonly used at Queen Victoria's receptions, but it proved far too regal for American tastes. This mode of receiving was soon abandoned, but it lent credibility to political opponents' charges that Van Buren had a "royal" view of the presidency.

Q: What improvements did Van Buren make to the Executive Mansion that led to the charges of "living like royalty"?

A: When Jackson was president, he used most of the congressional appropriation for the house to complete and furnish the East Room and to purchase silver and china services. After eight years of hard use by "the people," many of the mansion's public rooms were in shabby condition.

When Van Buren arrived, he began a thorough cleaning, refurbishing, and reupholstering of worn furniture. He had new wallpaper purchased for all the state rooms, and the chandeliers were restrung and regilded. Carpeting, bell pulls, rugs, stair runners, and hall lanterns were bought. Although very little new furniture was actually purchased, as observers watched throngs of carpenters, painters, and upholsterers coming and going in the Executive Mansion, they assumed that Van Buren was spending lavishly. In fact, he spent less than half of what Andrew Jackson had spent while in office.

During the redecoration, the color of the oval reception room was changed from its traditional red to a shade of blue, and its gold furniture was reupholstered in blue as well. Thus Van Buren established the Blue Room, which has remained a blue color from 1837 to the present.

Q: How did Van Buren's political enemies use his lifestyle and the mansion's refurbishing against him?

A: As public resentment mounted along with charges of a regal lifestyle, Congressman Charles Ogle from western Pennsylvania seized the opportunity to attack the president and win favor for the newly coalesced Whig Party. In 1840, several months before the election, Ogle took

the House floor, armed with purchase order accounts all the way back to the Monroe administration. It did not matter that they were not Van Buren's. Ogle thundered on for a three-day tirade, accusing the president of ordering golden spoons (untrue) and living in "a PALACE as splendid as that of the Caesar's" and residing in "magnificent splendor. . . . "How delightful it must be . . ." he continued, "to eat pâté de foie gras . . . from a silver plate . . . with a golden knife and fork."

The Blue Room. Martin Van Buren was the first to decorate this room in the color from which it later gained its name.

Ogle lost no time in championing the republican virtues of William Henry Harrison, soon to be the Whig candidate, and touting Harrison's "humble" origins in a log cabin. Here was a man who, instead of fine wines, wanted nothing more to drink than hard cider. The first salvo of the famous "Log Cabin and Hard Cider" campaign had been fired. The damage was irreparable. The perception of a lavish and exclusive lifestyle, while the public was shut out, contributed to Van Buren's defeat in the next election.

> " Democratic peacock in full court costume, strutting. "
> —*A Whig congressman's description of Angelica Van Buren*

William Henry and Anna Harrison

Q: What was the "Log Cabin and Hard Cider" campaign?

A: Foreshadowed by Congressman Ogle's tirade against Van Buren, the 1840 campaign was the first fully orchestrated "image" campaign in United States history—the prototype of modern political campaigns. Painting their candidate as a frontier Indian fighter, hero of the War of 1812, and man of the people, the Whigs took a slur by the opposition—that Harrison would be content to live in a log cabin and drink hard cider—and turned it to their political advantage.

"Old Tippecanoe," as Harrison was known for his victory over the Indians at the Battle of Tippecanoe, was in fact the son of Virginia landed aristocracy, born at Berkeley, one of Virginia's finest James River plantations. His father had been a member of the Continental Congress, a signer of the Declaration of Independence, and three-term governor of Virginia. Harrison himself became

William Henry Harrison was nicknamed "Old Tippecanoe" after his War of 1812 victory at the Battle of Tippecanoe. The name was widely used during the 1840 election campaign.

governor of the Indiana Territory and won further military honors defeating the British in a battle in the War of 1812.

The Whigs' well-organized campaign was based on image; partisan newspapers flooded the country with Log Cabin and Hard Cider editorials. In major cities, political supporters carried log cabins mounted on poles and staged torchlight parades complete with little suspended canoes that "tipped" as the torchbearers marched. Although lacking a substantive platform, the Whigs carried the day. Harrison won the election.

Q: What kind of inaugural ceremony was held for Harrison?

A: Harrison's Inauguration Day, March 4, 1841, was cold and stormy. The general rode a magnificent white horse amid marching militias, floats with log cabins, and cheering Whig supporters. This "frontiersman" delivered an inaugural address filled with classical allusions and Latin phrases, lasting one hour and forty-five minutes—the longest inauguration address in American history.

Q: What family members accompanied Harrison to the nation's capital?

A: Harrison asked his daughter-in-law, Jane Irwin Findlay Harrison, widow of his eldest son, William Henry Harrison Jr., to serve as interim first lady. Her adoptive parents, General and Mrs. James Findlay of Cincinnati, accompanied her so

Anna Symmes Harrison

that Mrs. Findlay could guide her daughter through the intricate social etiquette of Washington. Mrs. Thomas Taylor of Richmond, Harrison's niece, was also among the group. The women came equipped with trunks of fashionable clothing—much of which was never worn.

Anna Symmes Harrison did not go to Washington because she was recuperating from an illness. She and her husband decided that she should not make the long and tiring trip during the winter, but wait until May when the weather would be warmer. Because her husband died after only one month in office, Anna Harrison never traveled to Washington.

Q: How did the president become ill, and what medical treatment did he receive?

A: Harrison called Dr. Thomas Miller to the White House on March 26, complaining of chills and fever. Miller relied on old-fashioned remedies: "bleeding," to rid the body of illness, and "cupping," which involved applying heated cups to the skin to create suction and "cleanse" the body of impurities. These practices probably hastened the president's death. Harrison was also dosed with laudanum (opium) and shots of hot whiskey—to no avail. On April 4, 1841, one month after his inauguration, Harrison became the first U.S. president to die in office.

Q: What was significant about Harrison's funeral?

A: Alexander Hunter, a prominent Washington merchant, was asked to handle the mourning and funeral arrangements. There were not yet established ceremonies for official state mourning, so Hunter borrowed heavily from the rituals of royal funerals. His basic decisions formed the model that, with few changes, set the precedent for all future presidential funerals. Harrison lay in state in the East Room of the White House, where his funeral was also held.

William Henry Harrison on his deathbed, after enduring several popular treatments of the day: "bleeding," "cupping," and doses of laudanum.

> **I wish that my husband's friends had left him where he is, happy and contented in retirement.**
>
> —*ANNA HARRISON,*
> *upon hearing the news of her husband's electoral victory*

John Tyler

Q: **Why was President Tyler called "His Accidency" by his detractors?**

A: John Tyler was the Whig Party's vice-presidential candidate in the 1840

President John Tyler

election. He was nominated as a way to balance the ticket—Harrison was from the Northwest, Tyler from the South—to attract Southern voters. The famous campaign slogan, "Tippecanoe and Tyler, Too," was a reflection of this balancing act. Tyler was never intended to become president, even by his own party. Tyler had moved his family to Williamsburg, Virginia, some years before and planned to continue

living there during his vice-presidential term. Harrison's unexpected death after only one month in office was the "accident" that elevated Tyler to the presidency. John Quincy Adams—acerbic as ever—was the first to dub Tyler "His Accidency." John Tyler was the first vice president to succeed to the presidency through the death of the incumbent.

Q: **Who was the president's wife, and why was she unable to act as his official hostess?**

A: Letitia Christian Tyler was a Virginia beauty who was born and brought up on

Letitia Christian Tyler

a plantation not far from Tyler's home, twenty miles east of Richmond. Little is known of her life before she married. The couple wed in a ceremony at Cedar Grove planta-

tion, Letitia's home, on March 29, 1813. She gave birth to a large family of eight children, all of whom survived except for a daughter who died in infancy. In 1839, she suffered a stroke that left her partially paralyzed. After Tyler became president, it was decided that Letitia would move with the family to the Executive Mansion, but her physical condition did not permit her to act as her husband's hostess.

Vice president Tyler received news of Harrison's death while at his home in Williamsburg, Virginia. This image of a messenger passing a letter to the next president was engraved in wood by William Osborn Stoddard.

" She had everything about her to awaken love. "
—*Priscilla Cooper Tyler, about Letitia Tyler*

Q: Who served as Tyler's first lady during the early years of his administration?

A: Priscilla Cooper Tyler, wife of the Tylers' eldest son, Robert, served as the president's hostess. Priscilla, an acclaimed beauty, was a professional actress whom Robert had met in Richmond. Priscilla's father, famous tragedian Thomas Cooper, was known for his portrayal of Shakespeare's Othello. Yet, in the mid-nineteenth century, acting was considered a dubious profession, and actresses were reputed to be of questionable character. The Tylers nonetheless welcomed Priscilla into the family, and she developed a deep attachment to her mother-in-law. Robert and Priscilla lived in the Executive Mansion, where Robert served as private secretary to his father.

Priscilla handled the administration's entertaining in fine style, enlisting Dolley Madison as her adviser. The *New York Herald* reported about one of Priscilla's receptions that the "entertainment was magnificent [and] the wines superb."

Charles Dickens, shown above, was honored by the Tylers at a White House reception in 1842, as was Washington Irving.

Q: What was the only social event Letitia Tyler was able to attend while in the mansion?

A: Letitia witnessed the marriage of her third daughter, Elizabeth, to William Waller in the Executive Mansion on January 31, 1842. Dolley Madison also attended the wedding.

Q: What special reception marked the early Tyler years?

A: An elegant reception in the East Room in 1842 honored Washington Irving and Charles Dickens. More than three thousand people crammed the Executive Mansion to catch a glimpse of the two renowned literary figures.

Q: What tragedy struck the Tyler family during the president's administration?

A: Letitia's health continued to deteriorate, and in 1842 she suffered a second stroke. She died on September 10, 1842, the first presidential wife to die in the Executive Mansion. Her funeral was held in the East Room on September 12.

Q: Did President Tyler remarry?

A: The young, beautiful, and spirited Julia Gardiner became the president's second wife. Julia was born into an extremely wealthy family in 1820 and was brought up on Gardiner's Island, a thirty-three-hundred-acre island off the eastern tip of Long Island that her ancestors had purchased from the Indians. David Gardiner, her father, was a Yale-educated lawyer who practiced in New York City. He was elected to the New York state senate in 1824.

In 1839, nineteen-year-old Julia made the questionable decision (for a "lady" of her time) to appear in an advertisement for Bogert and McCamly's New York department store, touting, "Their goods are beautiful and astonishingly cheap." The advertisement featured Julia's likeness, labeled "The Rose of Long Island." Her mortified parents quickly whisked Julia off to Europe until the minor scandal died down.

Above: Julia Gardiner Tyler. President Tyler swept the fainting Julia Gardiner off of the frigate USS *Princeton* after a malfunctioning cannon killed her father. They became engaged shortly after and married seven weeks after the tragedy.

Right: Advertisement for Bogert and McCamly's New York department store featuring the young Julia Gardiner.

Q: What tragedy brought Julia and the president together?

A: In 1842, the Gardiners took their daughters, Julia and Margaret, to Washington for the winter social season. Suitors besieged Julia. The family was invited to the Executive Mansion and met the president, who, although still in mourning for his wife, became smitten with Julia. The Gardiners returned to Washington for the next social season, and the family became favorites at the Executive Mansion. Tyler, who had already proposed to Julia but had been rejected, invited the family to accompany him on an excursion to Mount Vernon aboard the new steam frigate the USS *Princeton*. During a firing demonstration, the breech of one of the *Princeton*'s guns exploded, killing Julia's father, the secretary of war, and several others. Within seven weeks of the tragedy, Julia accepted the president's proposal, despite their thirty-year age difference. The couple married on June 26, 1844, at the Church of the Ascension on New York's Fifth Avenue.

Members of Tyler's family were stunned by the hasty remarriage. Although his sons liked Julia from the beginning, it took his daughters a long time to adjust to their new stepmother. One daughter, Letitia Tyler Semple, always remained hostile to her father's new wife.

Q: How did Julia entertain as the new first lady?

A: The Executive Mansion came alive again with the young bride in residence. In her short eight months as first lady, Julia filled the house with dancing and fun. Her parties were lavish and formal. Taking herself quite seriously, she copied the practices of royal courts. Jessie Benton Frémont, wife of explorer John C. Frémont, recorded, "She received seated in her huge armchair on a slightly raised platform. . . . she wore three feathers in her hair and a long trained velvet dress." Her sister, Margaret, and young women friends served as her "attendants."

Julia used entertaining as a way to lobby for her husband's agenda and was particularly fervent in advocating the annexation of Texas. When annexation eventually took place in the latter part of Tyler's administration, Julia threw an elegant party to celebrate.

Q: What happened to the Tylers after the presidency?

A: The Tylers returned to their Virginia plantation, Sherwood Forest (a wry reference to his "outlaw" status with the Whig Party), where their happy marriage produced seven children. In an attempt to preserve the Union prior to the Civil War, Tyler was elected president of a Peace Convention in 1861. After its failure,

Tyler and Julia became ardent secessionists. Tyler even served as a representative to the Confederate Congress.

Tyler died in Richmond in 1862, leaving Julia a widow with seven children. She fled Virginia as the Civil War raged and took several of her children with her to the Gardiner home in New York. She spent the remainder of her life defending her husband and the Confederacy, trying to keep Sherwood Forest, and directing her children's education. She converted to Roman Catholicism in later life and died in 1889 at sixty-nine years of age.

Julia Tyler introduced the custom of having the band play "Hail to the Chief" when the president made an appearance.

Q: What modern practice did media-savvy Julia pioneer?

A: With an innate sense of the importance of positive publicity, Julia charmed the *New York Herald*'s Washington correspondent, F. W. Thomas, into publishing favorable press notices of her parties. Thomas referred to her in his accounts as "the Lovely Lady Presidentress." Julia, in effect, made Thomas an unofficial press agent for a first lady.

> "Nothing appears to delight the President more than . . . to hear people sing my praises."
>
> —*Julia Gardiner Tyler*

James and Sarah Polk

Q: **Why was James K. Polk considered a "dark horse" candidate for president?**

A: The term "dark horse" describes a candidate who has only an outside chance of being chosen as the party's nominee. Polk, a Tennessee politician and protégé of Andrew Jackson, had been a lawyer, state senator, U. S. congressman, Speaker of the House, and governor of Tennessee. While recognized as an able politician, Polk was outshone by others of his time, such as Henry Clay and Daniel Webster. Yet, in 1844, he was nominated for president by the Democratic Party.

James K. Polk, the "dark horse" president, so called after his unlikely victory over the charismatic Henry Clay. Although often overlooked, he was a strong executive, ranked by presidential scholars as one of the "near great" presidents, along with Jefferson, Jackson, Theodore Roosevelt, Wilson, and Truman. In their assessment, the three "great" presidents were: Washington, Lincoln, and Franklin Roosevelt.

Q: **What kind of education fitted Sarah Polk for the role of a political wife?**

A: Polk's wife, born Sarah Childress, was the daughter of a prominent Tennessee family. Her father often held political gatherings in their home, so Sarah was exposed to politics at an early age. Her political interests shaped her life as Polk's domestic and political partner. James and Sarah married on New Year's Day 1824, at the bride's home.

Sarah Polk's family believed in educating their daughters as well as their son. Her father made certain that she had an excellent education. After Sarah attended the Abercrombie School in Nashville, her father sent her and her sister, Susan, to the Moravian Female Academy in Salem (now Winston-Salem), North Carolina, which was then the finest school for women in the South. Escorted by their older brother, the sisters made the arduous journey of five hundred miles by horseback. Sarah's level of education was highly unusual for a woman of her time.

When Polk began courting Sarah, she knew she was choosing a political life. A clerk of the state senate at the time, Polk announced his candidacy for the Tennessee legislature before they married. Attributing his ambition partly to Sarah, he explained, "Sarah wouldn't have married me if I'd been satisfied with a clerkship." His family agreed, commenting that Sarah was a woman with "a great deal of spice and more independence of judgment than was fitting" for a woman.

Q: **Did the Polks have children?**

A: Although they loved children, the couple never had any of their own.

Sarah Childress Polk

After the death of both their fathers, Polk became the head of two families—his own and his wife's. James and Sarah assumed an increasingly large role as substitute parents for their growing nieces and nephews, and for Polk's younger brother.

Q: Where did the Polks live while he was a Tennessee congressman and Speaker of the House?

A: The Polks resided in boardinghouses when in Washington for congressional sessions during his thirteen years in Congress. Without the responsibilities of rearing a family and managing a household, Sarah devoted her excellent mind and education to the advancement of her husband's career. She became his political confidante and adviser. A well-known Washington hostess, she was as much admired for her political acumen as for her entertainments, and was an experienced political wife when they entered the Executive Mansion in 1845.

Q: What comment did one of Polk's opponents make about Sarah?

A: The gentleman, aware of Sarah's political partnership with her husband, said he hoped that if James were elected president, Sarah would take up housekeeping like a "normal" woman. Sarah retorted that if James were elected, she would "neither keep house nor make butter." Indeed, she did not. The Polks shared an upstairs office in the Executive Mansion, where she served as his adviser, helped him write speeches, and often edited those she did not write.

Q: What family members resided with the Polks during his term of office?

A: The Polks surrounded themselves with relatives, many of whom stayed in the house more than six months at a time. James Knox Walker, Polk's nephew and private secretary, personally paid by the president, had two bedrooms upstairs with his wife and two children. Walker's wife, Augusta, aided Sarah. Two more children were born to the Walkers while they lived in the mansion. Sarah's flirtatious niece from Tennessee, Joanna Rucker, attracted crowds of young people to the Polk receptions. She left a number of lively letters describing social life at the mansion. A far cry from the bleak assessment of Abigail Adams fifty years earlier, her impressions were nearly rhapsodic: "I reached the White House by moonlight. . . . I thought it was a beautiful place but my imagination had never led me to believe it was as beautiful as it is."

The façade of the White House as it appeared in 1848. The Polks installed gas lamps inside the Executive Mansion and on Pennsylvania Avenue, as seen in this illustration.

" **Wealthy, pretty, ambitious and intelligent.** "

—ANDREW JACKSON
about Sarah Childress Polk

Q: What took place at the Polk inaugural balls that heralded a change in social entertainment at the Executive Mansion?

A: When the Polks arrived at Carusi's assembly rooms, site of their inaugural balls, all dancing and music suddenly stopped, since the new first lady disapproved of it.

Sarah was a devout Presbyterian whose religious convictions led her to ban dancing, card-playing, and hard liquor (but certainly not wine) from the Executive Mansion, believing that they were a dishonor to the national home. She made up for their absence with formal, lavish dinners, despite the Polks' "frontier" roots in Tennessee. Sarah claimed that restrained graciousness and intelligent discussion of current political events were her forte.

The James K. Polk dessert china, featuring a different flower on each plate, the shield for the United States, and the nation's motto: "Out of many, one." It is considered by many to be the most beautiful pattern in the history of the White House.

The inauguration of James K. Polk. At the time of his election, the forty-nine-year-old Polk was the youngest man to become president.

Q: With dancing, card-playing, and hard liquor banned, how did Sarah entertain her guests?

A: The Polks held receptions on Tuesday and Friday nights and, in addition, gave dinners for the cabinet, Supreme Court, Congress, and foreign diplomats. Sarah also redecorated the state rooms under the able guidance of William Corcoran. They purchased an exquisite state service of French porcelain. Sarah's choice of French cuisine and the many courses served at state dinners were reflected in the distinctive and prolific number of serving dishes.

A detailed description of a Polk "dinner" at the mansion in December 1845 was recorded by Mrs. James Dixon, wife of a Connecticut congressman. "As the furniture is all new and fresh and all the decorations newly gilded, it was very splendid. Sit! I guess we did sit—for four mortal hours, I judged one hundred fifty courses, for everything was in the French style and each dish a separate course.

"Soup, fish, green peas, canvas back duck, turkey, birds, oyster pies, cotolettes di mouton, ham deliciously garnished, potatoes like snowballs, croquettes, poulet, in various forms, duck and olives, pâté de foie gras, jellies, orange and lemon charlotte rouse [sic], ices and 'pink mud' oranges, prunes, sweetmeats, mottos and

" I love you, Sarah, for all eternity, I love you. "
—*JAMES POLK'S LAST WORDS*

everything one can imagine, . . . The china was white and gold and blue with a crest, the eagle, of course, and the dessert plates were a mazarine blue and gold. . . . The glassware was very handsome, blue and white, finely cut, and pink champagne, gold sherry, green hock, madeira, the ruby port, and sauterne, formed a rainbow around each plate."

Q: Who was an intimate friend of the Polks?

A: The Polks were close friends with Dolley Madison, who had returned to Washington after her husband's death. Despite an impoverished widowhood, Dolley continued to reign as queen of Washington society. Dolley, who had always been known for her stylish mode of dress (and for a fondness of turbans) may have influenced Sarah's fashion sense, who also adopted the wearing of turbans.

Q: What major American war took place during the Polk administration, and what were its results?

A: Polk supported American territorial expansion and acquisition of lands to the west. The popular slogan exciting the nation was "manifest destiny"—the inevitable triumph of the nation's westward growth. Polk stationed General Zachary Taylor in Texas with American troops, virtually daring the Mexicans to attack. Once the fighting began, the Mexican War became the vehicle for an enormous land grab by the Americans. Taylor became a war hero, which propelled him into the presidency in the

next election. Polk signed the Treaty of Guadalupe Hidalgo, ending the Mexican War, on July 4, 1848. It added more than five hundred thousand square miles to the United States, including what are now the states of California, Nevada, and Utah, most of Arizona, and parts of Wyoming, Colorado, and New Mexico.

Q: What tragedy occurred as the Polks were returning to Tennessee after the end of his administration?

A: Polk, an obsessive worker during his presidency, was often plagued by illnesses brought on by exhaustion. On the journey home, huge and enthusiastic crowds awaited the Polks at every stop. Receptions, balls, parades, and bands greeted them, each site trying to outdo the others in hailing the retiring president. The Polks were deluged with congratulatory visitors, shook thousands of hands, and barely got any rest. Exhaustion took its toll. Once they arrived in Nashville, it was apparent that Polk was seriously ill. He died on June 15, 1849, and was buried at Polk Place, his home in Tennessee.

Bombardment at Veracruz during the Mexican War on March 25, 1847. The Treaty of Guadalupe Hidalgo, which ended the war, added more than five hundred thousand square miles to the United States.

CHAPTER 4

SECTIONALISM AND SLAVERY

The controversy over whether new lands should be admitted into the Union as slave states or as free states grew ever more bitter by the middle of the nineteenth century. An attempt to appease both the North and the South with the Compromise of 1850 raised as many problems as it solved. That year, California was admitted as a free state, but a stringent Fugitive Slave Act, which required citizens to assist in the recovery of fugitive slaves, inflamed passions in the North. The Kansas-Nebraska Act of 1854 repealed the Missouri Compromise and reopened the question of the spread of slavery into the West. Although many in Congress favored "popular sovereignty"—permitting each state to decide for itself whether to be slave or free—the furious competition between opposing factions turned violent and bloody. The Dred Scott decision of 1857, in which the Supreme Court held that slaves had no rights, further inflamed the Northern abolitionists. In 1861, when Southern forces fired upon a ship sent to resupply a federal garrison at Fort Sumter, South Carolina, a catastrophic civil war became inevitable.

Above: Henry Clay, shown here addressing the Senate in 1850, introduced a series of resolutions in an attempt to seek a compromise between North and South.

Left: More than 80,000 people flocked to the inauguration of Franklin Pierce. A driving snowstorm drove off all but about 20,000 spectators.

Zachary and Margaret Taylor

Above: Zachary Taylor encamped with his army at Walnut Springs within three miles of Monterrey, Mexico, where the Battle of Buena Vista was fought. Using heavy artillery, the general's 5,000 men turned back the 14,000 Mexican troops led by General Santa Anna. This Mexican War victory endeared Taylor, already popular with his men, to the entire nation.

Right: Beaded bag belonging to Margaret Taylor.

Q: Why was Zachary Taylor known as "Old Rough and Ready"?

A: Taylor, a career military army officer, was given this affectionate nickname by the soldiers he led. Always ready to fight along the frontier, he had been stationed at a series of outposts at the edge of the wilderness throughout his career. Not a "spit and polish" officer, he was heavy and unkempt and wore oversized, comfortable clothing rather than the tight military uniforms that fit the body. His scruffy appearance lent credibility to the nickname. Although Taylor earned his reputation fighting battles in the Indian wars, his victories in the Mexican War propelled him to the status of national hero.

As it had eight years earlier, the Whig Party selected a war hero as its candidate in 1848, in an attempt to quell the growing sectionalism that threatened to tear the nation apart. The Whigs hoped that Taylor's military record would attract Northern voters and his status as a

slaveholder would win over the South. When the South threatened to secede over the Compromise of 1850, Taylor, an ardent nationalist, threatened to lead the army himself to preserve the Union.

Q: Who was Zachary Taylor's wife?

A: Margaret Mackall Taylor was born into a prosperous and prominent Maryland planter family. On a visit to her sister in Kentucky in 1809, she met Lieutenant Taylor. After a short courtship, the couple married in June 1810. "Peggy" Taylor embarked on the life of a military spouse, enduring the hardships of remote frontier forts for the next forty years.

Peggy and Zachary had six children: one son and five daughters. Two daughters died of what Taylor called "a violent billious fever" when they were young children—a devastating blow to both parents. Although Peggy accompanied her husband to his military assignments whenever possible, she was determined that her four surviving children would have the best education available and sent them east for schooling. Yet, Peggy missed her children during their absences and was often lonely.

By the time her husband became president, Peggy was sixty-one years old. The

rigors of frontier life had debilitated her health, which deteriorated further during the White House years. Her condition, described as "delicate," did not permit her

Margaret Mackall Taylor

to participate in the formal social life of Washington, which held little appeal for her. Devoutly religious, she sometimes attended church services at Saint John's Episcopal Church across from the Executive Mansion. She spent most of her time in the family rooms on the second floor, a space she considered to be the center of her world. Surrounded by mementos, she welcomed her inner circle and entertained family, friends, and grandchildren. A close family friend, Varina Davis, recalled, "the most pleasant part of my visit to the White House [is] to be passed in Mrs. Taylor's bright pretty room, where the invalid full of interest in the passing show in which she has not the strength to take her part, talked most agreeably and kindly to the many friends admitted to her presence." Peggy was content to turn over the duties of hostess to her vivacious, twenty-five-year-old daughter, Betty Taylor Bliss.

Q: **To what historical figure was one of the Taylors' daughters married?**

A: At the age of sixteen, the Taylors' second daughter, Sarah Knox, known as Knox to her family, married Jefferson Davis. Taylor intensely disliked Davis, who had served under him in the Black Hawk War; therefore, the 1834 wedding took place with the Taylors' knowledge but without their blessing. After the wedding, Sarah and her mother kept in touch through letters, but a short three months later, both Sarah and Davis contracted malaria. Davis re-covered; Sarah died in her husband's arms. Davis later served with Taylor in the Mexican War, and the two men reconciled. After Davis married a second time, to Varina Howell, the Davis and Taylor families became intimate friends. In these antebellum years, Jefferson Davis, future president of the Confederate States of America, was a frequent White House guest.

Left: Few, if any, photos were taken of Peggy Taylor. This engraving is reported to be one of the rare images adapted from a photograph in a privately owned collection.

Below: Betty Taylor Bliss. "Miss Betty," as she was known to the press and public, filled her role as official hostess with poise and humor. One observer thought that her manner blended "the artlessness of a rustic belle and the grace of a duchess."

" **My wife was as much a soldier as I was.** "
—*Zachary Taylor*

Above: William Bliss and Zachary Taylor. During the Mexican War, Colonel Bliss was chief of staff to General Taylor. Noted for his efficiency, Bliss later served as the president's private secretary. Well-matched in popularity with his wife, Betty, the public found him cheerful and intelligent.

Taylor's beloved mount, Old Whitey, appears alongside the president in many depictions of him. Stories about "Old Zack" fighting side by side with his men and the relaxed way he sat atop Old Whitey while shots buzzed around his head quickly spread throughout the nation after the Battle of Buena Vista.

Q: **Whom did Taylor's other daughters marry?**

A: The Taylors' eldest daughter, Ann, married Robert Wood, a medical doctor who became a consulting physician to the president. The Wood family lived in Baltimore but frequently visited the White House with their four children. Robert and Ann's eldest son, John, who was eighteen when his grandfather was elected president, was a student at the Naval Academy. Bob, their younger son, who had resided with his grandparents before the White House years, was Zachary and Peggy's favorite grandchild. Taylor arranged an appointment for him at West Point. Becky, one of the Woods' daughters, lived at the White House when she was not in boarding school.

The Taylors' youngest daughter, Betty, married Colonel William Bliss, the president's longtime military aide. "Perfect Bliss," as he was called by family and friends because of his unflappable demeanor, managed Taylor's accounts and oversaw the White House, where he and Betty lived with their children. Bliss and the president were extremely close, and the Taylors were delighted with his marriage to their daughter.

Standing in for the ailing Peggy, Betty Bliss, who laughed easily, was a popular hostess. She entertained at elegant dinners twice a week on Wednesdays and Saturdays and held receptions on Tuesday and Friday afternoons, as well as Friday evenings. Weekly morning receptions and afternoon tea parties were part of the social whirl. Taylor's homespun manner and his decision to once again open the Executive Mansion to the people encouraged a crush of visitors to public receptions.

Q: **Who was "Old Whitey"?**

A: Old Whitey was Taylor's trusted horse from his military days. The same mount Taylor had ridden on his famous march through Mexico, Old Whitey went to the White House with the family. Now shaggy, he was turned loose to graze on the White House lawn, where he became a favorite with tourists, who admired him so much that they often snipped hanks of hair from his tail to keep as souvenirs.

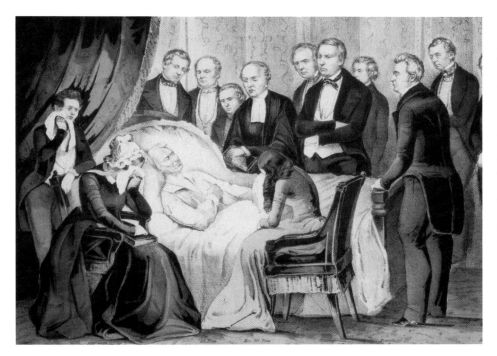

Death of General Zachary Taylor. His family gathered at the president's bedside when, after a sudden gastric illness, he died on July 9, 1850. His hysterical wife begged him not to leave her, repeating that he had survived far worse threats to his life on the battlefield. Too devastated to attend the East Room service, Peggy listened to the funeral dirges and drum marches while lying upstairs on her bed, shaking and sobbing with grief.

Q: How did Taylor's presidency end?

A: Taylor was the second president to die in office. In 1850, he participated in several Fourth of July celebrations, including breaking ground for the Washington Monument. There he sat for hours in the blistering sun listening to patriotic speeches. He returned to the White House ravenously hungry and consumed quarts of ripe cherries and iced milk. Later that evening, when he developed severe stomach cramps and a high fever, his son-in-law, Dr. Wood, was summoned from Baltimore. The Taylor family, including the Blisses and the Woods, and Jefferson and Varina Davis gathered in his bedroom. Taylor died five days later. Peggy Taylor and her daughters, overcome with grief, did not attend the funeral in the East Room.

Although the cause of death was officially listed as gastroenteritis, rumors circulated that the president had been poisoned by arsenic. Nearly 150 years after his death, a historian persuaded Taylor's descendants to allow his remains to be exhumed from a Louisville cemetery and analyzed by the Kentucky medical examiner. After reviewing the test results, the examiner concluded that the arsenic levels in hair and nail samples were far lower than they would have been if the president had been poisoned.

> **I have always done my duty. I am ready to die. My only regret is for the friends I leave behind me.**
> —*ZACHARY TAYLOR*

Millard and Abigail Fillmore

Right: Abigail Fillmore believed that women should work as hard as men to cultivate their minds. Her fragile health kept her from fulfilling many of her hostessing duties, but she brought culture to the White House, founding its first library and also entertaining authors and musicians, including singer Jenny Lind, who found the Fillmores intelligent and unpretentious.

Below: The Fillmores' outgoing daughter, Mary Abigail, took over many of the ailing first lady's duties. A talented musician, Abby played the piano and the harp, which she brought with her to the White House.

Q: Who were the Fillmores?

A: Fillmore's son, Millard Powers, called Powers, studied law at Cambridge before moving into the White House to work as his father's official private secretary. Fillmore's daughter, Mary Abigail, known as Abby, also lived in the White House after her graduation from boarding school, where she studied to be a teacher. Fluent in German, French, and Spanish, Abby was also musically gifted and entertained family and guests by playing her harp. The president's father, Nathaniel, known as "Old Nate" by the press, did not live in the White House, but earns a footnote in history as the first father to visit his son as president. He received guests with the Fillmores at one of their weekly receptions. At eighty years old, he appeared a wonder of health, tall and straight, with a thick head of white hair. Old Nate was not impressed with the White House,

however, complaining, "I don't like it here, it isn't a good place to live; it isn't a good place for Millard. I wish he was at home in Buffalo!"

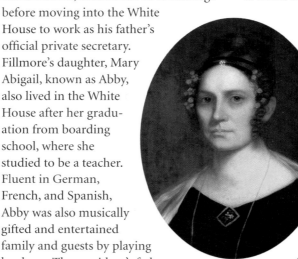

Abigail Powers Fillmore

Q: Who was the first lady?

A: Abigail Powers Fillmore was from western New York State. She and Fillmore met in their late teens while he was briefly her student. They were drawn together by their mutual love of books and learning, a passion and intellectual partnership they shared throughout their lives. The first of the first ladies to continue working after marriage, Abigail nonetheless took an active interest in Millard's political career and was well informed on political topics. Like many women of her era, however, she kept her politics private when advising her husband.

By the time Fillmore assumed the presidency, Abigail was in precarious health, suffering from an array of ailments: a persistent cough, back and hip problems attributed to rheumatism, and an ankle injury that had never healed properly and kept her from standing or walking for long periods. Citing delicate health, she turned over many of her social duties to her teenage daughter, Abby. Because the first lady, the daughter of a Baptist minister, did not approve of drinking, the Fillmore administration was "dry." The Fillmores nonetheless entertained regularly, holding weekly morning receptions and Friday-evening levees. They gave large dinners for thirty-six every Thursday evening and smaller dinners on Saturdays. Abby often presided at these social events.

Q: For what White House innovation is Abigail best remembered?

A: The Fillmores' personal library boasted more than four thousand books, and the intellectual Abigail was astonished to find that the White House had no library. Appalled, she persuaded her husband to prod Congress for an appropriation to create one. With the $2,000 Congress provided, she turned the oval room in the family quarters into a library and stocked the newly built shelves with the Bible, Shakespeare, a ten-volume set of American biographies, Burns, reference works on anatomy, law, astronomy, and histories of the world. The Fillmores entertained family and friends in this comfortable room, which also housed Abigail's piano and Abby's harp.

Millard Fillmore

The first lady sought to make the White House a place of culture and invited authors Washington Irving and William Thackeray to state receptions. When the musical Abigail was enchanted by Jenny Lind during the singer's Washington performance, she also invited the "Swedish Nightingale" to dinner at the White House.

Q: What tragedies followed Millard Fillmore into private life?

A: Fillmore was bitterly disappointed when he did not receive his party's nomination for a second term. The day of Franklin Pierce's inauguration was bitterly cold and snowy. At her husband's side throughout the outdoor ceremony, Abigail became thoroughly chilled. She developed bronchial pneumonia and died in the Willard Hotel on March 30, 1853. Her body remained at the Willard until the former president accompanied her coffin on the train home to Buffalo for burial. A little more than a year later, he suffered another terrible loss when Abby died suddenly of cholera. Fillmore sought happiness in a second marriage to a widow, Caroline McIntosh, in 1858.

Above: Caroline McIntosh was a wealthy, childless widow before her marriage to Fillmore.

Left: A man without great political achievements, Fillmore was a lawyer in Buffalo, and then held state offices and served eight years in the U.S. House of Representatives before becoming president after the unexpected death of Zachary Taylor.

> **Nothing brings out the lower traits of human nature like office-seeking. Men of good character and impulses are betrayed by it into all sorts of meanness.**
> —MILLARD FILLMORE

Franklin and Jane Pierce

Q: Why was Pierce another "dark horse" presidential candidate?

A: New Hampshire's Franklin Pierce had been a promising politician, a successful lawyer, congressman, senator, and general in the Mexican War. His wife, Jane Appleton Pierce, disliked both politics and Washington. She particularly disliked her husband's heavy drinking when in the company of other politicians. Although she accompanied her husband to Washington when he was elected to the Senate, she made clear her preference that he find another profession. After completing his senatorial term in 1842, Pierce retired from public office and resumed law practice. Although he remained active in the Democratic Party, he held no public office, making him an unlikely candidate for his party's nomination. After forty-nine ballots, however, with no clear favorite emerging, the Democrats nominated Pierce as a "dark horse" compromise candidate.

Q: What tragedy confirmed Jane Pierce's loathing of politics?

A: Jane, always in frail health, had enjoyed a happy period in her marriage while her husband practiced law. Despite losing two small sons, one at three days old, the other at four years old, she delighted in rearing their third son, Benjamin. She hoped that her husband would never again return to politics. Pierce, while secretly courting the presidency, had greatly minimized the likelihood of his nomination at the convention. When news of his nomination arrived, Jane fainted. She spent the campaign days praying for his defeat.

After Franklin's unlikely election, the Pierce family visited relatives in Massachusetts over the holidays before moving into the White House. On January 6, 1853, they boarded a train to New Hampshire, but after traveling only a short distance the train derailed. Although Franklin and Jane were uninjured, eleven-year-old Benny was crushed in the wreckage. He died before their eyes. This disaster dealt a terrible blow to both parents, but Jane never recovered. Morbidly religious, she swung between the conviction that Benny's death was God's retribution for their return to politics and the belief that God had taken Benny

Jane Pierce

Above: Franklin Pierce. Despite their state of mourning during much of their time in the White House, the Pierces updated the mansion, including a furnace, a tile-covered bathroom with hot and cold running water, ornate mirrors (still in use) and handsome china.

Right: Jane Pierce was a shy, reclusive woman, prone to morbid depressions. She never supported Franklin's political career nor was she able to mingle easily in society.

> " I hope he won't be elected for I should not like to be at Washington and I know you would not either. "
> —*BENNY PIERCE, IN A LETTER TO JANE*

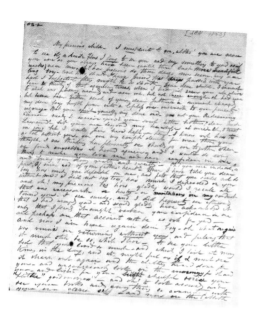

to remove any distraction to her husband's presidency. The already-fragile Jane sank into a severe depression that clouded the rest of her life.

In deference to the Pierces' loss, the inaugural balls were canceled. Taking refuge in her overwhelming grief, the first lady was in deep mourning during her first year in the White House. She secluded herself upstairs in the mansion, often writing letters to her dead son.

Q: Who helped the president and first lady in the White House?

A: After a year of seclusion, Jane began to receive guests at Friday afternoon receptions and joined her husband at official dinners. Until then, the president entertained at state dinners, either alone or joined by Jane's girlhood friend and aunt by marriage, Abigail Kent Means.

Abby helped soothe Jane's crippling grief and bolster her debilitated health. In the family quarters, the Pierces hosted a large group of family on whom they relied. Pierce's brother, Henry, visited, as did his nephews, Frank and Kirk. Jane's sisters, Mary Aiken and Elizabeth Packard, visited with their husbands and children. Jane's aunt Mary Mason, with her husband, Jeremiah, came to the White House with their two children. Sisters, aunts, uncles, nieces, and nephews provided assistance and much-needed solace.

Pierce was in the constant company of his private secretary, Sidney Webster, a young man in his early twenties who had read law in Pierce's Concord office. Among a group of young lawyers who had promoted Pierce's candidacy, Webster became his indispensable assistant.

Above left: Front of letter, dated January 23, 1853, from Jane Pierce to her dead son Benny. Benny was killed in a train accident only days before his father's inauguration as president.

Below: *The President's Levee at the White House.* The March 11, 1854, issue of *Gleason's Pictorial* illustrated a scene from Franklin Pierce's somber inaugural reception.

James Buchanan

Q: What factors made James Buchanan an attractive candidate for the presidency?

A: James Buchanan had been a successful lawyer and had served as a congressman and senator from Pennsylvania. He had also served as James Polk's secretary of state and had enjoyed a distinguished diplomatic career as U.S. minister to Russia and Great Britain. His absence from the country while minister to Great Britain had exempted him from participation in the vitriolic sectional debates of the 1850s. The Democratic Party hoped Buchanan would attract votes from both sections that would produce victory. But as president, Buchanan is deemed a failure, overwhelmed by the forces impelling the nation toward a bitter civil war.

Above: While in his twenties, Buchanan became engaged to Ann Caroline Coleman, the daughter of a wealthy iron manufacturer. When she committed suicide just several days after abruptly breaking off their engagement, Buchanan vowed never to marry.

Above: Harriet filled the White House with gaiety, a welcome relief from the sadness of the Pierce administration.

Q: Who was the only bachelor president of the United States?

A: James Buchanan was the nation's only unmarried president, remaining a bachelor throughout his life. In the absence of a wife, the president's niece Harriet Lane acted as official White House hostess. Harriet was the daughter of Buchanan's sister, Jane. Both Jane and her husband had died by the time Harriet was eleven years old. She and her younger brother, Elliott, were raised by Buchanan, who treated his wards as if they were his own children. Harriet received an excellent education at the Georgetown Visitation Convent school while Buchanan served as secretary of state under Polk, but she was more interested in and influenced by the education she received in Washington society and at the Court of Saint James's when her uncle served as minister to Great Britain. The "school" of society trained her well to perform the duties of first lady.

Harriet Lane

Q: What member of the Buchanan family died in the White House?

A: As was the custom of presidents-elect, Buchanan arrived in Washington prior to the inaugural festivities. While staying at the National Hotel, he and nephew Elliot fell deathly ill. Their condition, dubbed the "National Hotel disease," was caused by bacteria carried by rats in the hotel's water system. Buchanan

was still quite sick during the inaugural ceremonies and was forced to forgo any public reception at the White House. The malady persisted for six weeks. Elliott appeared to recover from the dysentery-like disease by April, but had a sudden relapse and died. The loss stunned both the president and Harriet.

Q: What other family members lived at the White House?

A: Buchanan came from a large family that included ten brothers and sisters; the president had twenty-two nieces and nephews and fifteen grandnieces and grandnephews. Along with Harriet and Elliot, another orphaned nephew, James Buchanan Henry, or "Buck" as he was known, was the president's private secretary. Buchanan was a strict disciplinarian who demanded that his nephew, by then a Princeton graduate, eat his vegetables. Buck, who managed the president's finances and all his presidential correspondence, felt incessantly watched by his uncle. When Buchanan forbade him to grow a mustache, it was the last straw. Buck quit his job, married, and moved to New York to practice law. After Buck left the White House, still another nephew, James Buchanan II, replaced him as the president's secretary.

Above: James Buchanan Henry. Buchanan's nephew Buck was the first presidential secretary to earn a federal salary.

Above left: In 1858, *Harper's Weekly* printed this depiction of a presidential reception at the White House. Harriet Lane guided its social life with enthusiasm and discretion.

"Public policy clearly indicates the propriety and desirability of the President's private secretary being . . . a blood relation, upon the ground that the honor and interests of the President . . . can be most safely entrusted to one having an interest in his good name and fame, and therefore more guarded against temptation of any kind."

—*James Buchanan Henry*

Q: How did Harriet perform her duties as first lady?

A: At twenty-six, Buchanan's "mischievous romp of a niece" had been well trained as a society belle, in the fashionable circles of both Washington and London. Considered beautiful by the standards of the day, Harriet had mounds of fair hair and porcelain skin. She had many suitors while in the White House but rejected them all. Her vivaciousness and gaiety, as well as her social acumen and tact, combined to make her an extraordinary presidential hostess.

Despite the growing divide in the nation and impending civil war, White House social life was a whirl of regal style and glittering dinner parties and receptions. Harriet became the nation's darling and was hailed in the press as "our Democratic Queen." She hosted elegant state dinners, which were held once a week. The dinners for forty, to which Supreme Court justices, the diplomatic corps, and noted visitors from home and abroad were invited, were presented in the style of a European court. In addition, Harriet sent out invitations in her own name to daytime receptions and teas. She and several women friends would pose in tableau, holding large bouquets of flowers, reminiscent of previous youthful first ladies. Harriet also wanted to host balls, but Buchanan declined them, thinking that much of the country considered dancing at the White House sinful.

Q: What special visits marked the Buchanan administration?

A: The first special occasion occurred in May 1860, when a large delegation of Japanese dignitaries visited the White House for the signing of the first commercial treaty with a nation of the Far East. Harriet wrote to a friend about the visit, "They are really a curiosity. All the women seem to run daft about them." The dignitaries brought to the White House an entire roomful of gifts, which were placed on display to the public. They included "saddles beautifully embroidered and embossed with gold and silver, bed curtains and screens, two princely swords, kimonos, lacquered ware, writing cases and a superb tea set with pearls and gold."

Far right: The press eagerly followed the itinerary of the Prince of Wales during his October 1860 visit to the United States.

Below: The president and Harriet inspect some of the gifts presented to the White House by the Japanese delegation. The magnificent display included swords, saddles, textiles, and furniture.

" From the semi-official position which she has so long sustained with so much honor to herself and credit to her country, [she] may be justly termed the first lady in the land. "

—FRANK LESLIE'S ILLUSTRATED NEWSPAPER, ABOUT HARRIET LANE

HARPER'S WEEKLY.
JOURNAL OF CIVILIZATION.
VOL. IV.—No. 197.]   NEW YORK, SATURDAY, OCTOBER 6, 1860.   [PRICE FIVE CENTS.

HIS ROYAL HIGHNESS ALBERT EDWARD, PRINCE OF WALES.—[FROM A RECENT PHOTOGRAPH.]

Harriet's crowning social achievement was the visit of Albert Edward, the nineteen-year-old Prince of Wales (later King Edward VII of Great Britain). An elegant dinner was prepared with card games afterward, a first in the Buchanan White House. Harriet arranged a boat trip down the Potomac River aboard the Coast Guard cutter *Harriet Lane* to Mount Vernon for a wreath laying at George Washington's grave, a high point of the prince's Washington visit.

Q: How did Buchanan deal with the impending Civil War?

A: The president and his cabinet could produce no decisive course to forestall the war. As his administration drew to a close and the election of Abraham Lincoln, a Republican, appeared inevitable, Southern states began to seize federal property. Buchanan's attempts to resupply federal forts were met by hostility, but he was reluctant to use military force. While denying that states had the legal right to secede, he held that the federal government could not legally prevent them. His vacillation continued until he left office, as Southern states began to secede from the Union.

Q: What happened to Harriet Lane after her White House years?

A: At thirty-six, Harriet Lane married a prominent Baltimore banker, Henry Elliott Johnston, in January 1866. The couple had two sons. The elder son, James Buchanan, died in 1881, and the second son, Henry Elliott, died in 1882. Her husband died in 1884. A wealthy widow, Harriet was an art collector and philanthropist. After her death, she bequeathed her art collection to the Smithsonian Institution, where it became the core collection of the Smithsonian American Art Museum (formerly the National Collection of Fine Arts). She also left a large sum to endow a pediatric facility specializing in children's diseases to the Johns Hopkins University Hospital in Baltimore. The Harriet Lane Clinics at Johns Hopkins serve thousands of children today and are part of the Children's Miracle Network, a national consortium of pediatric hospitals.

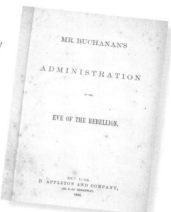

MR. BUCHANAN'S
ADMINISTRATION
ON THE
EVE OF THE REBELLION.

NEW YORK:
D. APPLETON AND COMPANY,
443 & 445 BROADWAY.
1866.

Above: After his 1856 election, hopes ran high that James Buchanan would maintain the nation's unity. He failed entirely. In 1866, he published the first presidential memoir, in part to justify his place in history.

Below: In her later years, Harriet Lane turned to philanthropy, including the endowment of a pediatric facility at Johns Hopkins University Hospital.

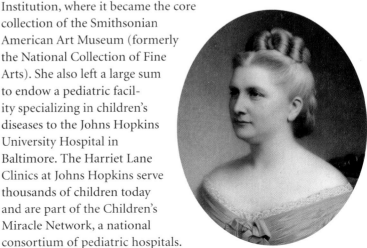

CHAPTER 5

CIVIL WAR AND RECONSTRUCTION

The four presidential administrations from Abraham Lincoln through Rutherford B. Hayes confronted the greatest threats that the United States has ever faced: civil war and disunion. From 1861 through the 1880s, the public and private lives of White House families revolved around winning the war, preserving the Union, and "reconstructing" Southern society and its shattered economy.

Mary Todd Lincoln, vilified as a spy and a traitor because of her Southern family, lost her husband to the Civil War, which first absorbed his time and his energy, and then ultimately cost him his life. Andrew Johnson's attempt to follow Lincoln's conciliatory policy toward the South angered Congress, which retaliated by impeaching him. Although he was acquitted, his power was effectively diminished. Ulysses S. Grant allied himself with the Radical Republican Congress and its wealthy backers, assuring himself two presidential terms and national acclaim. Another Republican president followed him, Rutherford B. Hayes, who won a hotly contested election through an unsavory political "deal" reached by a congressional electoral commission, but who nevertheless ended military occupation of the South.

Above: On April 12, 1861, Confederate batteries opened fire on Fort Sumter in Charleston Harbor, the opening salvo of the bitter Civil War.

Left: The 1876 Centennial Exhibition in Philadelphia was designed to introduce the United States as a new industrial power, soon to eclipse the might and production of every other industrialized nation.

Abraham and Mary Todd Lincoln

Q: What was Lincoln's background?

A: Born into frontier poverty in Kentucky on February 12, 1809, Lincoln

lost his mother, Nancy Hanks, during his childhood. He struggled to gain a rudimentary education and worked on a farm, split rails for fences, and clerked in a store. After studying law, he rode the court circuit in Illinois as a frontier lawyer and served eight years in the state legislature. He gained national prominence in 1858 as a Republican senatorial candidate against Stephen A. Douglas. After their famous Lincoln-Douglas debates over the extension of slavery, Lincoln lost the election but gained a national reputation that favored his presidential nomination in the 1860 campaign. Lincoln's election triggered the secession of Southern states from the Union and civil war.

Despite his rise to the nation's highest position, Lincoln was prone to introspection and self-doubt, struggling with debilitating bouts of depression throughout his life, a struggle that may have contributed to his empathy and compassion as president.

Q: Who was Lincoln's first lady?

A: Mary Todd, born on December 13, 1818, was the daughter of a wealthy and socially prominent slaveholding family

Above: During the campaign, the Republicans dubbed Lincoln the "Rail Splitter" to emphasize the power of "free labor," whereby a common farm boy could work his way to the top by his own efforts.

Right: Although Mary Lincoln was an ardent Unionist, she was suspected of supplying secret information to the Confederacy because she had been born in the South and her brothers and male family members served in the Confederate military.

in Lexington, Kentucky. Her mother died when Mary was six years old, and her father's remarriage to Elizabeth Humphreys brought into the family a stepmother whom Mary and her older sisters despised. With half-siblings being born in rapid succession, Mary felt lost in the family shuffle, engendering in her lifelong insecurities. She received an excellent education, but after her teenage years she moved to Springfield, Illinois, to live with her sister Elizabeth and brother-in-law Ninian Edwards. In the state capital, where lawyers and legislators abounded, Mary was a belle with many suitors. She chose Lincoln and, after a stormy courtship that included a broken engagement, married him at her sister's home in November 1842.

Mary Lincoln was an emotionally volatile woman. Modern scholars speculate that she suffered from bipolar disorder, a condition that would have been aggravated by the staggering series of losses of those she loved.

Q: How did Lincoln's "frontier" image affect the presidential couple?

A: Lincoln's campaign portrayed him as the rough and ready frontiersman, born in a log cabin, a rail splitter and an Indian fighter. This frontier image of a self-made man of the people, a rugged individualist who could handle any difficulty, was enhancing for a politician, but for his female partner such an image was deadly. To a Victorian-era public it suggested an unrefined, ignorant, corncob-pipe smoking woman—the antithesis of the qualities Americans sought in a "lady," especially a president's wife. Vilified as uncouth even before her arrival in the capital, Mary was the object of scorn among Washington society leaders.

Broadcloth coat, part of Lincoln's office suit. His contemporaries often commented on his "un-statesmanlike" appearance, although he rarely gave notice to what he wore. At his 1860 appearance at New York's Cooper Union, one observer noted: "At first sight there was nothing impressive or imposing about him; his clothes hung awkwardly on his giant frame."

The Lincolns greet Union generals, cabinet members, and others at an 1865 reception. Mary sought to counter her frontier image with elegant entertainments.

> " They say Mrs. L. is awfully western, loud and unrefined. "
> —HARRIET LANE, ABOUT MARY LINCOLN

Q: How did Mary seek to establish herself as leader of Washington society?

A: Mary understood that Washington society watched carefully and judged critically. Her tenure as first lady was one of well-meant intentions versus negative public perceptions. To dispel notions that she lacked social grace, she attempted to establish herself as the premiere hostess of the nation's capital. Taking cues from her predecessors, whose social entertainments were often displays of political power, Mary engaged New York catering firms to create lavish presentations meant to highlight the prestige of the presidency at a turning point in history. But her elaborate displays were perceived as self-aggrandizing, and worse; many felt she displayed a callous disregard for the fighting and dying men on the battlefield. In declining an invitation to the White House, Senator Benjamin Wade angrily responded, "Are the President and Mrs. Lincoln aware that there is a Civil War?" Yet, when she curtailed entertaining, she was attacked for *not* upholding the prestige of the presidency.

Perhaps to camouflage her insecurity and counter critics who regarded her as provincial, Mary dressed extrava-

gantly. Her notorious shopping sprees in New York were criticized by the press. She hired Elizabeth "Lizzie" Keckly, a talented African American designer, seamstress, and former slave who had purchased her own freedom, to create exquisite gowns for her. "I must dress in costly materials. The people scrutinize every article that I wear with critical curiosity," she said.

Q: In what state did the Lincolns find the White House?

A: Mary was shocked at the shabby condition of the White House, where she found broken furniture, peeling wallpaper, and soiled rugs. The president, keenly aware of the symbolic power of presidential style, also understood the symbolism of fine public buildings. In ordering the completion of the Capitol, he stated, "If people see the Capitol go on, they will know the Union will go on." Similarly, he wanted the Executive Mansion to look its best—another public statement that the nation would survive. With this in mind, Mary began to refurbish the mansion in splendid style. On shopping trips to New York and Philadelphia, she purchased furniture with abandon, greatly overspending the congressional appropriation. She then intrigued with the commissioner of public buildings and others to cover up the expenses in other government accounts. When her husband found out,

Elizabeth Keckly's soft-spoken, upbeat manner calmed the first lady in moments of crisis. In 1868, Keckly published *Behind the Scenes, or Thirty Years a Slave, and Four Years in the White House*. In the preface, she said she wrote the book to place Mary in a better public light, but divulged behind-the-scenes confidences of the Lincolns. Mary, feeling betrayed by her closest friend, never saw her again.

he was infuriated. Word leaked out to the press of her outrageous spending, and of her husband's anger, further damaging her reputation.

Q: Who made up the Lincoln "family" in the White House?

A: The Lincolns had four sons. Three sons accompanied them to the White House: Robert Todd, born in 1843; William Wallace ("Willie"), born in 1850; and Thomas ("Tad"), born in 1853. Their second son, Edward, born in 1846, had died of tuberculosis when he was three. Robert spent most of his father's White House years studying at Harvard. After graduation he entered the army, assigned as a member of General Ulysses S. Grant's staff. Lincoln's two private secretaries, John G. Nicolay and John Hay, although adults,

were like sons and companions to him, and both had bedrooms in the family quarters. Because of wartime emergencies, they were on call at all times. Lincoln would sometimes wake in the night, seek them out in their rooms, and talk or read poetry with them until he was able to fall back to sleep. Nicolay and Hay did not dine with the family; they instead took their meals at the nearby Willard Hotel.

As time passed, Elizabeth Keckly became far more to Mary Lincoln than a dressmaker. Although she did not live at the White House, Keckly was often there to attend to Mary's clothes. She became Mary's best friend and confidante during the presidential years, and Mary came to consider her one of the family.

The Lincoln family in 1861. Abraham and Mary seated at a table with their three sons: Robert, standing; Willie seated center; and Tad, on his father's lap. Robert, the only surviving son, enjoyed a successful career as secretary of war in the Garfield administration and as an executive for the Pullman railroad.

Lincoln shown seated between John G. Nicolay and John Hay. Lincoln's two private secretaries kept extensive notes and letters that have proved invaluable sources of information on life in the Lincoln White House.

> **Marriage is neither heaven nor hell, it is simply purgatory.**
> —*ABRAHAM LINCOLN*

Q: What family member died during the White House years?

A: The Lincolns' son Willie, then eleven years old, was stricken by what was diagnosed as a "bilious fever," probably typhoid. Both Willie and Tad were ill for several weeks as their parents frantically nursed them. Willie was the favorite of both Abraham and Mary, a precocious, likable, sensitive boy. His death on February 20, 1862, devastated them. Lincoln retreated to John Nicolay's office, where he broke down and wept. Mary was carried to her bedroom, suffering what Elizabeth Keckly called "paroxysms of grief." Willie's funeral was held in the East Room on February 24, with government and military officials in attendance. His coffin was placed in a temporary repository in Washington. Sometimes on his carriage rides, Lincoln would visit the tomb, lift the lid of the casket, and gaze at his son's face. Mary never really recovered from the loss of Willie.

Above: William Wallace "Willie" Lincoln, the Lincolns' third son, died in 1862 at the age of eleven. Julia Taft, a childhood friend of the Lincoln children, described Willie as "the most lovable boy I ever knew, bright, sensible, sweet-tempered and gentle-mannered."

Right: Lincoln with his son Tad. Tad was known as the mischievous Lincoln boy, and after Willie's death his parents indulged him. The president's secretary, John Hay, wrote, "He had a very bad opinion of books and no opinion of discipline."

Q: What characterized Tad Lincoln's life in the White House?

A: Both of his parents became more attached to Tad after Willie's death, and Tad and the president became almost inseparable. Perhaps fearing that another child would be lost, the president and first lady hesitated to discipline him. He had the run of the mansion, bursting in on the cabinet and interrupting meetings by tapping three times on the door.

Lincoln always responded because, he said, he had vowed never to go back on "the code." Tad loved to play soldier, so the secretary of war commissioned him as a "Union lieutenant," complete with his own miniature uniform. On one occasion, Tad hitched his pet goat to a dining room chair and trotted into a state room where his mother was entertaining guests.

The indulgent parents were amused by his antics, which provided them relief from the grim realities of war. "Let him romp," Lincoln insisted. Although Willie and Tad were tutored privately in the mansion (probably as a security precaution), there is evidence that Tad had a learning disability. Elizabeth Keckly noted in her behind-the-scenes book that, at almost twelve years of age, Tad had great difficulty reading and was hindered by a speech impediment. After Lincoln's assassination, Tad proved to be his mother's only comfort. His unfortunate death from tuberculosis at the age of eighteen was the final blow in Mary Lincoln's tragic life.

Just after the close of the Civil War, the Lincolns attended a special performance of the comedy *Our American Cousin*, at Ford's Theater accompanied by a twenty-eight year-old officer named Major Henry R. Rathbone, and Rathbone's fiancée, Clara Harris. As the group watched the play below, John Wilkes Booth stepped into the presidential box, aimed a Deringer pistol, and fired, mortally wounding the president.

Q: **What was the ultimate tragedy of the Lincoln years?**

A: On Good Friday, April 14, 1865, the Civil War had just ended and the Lincolns were to celebrate and relax by attending the comedy *Our American Cousin* at Ford's Theater in Washington. As they watched the play, the renowned actor John Wilkes Booth, a Southern sympathizer, entered the presidential box and shot Lincoln in the back of the head at near point-blank range. Booth then struggled with Henry Rathbone, one of the Lincolns' companions that evening, before jumping eleven feet to the stage below, reportedly shouting, *"Sic semper tyrannis!"* (Thus always to tyrants). Although Booth reportedly snapped the fibula bone in his left leg just above the ankle, everything happened so fast that no one had time to stop him from escaping the crowded theater. The mortally wounded president was carried across the street to William Petersen's boardinghouse, where he died at 7:21 the next morning. Mary, hysterical with grief, had to be escorted from the room.

Lincoln's body was taken first to the White House, where it lay in state until the funeral on April 19; it was then taken to the Capitol rotunda to lie in state until April 20. On April 21 his body was placed on a funeral train that passed through many Northern and Midwestern cities, where elaborate mourning ceremonies were staged. The journey to Lincoln's final resting place in Springfield, Illinois, took twelve days.

Lincoln's top hat, worn the night he was shot.

> **Now he belongs to the ages.**
> — *SECRETARY OF WAR EDWIN M. STANTON,*
> *UPON LINCOLN'S DEATH*

Andrew and Eliza Johnson

Q: How did Andrew Johnson become president?

A: Andrew Johnson was vice president during Lincoln's second term and became president upon Lincoln's assassination. Johnson took the oath of office in the parlor of the Kirkwood House, a hotel on Pennsylvania Avenue, at 10 A.M. on April 15, 1865, the day Lincoln died. The government feared that there was a plot to kill other members of Lincoln's administration, and rushed to swear in the new president as quickly as possible. Johnson, who was boarding at the Kirkwood House, accepted an offer from Congressman Samuel Hooper to live in his house on Massachusetts Avenue until Mary Lincoln and her sons vacated the White House. While he waited for the grief-stricken widow to move, the new president set up his offices in the Treasury Department and began to recruit a staff. It was not until June 9, 1865, that Johnson moved into the mansion.

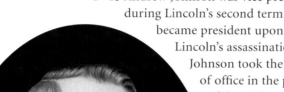

Above: Andrew Johnson was a self-educated man of humble origin. Upon his nomination as the vice-presidential candidate in 1864, *Harper's Weekly* wrote favorably that, "'Andy' Johnson, like Mr. Lincoln, is emphatically a self-made man."

Right: Ticket to Andrew Johnson's 1868 Senate impeachment trial.

Q: What political "first" occurred during the Johnson presidency?

A: Throughout his presidency, Johnson was locked in a fierce political battle with the Radical Republican Congress, elected while Southern states were out of the Union. The central issues were how to bring the South back into the Union and how to deal with the newly freed slaves—and whether the policies would be carried out in a spirit of reconciliation or of retribution. Johnson followed Lincoln's conciliatory plan for reunion. Radical Republicans believed the South could not be "reconstructed" without harsh measures. After Johnson's veto of reconstruction measures, Congress retaliated by passing the Tenure of Office Act, which restricted Johnson's power to dismiss cabinet members without the Senate's consent. When Johnson dismissed Secretary of War Edwin M. Stanton in February 1868, Congress impeached him for "high crimes and misdemeanors."

U.S. SENATE
Impeachment of President
ADMIT THE BEARER
APRIL 17TH 1868.
GALLERY.
Geo. T. Brown
Sergeant-at-Arms

> **I feel incompetent to perform duties . . . which have been so unexpectedly thrown upon me.**
>
> —*ANDREW JOHNSON*

Left: The ladies' gallery of the Senate during the impeachment trial. Spectators jostled each other to get a glimpse of the historic proceedings. Andrew Johnson was the first president to be impeached, and the only one until Bill Clinton 130 years later. Both presidents were acquitted.

Below: Rumors persist that Eliza Johnson taught Andrew to read and write. She acknowledged that she had encouraged his education, but maintained that he "was an apt scholar and acquired all the rest for himself."

The public clamored for tickets to the Senate trial to watch the political drama. Johnson was acquitted by one vote. He remained president and considered the outcome a victory for presidential authority, but he was virtually without power. Congress passed a series of harsh reconstruction measures and divided the South into five districts occupied by the military as a conquered nation.

Q: Who was Andrew Johnson's wife?

A: Eliza McCardle met Andrew Johnson when he arrived in her hometown of Greeneville, Tennessee, from Raleigh, North Carolina, to set up his own tailoring business. Eliza and Andrew married in May 1827, when she was only sixteen and he just eighteen years old. While rearing their family of five children, she also helped him hone his oratorical skills as he rose in his political career. Before the Civil War, Eliza developed tuberculosis, and the hardships brought on by the conflict further weakened her. By the time of her husband's presidency, her health had deteriorated, and, as had several first ladies before her, she relinquished her hostessing duties to a daughter. Nonetheless, she participated actively in family life from the rooms on the White House second floor and was a source of constant support for her husband during his impeachment.

Eliza McCardle Johnson

Q: Who made up the Johnsons' White House family?

A: Andrew and Eliza enjoyed the company of a large family, which included their daughter Martha Johnson Patterson, her husband, Tennessee senator David Patterson, and their two children, Mary Belle and Andrew; the couple's younger widowed daughter, Mary Johnson Stover, and her three children, Lillie, Sarah, and Andrew; and the Johnsons' youngest son, Andrew. Johnson had chosen William Browning as his secretary, a man who had served him ably as vice president. But when Browning died unexpectedly, Johnson asked his thirty-three-year-old son and favorite child, Robert, to act as secretary. This was a problematic choice because Robert had a serious drinking habit. Although he performed his professional duties well, rumors of his drinking binges circulated around Washington and reached the ears of the president. Robert, a former colonel in the Union forces, died four weeks after his father's term ended.

Above right: The Stover children, Andrew, Lillie, and Sarah.

Below left: Mary Belle Patterson.

Below right: Andrew J. Patterson. The Johnsons' five grandchildren were schooled in a basement room of the White House, and took dancing lessons at Washington's famed Marini Dancing Academy. They were the center of attention at the special "juvenile soiree" at the White House on Johnson's sixtieth birthday party.

The president was devoted to his grandchildren and would watch them play on the South Lawn, permit them to interrupt business in his office, take them on picnics in Washington's Rock Creek Park, and tell them bedtime stories in the evening. The cramped family quarters and lack of privacy on the second floor of the mansion did not seem to bother this close-knit family. The grandchildren, who attended school in one of the basement rooms of the mansion, would scamper to their grandmother's room after classes ended to play and talk with her.

Q: Who was President Johnson's official hostess in the White House?

A: Although both of Johnson's daughters acted as hostesses, Martha Patterson assumed responsibility for entertaining and managing the household. Martha had attended the Georgetown Visitation

Convent school in Washington while her father served in Congress. The Polks and Andrew Johnson were fellow Tennessee politicians, and Sarah Polk had often invited Martha to spend weekends at the White House and participate in its social events. These experiences were helpful in Martha's new role as hostess.

Despite the ugly political battle between the president and Congress, the Johnson family continued entertaining socially and maintained a cheerful and united front for the public. Martha and her sister, Mary, held public receptions every Monday afternoon, and the president held levees twice a month during the winter social season. The Johnsons also held three or four state dinners a month for approximately forty guests on Tuesday evenings in the State Dining Room. Professional chefs, butlers, and waiters were hired for these occasions.

Martha Patterson

Q: What special parties marked the Johnson administration?

A: In August 1866, the Johnsons held a special dinner for Queen Emma, widow of King Kamehameha IV of the kingdom of Hawaii. After dinner, the White House was opened to the public so that all who

wanted to greet the queen could do so. The dinner was made more notable because it was one of only two official events that Eliza attended while in the White House.

The other spectacular event was the president's sixtieth birthday party on December 29, 1868. Knowing her father's love of children, Martha planned a "juvenile soiree," the first children's ball held in the White House. The president greeted his four hundred young guests in the Blue Room, which one observer commented "looked like a fairyland." Dancing in the East Room was led by the Marini Dancing Academy and included the Highland fling, the Spanish fandango, the Virginia reel, and polkas, waltzes, and square dances. Afterward, the children enjoyed "gorgeous refreshments of ice cream and cakes and beautiful glace fruits." According to Johnson's account books, the party cost $450, more than the typical state dinner.

As acting first lady, Martha Patterson oversaw a refurbishing of the White House, which had been vandalized during Mary Lincoln's months-long seclusion after the assassination. Martha brought the long-forgotten portraits of former presidents out of storage and displayed them on the ground floor.

Queen Emma. Eliza Johnson made only two public appearances during her husband's term of office—one at a reception for Queen Emma, widow of Alexander Liholiho, who ruled the kingdom of Hawaii as Kamehameha IV.

> "We are plain people, from the mountains of Tennessee, called here for a short time by a national calamity. I trust too much will not be expected of us."
>
> —MARTHA PATTERSON

Ulysses and Julia Dent Grant

Ulysses S. Grant was born in 1822, the son of an Ohio leather tanner. After attending West Point he was assigned to a series of army posts, and fought in the Mexican War. After fifteen years of service, he resigned from the army, but at the outbreak of the Civil War, he rejoined. He rose quickly to the rank of general and, in 1864, Lincoln appointed him general-in-chief of the Union army.

Q: How did Ulysses S. Grant become president?

A: "Let Us Have Peace," Grant's famous post–Civil War phrase, became a national motto. As general-in-chief of the armies of the United States, Grant personified the victorious Union. During the Johnson administration, he had aligned himself with the Radical Republican Congress in taking stringent reconstruction measures in the South. His belief that the elected representatives in Congress were the ultimate expression of the people's will made him the logical choice as the Republican candidate. He was swept into office on a tide of

After so many years of hardship and stress as the wife of an army officer, Julia Grant rejoiced in her husband's renown as a victorious general. As first lady, she entertained extensively, and her White House tenure was marked by Gilded Age splendor.

euphoria, hailed as the hero who won the war and preserved the Union. At forty-six, Grant was the youngest man elected to the presidency during the nineteenth century.

Q: Who was Grant's first lady?

A: His wife, Julia Dent, served as first lady, a role she clearly relished. Julia met the future president in 1844 when he visited her family's home, White Haven in Missouri, with his West Point roommate, Fred Dent, Julia's brother. The couple married on August 22, 1848, after Grant had served in the Mexican War. The Dents were slave-owning Southerners, but Julia's loyalties were always with her husband's Union sympathies. She endured hardship at a succession of drab frontier army posts, gave birth to three sons and one daughter, and saw her husband fail at a series of jobs. Yet her faith in his potential greatness never wavered.

That faith was rewarded when Grant became a war hero and ultimately was elected president. Basking in the glow of postwar White House life, Julia was determined to return elegant entertaining to the mansion. She outdid

Julia Dent Grant

> **It was my fortune, or misfortune, to be called to the office of Chief Executive without any previous political training.**
>
> —*Ulysses S. Grant*

Mary Lincoln's lavishness yet escaped the public censure heaped on Mrs. Lincoln. In the dawn of the Gilded Age, it had become fashionable to move in the social circles of millionaire Republicans. Julia chose as her mentor in matters of social style Mrs. Hamilton Fish, wife of Grant's secretary of state and veteran of New York high society.

Julia organized grand dinners every Wednesday night, a twenty-nine course meal for thirty-six guests prepared by an Italian steward, Valentino Melah, a former steward at the Everett House in Boston and New York's Astor House. The banquets cost between $700 and $1,500 each—an enormous sum at the time.

Q: What family members lived in the White House?

A: The Grants brought their children Ulysses Jr. ("Buck"), Ellen ("Nellie"), and Jesse with them. Fred, the oldest son, was a student at Harvard and, after graduating, went on active duty with the army. Julia's father, Frederick Dent, also moved into the White House. In his early eighties, the unreconstructed Southerner and former slaveholder delighted in provoking the Grants' "Yankee" friends and gleefully baiting the president's father, Jesse, who visited the family often but stayed in a hotel. The president's mother, Hannah, never visited Washington.

After graduating from Harvard, Buck Grant worked as his father's aide. General Orville Babcock, who had held a high position on Grant's wartime staff and was also a close friend, served as Grant's private secretary. Babcock then headed the office of Public Buildings and Grounds. Babcock was given an upstairs room in the White House. Another Grant intimate, General William Belknap, a respected Civil War hero, became secretary of war. Both Babcock and Belknap were involved in the notorious scandals that riddled the Grant administration. Grant, a man of integrity himself, lacked the ability to discern corruption in those around him. He allied his administration with Republican backers of enormous wealth, whose power, ruthlessness, and excesses defined the postwar Gilded Age.

Fred Grant married during his father's presidency, although the ceremony was not held in the White House. Fred's daughter Julia, the first grandchild, was born there, however. The first lady arranged for her granddaughter, who was named after her, to "receive" at the 1877 New Year's Day reception, as thousands of visitors streamed by, catching a glimpse of the baby dressed in antique lace.

Julia's father, Frederick, died in the mansion at age eighty-nine, in December 1873, "a clear case of life worn out purely by time," wrote the president. Dent's funeral was held in the East Room.

Ulysses and Julia Grant with their four children, Jesse, Nellie, Fred, and Buck, from an 1868 print.

Q: What kind of press coverage did the Grant family receive?

A: As president, Grant took advantage of the increased press coverage of the White House in the postwar years. He adopted a policy of "being seen in public" to restore normality to a nation torn by bitter war and assassination. The entire family participated. Every morning, to the delight of White House spectators and newspaper correspondents, Buck, Nellie, and Jesse went off to school in a wicker pony cart painted yellow. The first lady was driven around town in the Grants' elegant coach, calling on other Washington political wives. Grant, who loved horses, was often seen driving his carriage through the streets of the capital.

Above: Named after his father, Ulysses S. Grant Jr. was known as Buck, after the Buckeye State of Ohio, where he was born.

Below: Ulysses and Julia arrive at Grant's 1869 inaugural ball in the Treasury Department, the first of many extravagant social events held during Grant's administration.

Q: What changes did the Grants make in the White House?

A: Congress doubled the president's salary to $50,000 a year and appropriated money for a redecoration of the mansion. The grand staircase in the entrance hall was replaced by a wider and more massive one of walnut, to accommodate the wide gowns and grand entrances of the era. The entrance hall was redecorated to "epitomize the Republican Party as savior of the nation" with flags, Union shields, and eagles, "a riot of Fourth of July red, white, and blue," culminating in two painted panels with cameo portraits of Washington and Lincoln. The Blue Room was redone in a "New Grecian" style. A more ornamental room than before the redecoration, the East Room featured Corinthian columns and heavy beams that spanned the room. The ceiling was treated as an artificial sky, shading from azure to pink and gold with white clouds.

One of Grant's favorite pastimes was billiards, which had lost its unsavory associations and was considered a wholesome family recreation. A billiard room was built on the west terrace, a room rich in wood paneling, wainscoting, and timber framing that produced an immense, great hall effect. The Grants often invited guests to play billiards and games continued for hours. This room became the most popular room in the house.

Q: What lavish social event crowned the Grant administration?

A: The wedding of the Grants' eighteen-year-old daughter, Nellie, to Englishman Algernon Sartoris on May 21, 1874, was a lavish affair. Press coverage of her elaborate trousseau, the elegant gifts sent from around the world, the sumptuous wedding feast, and the more than 250 guests captivated the American public. The marriage took place in the East Room at eleven in the morning, with the bride

appearing in a white satin wedding gown with a six-foot train. Six bridesmaids dressed in matching white satin dresses attended her. Methodist minister Otis Tiffany performed the ceremony on a dais covered with Turkish carpets over which a tall floral arch was erected. A large wedding bell of white roses hung suspended from the arch. The wedding feast was held in the State Dining Room, while the gifts were displayed in the oval room upstairs. The couple left for New York to sail to their new home in England. The fairy-tale marriage later ended in divorce.

Q: What did the Grants do after leaving the White House?

A: The Grants embarked on a two-and-a-half year, triumphal around-the-world tour. At every port of call they were received like visiting royalty and showered with extravagant and exotic gifts. They settled in New York, but Grant's business investments failed, and he developed throat cancer. To provide for Julia and the family, he decided to write his memoirs, the first ex-president to do so. In a race against death, he completed them a few days before he died in 1885. Mark Twain published Grant's book, which became a best seller. It earned almost $450,000—and made Julia a wealthy widow. She moved back to Washington, scene of her social triumphs, where she lived until her death in 1902.

"The Wedding at the White House" from *Frank Leslie's Illustrated Newspaper.* The press adored Nellie, the Grants' only daughter, who spent her teenage years in the White House. The newspapers portrayed her as a kind of American "princess."

Grant's Tomb on Riverside Drive in New York City. On April 27, 1897, the seventy-fifth anniversary of Grant's birth nearly a million spectators gathered for the parade to the dedication ceremony of the tomb. Julia died in 1902 and was buried beside her husband.

"My life at the White House was like a bright and beautiful dream . . . quite the happiest period of my life."

—JULIA GRANT

Rutherford and Lucy Hayes

Q: How did Rutherford B. Hayes become president?

A: The election of 1876, the centennial year of American independence, was among the most bitterly contested in the nation's history. Hayes, the Republican candidate, ran against Democrat Samuel J. Tilden, governor of New York. Much was at stake: Republican control of the South and the enforcement of the Thirteenth, Fourteenth, and Fifteenth amendments guaranteeing citizenship and voting rights to newly freed African Americans. At the conclusion of the election there was no clear winner. Tilden won the popular vote, but the electoral college vote was disputed. From November 1876 until March 2, 1877, no one knew who would be president. In January 1877, Congress set up an electoral commission of eight Republicans and seven Democrats, who awarded all the disputed electoral votes to the Republicans, declaring Hayes the winner by the electoral vote of 185 to 184. Because of the contested election, many feared an outbreak of violence. To further heighten the tension, inauguration day fell on March 4, a Sunday, when no official ceremonies could be held. Grant's term ended at noon

Right: The Hayes inauguration followed months of uncertainty during which a congressional electoral commission determined the outcome of one of the most fiercely disputed presidential elections in American history.

Below: Rutherford B. Hayes, with a reputation for dignity and honesty, was elected president after the tumultuous, scandal-ridden years of the Grant administration.

on the fourth, but because the swearing-in did not occur until noon, Monday, March 5, the presidency was technically vacant for a day. Fearful of a possible coup, Grant insisted that Hayes not wait.

The Grants sent out invitations for thirty-eight guests to attend a dinner party honoring President-elect and Mrs. Hayes at the White House for Saturday night, March 3, 1877. During a break in the dinner, President Grant and Rutherford Hayes slipped away to the Red Room, where Chief Justice Morrison Waite administered the presidential oath to Hayes. This was the first time a president-elect had taken the oath of office in the White House. The public swearing-in ceremony took place at the Capitol the following Monday.

Because of the unusual circumstances, no inaugural parade or balls were held. There was a torchlight parade on the evening of March 5, organized by Hayes supporters, followed by a reception in Washington's Willard Hotel.

Q: Who was the president's first lady?

A: Lucy Webb Hayes, the president's wife, served as first lady, the first to earn a college degree. Born in 1831, she was the daughter of a medical doctor who died when Lucy was very young. Her father's antislavery beliefs shaped the family's reform sentiments. When Lucy was thirteen, her mother took her two older brothers to Ohio Wesleyan University for their studies. Although girls were not allowed to officially enroll at the university, Lucy nonetheless took college courses and became the first female student. She later transferred to Cincinnati Wesleyan Female College, one of the first colleges to grant degrees to women, and graduated in 1850.

Lucy met Hayes in Cincinnati, where he practiced law, and they married in her home on December 30, 1852. The couple had eight children, three of whom died in early childhood. Their four surviving sons were Birchard (called Birch), James Webb (called Webb), Rutherford ("Ruddy"), and Scott Russell. Fanny, their only daughter, also survived. Lucy visited her husband often during his Civil War service and nursed him back to health after he was severely wounded.

Lucy Webb Hayes

Always supportive of his political career, she gained valuable social experience while Hayes was governor of Ohio.

Q: What family members lived in the White House?

A: The Hayes family circle included their five children. Birch, who was twenty-four and a Harvard law student, and Ruddy, nineteen, also a college student, did not spend much time in the White House until the final year of their father's term. Ruddy then served as an aide to the president. Webb, twenty-one, was the closest to his parents and served as his father's private secretary. Fanny was nine and Scott six when the family entered the mansion. Emily Platt, the president's niece who also lived with the family, served as a social secretary.

Below left: Although Harriet Lane had been referred to as "first lady," when a reporter described Lucy Hayes as the "first lady of the land," in an account of President Hayes's inauguration, the rest of the press picked up the term. Since then, each president's wife has been known by this title.

Below: The Hayes family at Spiegel Grove, Ohio, from left to right: Birchard Austin Hayes; his wife, Mary Sherman Hayes; the president; Scott R. Hayes; Rutherford Platt Hayes; the first lady; Fanny Hayes; and Webb Cook Hayes.

"A heart as true as steel . . . Intellect she has too . . . By George! I am in love with her!"
—*Rutherford B. Hayes, about Lucy Hayes*

Q: What was life in the White House like during the Hayes administration?

A: Young Fanny and Scott, who were tutored in a small schoolroom created for them in the family quarters, brought a lively atmosphere to the White House during their father's administration. The pair often roped visiting officials into their games of hide-and-seek in the state rooms, and Fanny played with her large dollhouse near the staircase on the second floor. The children's pet goat often hauled Scott around the White House lawn in a cart.

In 1879, the family-oriented Hayeses were the first to invite the children of Washington to roll Easter eggs on the White House lawn, to the delight of Fanny and Scott. Congress had banned this activity from the grounds of the Capitol.

Both the president and the first lady thought that continuing the religious devotions that they had followed in their own home would set a moral example for the nation. The family attended Foundry Methodist Church in Washington on Sunday mornings. They held morning prayer services in which the Bible was passed among family members, who each read a verse. The service concluded with everyone saying the Lord's Prayer. On Sunday evenings, the Hayes family, their many guests, and any visiting cabinet members gathered around the piano to sing hymns.

Q: Who was "Lemonade Lucy"?

A: Both the president and the first lady opposed the drinking of alcohol and banned the serving of liquor and wine, much to the consternation of the diplomatic community. Although Hayes made the decision, Lucy, as his hostess, received most of the ridicule in the press. Evidence suggests that their position may have been politically motivated in part by a desire to please a temperance constituency. Although she was not referred to by this derisive nickname while first lady, historians later dubbed her "Lemonade Lucy" for her refusal to serve alcohol.

Q: What was the most important social event of the Hayes administration?

A: The celebration of the Hayeses' twenty-fifth wedding anniversary was a magnificent affair, which began on

Lucy Hayes in White House conservatory with Carrie Davis (daughter of artist Theodore Davis, who created the Hayes White House China), Scott Hayes, and Fanny Hayes.

their anniversary, December 30, 1877, and continued into New Year's Eve. On Sunday afternoon Rutherford and Lucy renewed their vows in the Blue Room, an event made more special by the attendance of their children and many of the original wedding guests. The ceremony was performed by Dr. L. D. McCabe, the same minister who had married them twenty-five years earlier. Lucy wore her 1850s white satin wedding gown and was attended by the same bridesmaid.

On New Year's Eve, a public reception was held. Mendelssohn's "Wedding March" began at 9 P.M. as the president and first lady descended the staircase together and formed a receiving line in the East Room to welcome their friends and guests. Following the ceremony, the president presented his two young children, Fanny and Scott, to be baptized, after which a sumptuous dinner was served.

Q: What special service of state china did the Hayeses order?

A: Lucy wanted a distinctively "American" service featuring the flora and fauna of the United States, a theme emphasizing post–Civil War reunification, and commissioned *Harper's Weekly* artist Theodore Davis to design it. The most elaborate and distinctive of presidential porcelains, it contained uniquely shaped serving and dining plates for each separate course. New molds had to be created for the shapes, and the factory developed a process called "decalcomania" to transfer the vibrant colors onto the china, which required multiple firings for each plate. The Hayes china remains a singular expression of the nineteenth-century search for a truly "American" service.

Above left: Cuff links adorned with Lucy's silhouette. A brooch with Hayes's image completed the set, which the couple exchanged as twenty-fifth anniversary gifts.

Below left: Portrait of the Hayeses on their wedding day, December 30, 1852.

Below: The new shapes and multiple firings drove the expense of the Hayeses' service to exorbitant levels. Haviland, the French manufacturer, charged only a fraction of the actual cost, recouping its losses by making duplicate services for sale to wealthy Americans.

"In avoiding the appearance of evil, I am not sure but I have sometimes unnecessarily deprived myself and others of innocent enjoyments."

—RUTHERFORD B. HAYES

CHAPTER 6

THE GILDED AGE

The years between Reconstruction and the turn of the twentieth century, often referred to as the "Gilded Age," as humorist Mark Twain dubbed it, saw rapid industrialization, urbanization, scientific and technological innovations, the construction of transcontinental railroads, and the rise of big business. In these years, presidential administrations firmly allied themselves with the Republican Party— and with the industrial capitalists who consolidated their wealth through high tariffs that "protected" American products from foreign competition. Waves of foreign immigration supplied cheap labor, but low wages, long hours, and unsafe working conditions fueled growing labor unrest and sparked a demand for reform. When the U.S. battleship *Maine* was blown up in the harbor of Havana, Cuba, the press and public assumed that Spain was responsible and clamored for war under the rallying cry, "Remember the *Maine*!" Victory in the Spanish-American War in 1898 brought influence over Cuba and new territories in Hawaii, the Philippines, and Puerto Rico. It also brought the nation into the age of imperialism and made the United States a world power.

Above: An advertisement for the Vitascope motion picture projector, marketed by the Edison Manufacturing Company. Moving pictures were just one of many new technological advances of the Gilded Age.

Left: Portrait of First Lady Caroline Scott Harrison by Daniel Huntington. The inhabitants of the White House reflected the opulence of the Gilded Age.

James and Lucretia Garfield

Above: James A. Garfield served eighteen years as a U.S. congressman from Ohio, only becoming the "dark horse" presidential candidate when the two wings of the Republican party could not agree on a nominee. One of the few politicians of the era untouched by scandal, Garfield easily won the 1880 election.

Above right: Lucretia Garfield. Their early marriage was a rocky one, filled with separations, doubts, and disappointment, as well as infidelity on James's part. By the time of the presidency, however, the Garfields were virtually inseparable.

Below right: The Garfield family. From left to right: Mary, Jim, Garfield, Lucretia, Irvin, and Harry. Seated at the front of the table are Eliza Garfield and youngest son, Abram. Eliza was the first mother of a president to witness her son's inauguration.

Q: How did James and Lucretia Garfield meet?

A: James Abram Garfield, last of the log-cabin presidents, was born in Cuyahoga County, Ohio, in 1831. Fatherless by the time he was two, he worked himself out of poverty driving canal boats, teaching English and the classics, and even working as a janitor through college. He attended Western Reserve Eclectic Institute (now Hiram College) and went on to Williams College in Massachusetts. After graduation from Williams, Garfield returned to the Eclectic Institute, where he again taught the classics. Within a year, he was the college's president.

Lucretia Rudolph was born in 1832 to a well-to-do farming family in Ohio's Western Reserve and attended Geauga Academy, where she first met Garfield. They renewed their friendship when they met again at the Eclectic Institute in 1851, where "Crete," as she was known, studied Greek under Garfield. Upon her graduation in 1855, Crete pursued a career as a teacher, also at the Eclectic Institute. She and Garfield, who was then attending Williams, began a rather stiff courtship, about which each expressed serious doubts. Garfield wrote, "There is no delirium of passion nor overwhelming power of feeling that draws me to her irresistibly." Only after Crete showed him her secret diary, in which she had confided the depth of her passion for him, did their November 1858 wedding take place.

Lucretia Garfield

Q: What was life like in the Garfield White House?

A: The Garfields had seven children, two of whom died in early childhood. Their surviving children, Harry, James Rudolph, Mary, Irvin, and Abram, lived with them in the White House. Garfield's eighty-year-old mother, Eliza Ballou Garfield, the first presidential mother to witness her son's inauguration, also moved with them to Washington. Although portrayed by the press during the campaign as the "sainted" Victorian mother, Eliza was a tough and often demanding woman.

The Garfield family enjoyed one another's company and were openly affectionate. Although the elder sons, seventeen-year-old Harry and fifteen-year-old Jim, spent months in a small hideaway upstairs studying to enter college, they would venture downstairs to rope the president into pillow fights and wrestling matches. Irvin also romped through the

mansion, riding his bicycle down the family staircase into the East Room, while Jim jumped on a springboard in the high-ceilinged salon. Crete wrote to a friend about her sons' roughhousing in the White House, fondly commenting that, "My live[ly] boys go tumbling through it with their handsprings and somersaults."

The happy days in the White House were cut short, however, when Crete fell gravely ill with malaria in May 1881. The distraught president took personal charge of her care, nursing her through bouts of fever and chills. Once Crete was past the crisis, her physician recommended recuperation at the seashore. The Garfields and several of their children boarded a train to Elberon, New Jersey, where Crete was to spend the summer recovering.

Q: What tragedy occurred just as the first lady was recovering?

A: Garfield, accompanied by his son Harry and Secretary of State James G. Blaine, arrived at Washington's Sixth Street Station on July 2, 1881, preparing to join Crete. As Garfield walked through the station, Charles Guiteau, an embittered office-seeker, fired two shots at him. One bullet grazed his arm, but the other lodged itself somewhere inside his body. Crete, barely well herself, returned immediately to Washington to nurse him. "You are not going to die," she declared. "I am here to nurse you back to life." Yet Garfield's doctors were unable to locate the bullet, and he lay immobilized, in excruciating pain, in the stifling summer heat of the White House. Finally, his doctors recommended sea air for his recovery, and Garfield was carefully moved by train to Elberon. On September 19, 1881, he died from an infection and internal hemorrhage. Most medical experts and historians now believe that Garfield would most likely have survived his wound had the attending doctors used sterile medical practice.

His wife and sons accompanied the president's body back to Washington for funeral services in the Capitol rotunda. Crete, hailed in the press as "the bravest woman in the universe," received more than $360,000 in donations from the American people to support her family.

After being shot on July 2, 1881, Garfield lay near death for eighty days before finally succumbing to infection. Unable to locate one of the bullets that lodged in his body, his desperate doctors turned to technology in hopes of easing his suffering. Alexander Graham Bell had invented a metal detector to find the foreign object, and brought it to the White House some three weeks after the shooting. Bell did not locate the bullet—which may have been a futile exercise at best.

> **The tyranny of our love is sweet. We waited long for his coming, but he has come to stay.**
> —*JAMES A. GARFIELD,*
> *on his marriage to Lucretia Rudolph*

Chester A. Arthur

Q: Who was Chester A. Arthur?

A: A crony of shady political boss Roscoe Conkling, Republican senator from New York, Chester A. Arthur had made his career, and his fortune, in the corrupt world of New York "party machine" politics. Born the son of a Baptist preacher in Fairfield, Vermont, in 1829, Arthur graduated from Union College in Schenectady, New York, and practiced law in Manhattan. Appointed collector of the Port of New York by Grant, Arthur had been a firm believer in the "spoils system," but as president he proved to be an honest advocate of civil-service reform. He was picked as James Garfield's vice president in 1880 to attract votes from Conkling's "Stalwart Republican" wing of the party. Upon news of the death of Garfield, Judge John R.

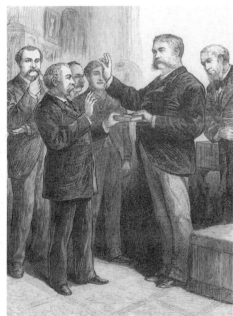

Above: Judge John R. Brady administering the presidential oath to Vice President Arthur at his residence in New York.

Right: Ellen Herndon Arthur did not live to become first lady. She died at age forty-two, just months before Arthur was elected as James Garfield's vice president.

Brady swore in Arthur as president at 2:15 A.M. on September 19, 1881, in the parlor of Arthur's elegant brownstone residence at 123 Lexington Avenue in New York City, where a small group of friends had gathered for the ceremony. Arthur, knowing for several weeks that Garfield was dying, had ordered a private train to stand by. The next morning he boarded the train for Elberon, New Jersey, where Garfield had died, to pay his respects to the family.

Q: Why did President Arthur's wife not serve as first lady?

A: Arthur was a widower when he became president. He had married Ellen Herndon in 1859, and the couple had moved in the most fashionable circles of New York society. Ellen, known as Nell, was a native of Virginia but grew up in Washington, D.C., and New York City. She was a strikingly beautiful woman whose cousin had introduced her to "Chet" Arthur, who was then establishing a law practice in Manhattan. Chet and Nell married that same year and had three children: a son who died when he was only two; a second son, Chester Alan, called Alan; and a daughter, Ellen, also called Nell. In January 1880, Ellen

Ellen Herndon Arthur

Honors to me now are not what they once were.
—CHESTER A. ARTHUR,
on his election as vice president after his wife's death

attended a benefit concert in New York City, while Arthur was busy with politics in Albany. In the chill of the winter night, she caught a cold while waiting for her carriage. By the time Arthur returned to New York, she was already unconscious. On January 12, less than a year before her husband was elected Garfield's vice president, Ellen died of pneumonia. She was only forty-two years old.

Still mourning the loss of his beloved Nell, Arthur placed a silver-framed oval photograph of his wife near his White House bedside, ordering the head gardener to place fresh roses in front of her likeness every day. He also donated a stained-glass window in her memory to Saint John's Church, across from the White House in Lafayette Park. He often looked at it at night from his bedroom window, where he could see it illuminated by candlelight inside the church.

Q: Who served as Arthur's hostess in the White House?

A: The president asked his youngest sister, Mary Arthur McElroy, to live with him in the White House and to act as his hostess during the winter social season and in the fall and spring. Molly, as she was called, was forty years old, a small woman with dark hair. She was the wife of a prominent Albany businessman and the mother of four young children. A college graduate, she possessed good judgment and a ready smile that endeared her to the citizens of Washington. She proved to be a gracious hostess.

Molly brought her two daughters, May and Jessie, to live with her in the White House. Her husband, John, remained in Albany with their sons, William and Charles. Making up the rest of the Arthur household was Arthur's daughter, Ellen. His son, Alan, attended college at Princeton, but he made frequent trips to Washington to join the family.

Above: Still mourning Ellen, at the White House, Arthur refused to give anyone the place that would have been his wife's. He asked his sister Mary Arthur McElroy to assume certain social duties and to help care for his daughter.

Left: Called "Nell" after her mother, the president's only daughter lived at the White House, but older brother Alan spent most of the White House years at Princeton.

Q: Why did Arthur not live in the White House when he first took office?

A: The assassination of President Garfield had postponed the redecoration slated to take place during his administration. Arthur, who was used to elegant living, immediately let it be known that he refused to live in the White House in its current shabby state, announcing, "I will not live in a house like this." He moved temporarily to a granite-faced row house on Independence Avenue across from the Capitol, the residence of Senator John P. Jones. After the first set of White House renovations were done, Arthur moved into the Executive Mansion on December 7, 1881, but drew up plans to redecorate to his own taste.

Below: Chester A. Arthur rose from relative obscurity to the presidency at the death of James Garfield. Political pundits predicted a flood of corruption during his term of office, but Arthur ran the presidency in an honest fashion.

Below right: Louis Comfort Tiffany's redecorated Red Room. In addition to repainting the walls and ceilings, Tiffany added an elegant cherry mantel, which was stained an amaranthine red and inlaid with stained glass.

Q: How did Arthur redecorate the White House?

A: Dismissing the furniture and decorations of the mansion as "department store" style, President Arthur commissioned Louis Comfort Tiffany to supervise the redecoration. Tiffany, the son of the famous New York jeweler, headed Associated Artists, a group of prestigious painters, decorators, and designers. Before Tiffany could begin work, Arthur had to dispose of the old furnishings. Twenty-four wagonloads of furniture—some of it priceless in association—were carted away and auctioned off, as was the nineteenth-century White House custom.

The Green Room, the Blue Room, and the East Room, remodeled in the first months of Arthur's presidency, remained unchanged. Tiffany would redecorate the Red Room, the State Dining Room, and the transverse entrance hall of the mansion, as completely as possible. The president moved to the Soldiers' Home during the

summer of 1882 so that Tiffany could work unencumbered. Wrote a reporter for *Century Magazine,* "The Red Room was painted a deep, purplish Pompeiian red, the wainscoting in a darker red . . . a delicate frieze an abstraction of stars and stripes. The ceiling . . . was covered with stars of shiny bronze and copper . . . so that they caught every flash of light. . . . The State Dining Room . . . was painted in 'glowing yellows,' [with] an elaborate painted and stenciled frieze around the ceiling." Tiffany's most famous and enduring addition was a stained "glass mosaic" screen, installed between the entrance hall and the transverse hall. Approximately ten feet tall, the glass screen of red, white, and blue stretched across the entrance hall, making the space "continually iridescent . . . with splashes of crimson, cobalt, and white, blue-white, rosy-white, and amber-white." The *Century* praised the entrance hall as the "most successful" of all Tiffany's interiors at the White House.

Q: What was the social style of the Arthur presidency?

A: "Arthur was the highest liver in the White House," reminisced a Washington market proprietor, and "gave a lot of personal attention to his dinners." A connoisseur of wines, he entertained constantly and elegantly, supervising the details of each event. He devised an I-shaped dining table to increase the capacity of state dinners from fifty to sixty-five. Music

Arthur on vacation in ritzy Newport, Rhode Island. Arthur is probably best remembered for being the most elegant and well-dressed president, reportedly owning some eighty suits. Nicknamed the "Gentleman Boss," he enjoyed parties and had an epicure's taste in food and drink.

at the White House attained distinguished levels, and the Marine Band became world renowned under the leadership of John Philip Sousa. Molly McElroy held weekly receptions, making them less formal than those of her predecessors, as well as "ladies" receptions for which she invited the young women of Washington society to receive guests with her in the Blue Room. Molly chose the Hayes china for state dinners, reordering specific individual replacements for the service. Arthur also reordered a large service of the Lincoln purple-bordered state china. Harriet Blaine, wife of the former secretary of state and a frequent White House guest, reported, "I dined at the President's Wednesday. The dinner was extremely elegant . . . the flowers, the damasks, the silver, the attendants, all showing the latest style and an abandon in expense and taste."

> "Since I came here I have learned that Chester A. Arthur is one man and the President of the United States is another."
>
> —*CHESTER A. ARTHUR*

Grover and Frances Cleveland

Q: **What was historic about Grover Cleveland's presidency?**

Below: Fireworks light up the night sky near the White House in celebration of Grover Cleveland's first inauguration.

Below right: Cleveland, a successful lawyer, had established a national name for himself as the reform mayor of Buffalo and as governor of New York.

A: Grover Cleveland was the first Democrat elected president since the Civil War and the only president elected to two nonconsecutive terms. He served from 1885 to 1889 and 1893 to 1897.

During Cleveland's first presidential campaign, the Republican opposition charged that he had fathered a child out of wedlock and was paying child support to the mother. Cleveland, a bachelor, admitted that he and other men in his political camp had been intimate with Maria Halpin, a widow in Buffalo. Although he acknowledged paying child support, Cleveland insisted that the child was not his and that he had claimed responsibility to spare the actual father, a married man, the embarrassment to his family. Tellingly, Halpin had named her son, born in 1874, Oscar Folsom Cleveland. Oscar Folsom had been Cleveland's Buffalo law partner and was the father of Cleveland's future bride, Frances Folsom. Cleveland's savvy managers "spun" this awkward scandal

to emphasize his honesty and integrity, and Cleveland gained support from a public disgusted with the widespread corruption of nineteenth-century politics.

Q: **Who was Cleveland's White House hostess before his marriage?**

A: Cleveland's unmarried youngest sister, Rose Elizabeth Cleveland, served as his White House hostess, assisted at times by his married sister, Mary Hoyt. "Miss Rose" was a scholar, teacher, and author. A professor at Buffalo's Houghton Institute and later at the Collegiate Institute, she spent her private time writing a book on George Eliot's poetry, which she declared "is not of a kind to suit the masses." Her celebrity helped promote her book and earned her a first royalty payment of $25,000. The intellectual Rose found standing in endless receiving lines at the White House a boring duty and admitted to amusing herself mentally by conjugating Greek verbs while greeting guests.

After Rose left the White House, she became editor of *Literary Life* magazine and enrolled in law school. She and her lifelong companion, Evangeline Marrs Simpson,

Grover Cleveland

> **"Sometimes I wake at night in the White House and rub my eyes and wonder if it is not all a dream."**
> —*GROVER CLEVELAND*

moved to Chicago and then to Tuscany, where they lived together discreetly. Rose died in Italy in 1918, a victim of the worldwide flu epidemic of that year.

Q: Who was Cleveland's bride?

A: Cleveland wed the young and beautiful Frances Folsom—"Frank" to her friends and family. The twenty-one-year-old bride was twenty-seven years younger than her groom. In fact, back when he was the law partner and friend of her father, Cleveland had purchased the baby carriage that was to be occupied by his future wife. Later, when Oscar Folsom was killed in a carriage accident, Cleveland served as administrator of his estate. Although he was never her legal guardian, Cleveland guided Frank's education through Wells College. He corresponded with her during her college years and regularly sent fresh flowers to her room. In the spring of 1885, Frances and her mother visited the White House, where friendship ripened into love. Lest the press hound his fiancée, Cleveland conducted the courtship in secret and proposed to Frank by letter shortly before she departed for a post-graduation trip to Europe. The trip, intended to broaden her education, became a shopping spree for her wedding trousseau in Paris, where she purchased her wedding gown from renowned couturier Charles Frederick Worth.

When rumors first circulated of an upcoming wedding for the president, many assumed that Cleveland was courting Frank's mother. That rumor was dispelled

Upon her engagement, Frances Folsom Cleveland became a national celebrity. Without her permission, her likeness appeared on a variety of everyday items, such as posters, dishes, salt and pepper shakers, playing cards, and advertising, making her the nation's first "pop culture" first lady. She even became a campaign symbol in Cleveland's second presidential campaign.

when the engagement was officially announced in May 1886. As Cleveland had feared, the bride-to-be was besieged by reporters upon her return from Europe. In an effort to maintain a measure of privacy, the couple resorted to subterfuge, with Frank and her mother slipping into the White House through service entrances and hiding behind dark veils. On one occasion, when Cleveland was scheduled to review a Memorial Day parade by the Grand Army of the Republic in New York City, his men spirited Frank off a tugboat in the harbor and into the Gilsey Hotel on Fifth Avenue, from where she watched the parade. Meanwhile, as a marching band playing patriotic tunes approached the president's reviewing stand, it suddenly broke into "He's Going to Marry Yum Yum," from the Gilbert and Sullivan operetta *The Mikado*. The country had quickly fallen in love with Frances Folsom.

Q: Where did Grover and Frances's marriage ceremony take place?

A: The Clevelands' wedding was the first marriage ceremony of a president to take place in the White House. Cleveland determined that he could best limit press coverage and maintain privacy from within the mansion. He personally wrote out the invitations to family, close friends, and cabinet members. On Wednesday, June 2, 1886, at 7 P.M., the Marine Band, under conductor John Philip Sousa, struck up the wedding march as Cleveland and his bride descended the grand staircase together. There were no bridal attendants. Following the East Room ceremony, the couple and their guests enjoyed a candle-light dinner in the State Dining Room.

Q: Where did the Clevelands live after the wedding?

A: Faced with unrelenting attention from the press, the Clevelands became the first presidential couple to maintain full-time alternative residences. The White House was their primary residence in the winter social season when the entertaining schedule was heavy, but Cleveland purchased a stone farmhouse near the present Washington Cathedral for the rest of the year. Commanding sweeping views of the city, it was converted into a large home surrounded by porches on two levels and painted dark green. Although Frances named it Oak View, the press nicknamed it Red Top, after its vast roof of red shingles. The area where the house was located became known as Cleveland Park.

After the president's 1888 defeat, the Clevelands sold Red Top, making a handsome profit of $100,000, for which they were criticized in the press. In their second White House term, the Clevelands again bought a large, private residence, this one named Woodley.

Q: What health problem threatened the president during his second term?

A: The president experienced pain in his mouth, which doctors diagnosed as mouth cancer. Not wanting to appear weakened at a crucial juncture in his presidency, Cleveland chose to have his surgery in secret. The cover story was given to the press that his wife, in the late stages of pregnancy, was vacationing at their summer retreat on Cape Cod while the president took a cruise aboard the *Oneida,* the

Ten days after the event, *Harper's Weekly* published this print of the Cleveland wedding on June 12, 1886, although it bore little resemblance to the actual ceremony because reporters were barred from the White House. For the ceremony, the East Room was profusely decorated with flowers from the mansion's greenhouses. After a candlelight wedding dinner, the couple departed by train to the mountains of western Maryland, where journalists used spyglasses to get a closer look at the honeymooners.

yacht of his close friend Commodore Elias Benedict. The operation was performed aboard the yacht while at sea. The president's malignancy was far more extensive than his surgeons had anticipated, and the entire left upper jaw, as well as part of the soft palate, was removed, replaced by an artificial device made of rubber. Cleveland enjoyed a full recovery, and the surgery remained secret until 1917, when the principal surgeon wrote a detailed account for the *Saturday Evening Post*.

The Clevelands with their second daughter, Esther, the only child of a president to be born in the White House. As it had been with her mother, the press was fascinated by Esther and her sisters.

Q: Who were the Clevelands' children?

A: The Clevelands' first daughter, Ruth, was born in 1891, between her father's two terms of office. Fondly nicknamed "Baby Ruth" by the press, she was a sickly child. Tragically, Ruth died in 1904, from diphtheria. The Clevelands' second daughter, Esther, was born on September 9, 1893, the only child of a president to be born in the White House. A third daughter, Marion, was born in 1895. After the presidency, the Clevelands had two sons, Richard Folsom, born 1897, and Francis Grover, born 1903.

The 1893 World's Fair, also known as the Columbian Exposition, was a glittering symbol of both technological progress and imperial expansion. President Cleveland, after completing his opening speech in front of the administration building, pushed a button to start the Columbian Fountain and hoisted an American flag up a pole.

"I have not had a life yet. It is all before me."
—*FRANCES CLEVELAND,*
on leaving the White House

Benjamin and Caroline Harrison

Q: What type of campaign did Benjamin Harrison wage for his election?

A: Benjamin Harrison was the only president who was the grandson of a former president. The campaign imagery of his grandfather, William Henry Harrison, had worked so well that Republicans resurrected it for his grandson's campaign. William Henry had been "Old Tippecanoe"; his grandson became "Young Tippecanoe." Miniature log cabins and barrels of "hard cider" abounded. Since the younger Harrison wore a top hat, his managers introduced campaign songs and slogans about "filling his grandfather's hat"—something like filling a predecessor's shoes. Republicans sang "The Same

Old Hat—It Fits Ben Just Fine," while Democrats chanted, "His Grandfather's Hat—It's Too Big for Ben." Three-inch novelty beaver hats were marketed with the slogan, "His Grandfather's Hat."

Q: What family members lived in the Harrison White House?

A: Four generations of the Harrison family moved into the White House, including the president and his wife, Caroline Scott Harrison; their daughter and son-in-law, Mary and J. Robert McKee, and the McKee children, Benjamin Harrison ("Baby") and Mary Harrison; the Harrisons' son and daughter-in-law,

Left: The Pension Building inaugural ball typified Gilded Age celebrations. Caroline Harrison and her daughter Mary McKee wore gowns deliberately produced in the United States for the occasion to emphasize Harrison's campaign theme of "Protection to Home Industries," the late-nineteenth century equivalent of "Buy American."

Right: Four generations of the Harrison family. Standing is Mary Harrison McKee. Her mother, Caroline, holds her son, "Baby McKee" and the Rev. Dr. John Scott holds her daughter Mary Lodge.

“ **I want to avoid everything that is personal and I want it understood that I am grandson of nobody.** ”

—*Benjamin Harrison*

Russell (who joined the family when business permitted) and Mary, and their daughter, Marthena. Another grand-daughter, Mary Lodge McKee, was born during these years. The Harrisons also asked Caroline Harrison's eighty-year-old father, the Rev. Dr. John Scott, who had performed their marriage ceremony, to live with them. Rounding out the family circle was Caroline Harrison's widowed niece, Mary Scott Lord Dimmick, who lived with the family and served as a secretary to the president and first lady.

Q: What family activities endeared the Harrisons to the public?

A: The Harrisons' family life capti-vated the American public, from their daily morning prayers to Mary McKee's walking Baby on the White House lawn to shake hands with the visitors to the grandchildren's cavorting on the grounds in their goat cart. Newspaper readers devoured reports about how the first lady had painted decorative flowers on Baby's porcelain bathtub. The child would lean out of the bathtub to "smell" the flowers and spill water all over the bathroom floor. Whether it was an anecdote about Baby leading the Marine Band or sneaking away with state papers, which he threw into a White House spittoon, or a report of the White House christening of the Harrisons' grand-daughter, Marthena, a ceremony pre-sided over by her great-grandfather, the Rev. Dr. Scott, who used water from the River Jordan, readers were enchanted.

Adding to the public's fascination was the abundance of photo-graphs of the first family now available. By the late nineteenth century, photographic technol-ogy had progressed to the point where taking pictures was relatively easy. Everything about the Harrison grand-children seemed fair game—their romps on the White House lawn, their nursery, their clothes. A number of photographers and photographic studios made favorites of Mary McKee and her children. A veritable industry had grown up around photographing the first family, a state of affairs that brought the presidency closer to the American people but trapped the presi-dential family in a fishbowl existence.

Harrison's son Major Russell Harrison with his daughter, Marthena, and Mary Lodge and Baby McKee on the White House lawn. The public was charmed by photo-graphs of the close-knit Harrison family.

Because Benjamin Harrison stood only five feet six inches tall, his Democrat opponents dubbed him "Little Ben." During the presidential campaign the Republicans countered the jibe by insisting that he was big enough to wear the hat of his grandfather, "Old Tippecanoe," the United States's ninth president.

Caroline Harrison's goal of modernizing the White House earned her both acclaim and ridicule as the "best housekeeper in the nation." Her interests did not stop at the renovation of the mansion, however. The Daughters of the American Revolution was formed in the 1890s after the "Sons" refused to admit women. Caroline gladly became its first president-general, believing that it would become a strong political force for women to bring them into mainstream politics and improve women's status.

Q: How did Caroline Harrison intend to improve the White House?

A: Even with the improvements undertaken during the previous administration, when the Harrisons entered the White House in 1889 they found the mansion overcrowded, infested with rats, and clearly in need of further renovation. A lover of history, Caroline understood the mansion's symbolism as a stage for national power and fully appreciated the house as the embodiment of the nation's past. She felt that a grander building was needed, "a home which may be creditable to the Executive of the greatest nation on the globe." Spurred by the centennial of the presidency, she secured Frederick Owen, a Washington engineer, architect, and friend, to draw up elaborate plans that embodied her vision for a White House expansion. The existing house would be saved and two wings would be added: a west wing for presidential offices and an east wing to be used as an art gallery, leaving the mansion itself as a residence for the president's family. The plan also proposed an expanded botanical garden.

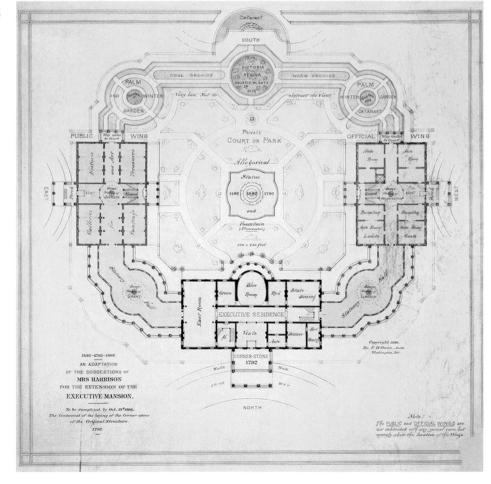

The proposed plan for extensions to the White House and grounds, including a garden. Congress rejected her plans for an expansion, but much of Caroline's vision was retained in later renovations.

Under the guise of entertaining, Caroline extensively lobbied members of Congress, invited congressional committees to view the plans, and successfully sought the support of the press. She believed the expansion "would be a fitting memorial to the growth of the republic during the first hundred years." A bill to adopt the plan sailed through the Senate but was not voted on in the House because one of the representatives chose to vent his personal anger at the president by thwarting his wife's hopes. Despite its rejection in her own time, Caroline's grand vision for the White House sowed seeds for the future that culminated in the extensive renovation of the mansion under Theodore and Edith Roosevelt.

Caroline did manage to secure $52,000 in congressional appropriations to refurbish and upgrade the mansion. In addition to a thorough cleaning, repainting, and repapering of the house, she oversaw an extensive inventory of the furnishings and china, including those hidden away for years in the attic and basement. Included in this general upgrading was the installation of electricity and a "modern" kitchen. Caroline, however, was afraid of the new electric lights and never used them, continuing to rely on gaslight.

Another element of her vision for an enhanced presidential residence included a new service of state china. In this she was successful. A talented artist, who held china painting classes in the White House for friends and wives of officials, Caroline personally designed the state service of porcelain for the Harrison administration to reflect American themes. Corn, typifying the nation's abundant produce, and goldenrod, her husband's favorite flower, were the gold decorative motifs on a deep-blue border, with the American eagle in the center of the plate, a "representation of the Arms of the United States . . . adapted from the eagle used on the center of the Lincoln plates."

Q: What rumors circulated after Caroline's death?

A: Caroline succumbed to tuberculosis on October 25, 1892, the second first lady to die in the White House. In 1896, the former president married Caroline's widowed niece, Mary Lord Dimmick, then in her thirties. Mary had lived with the Harrison family in the White House and assisted with the social functions as Caroline's health declined. She also served as an aide to the president. The Harrison children, Russell and Mary, adamantly opposed their father's second marriage and had little to do with him after he remarried. Rumors persisted that a romantic relationship had developed in the White House while Caroline was still alive, but little evidence exists to confirm or deny those rumors.

A *Washington Post* cartoon depicts Harrison walking with his bride, Mary Lord Dimmick, in front of the White House.

"After the heavy blow of the death of my wife, I do not think that I could have stood reelection."
—*Benjamin Harrison*

William and Ida McKinley

Q: What kind of election campaign did William McKinley conduct?

A: William McKinley ran a "front porch" campaign, an election technique in which the candidate remained at home, literally on his front porch, and

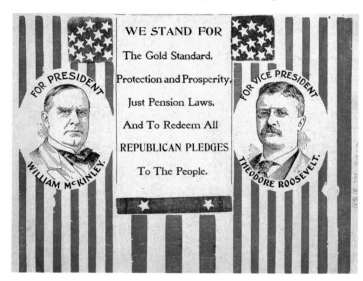

WE STAND FOR
The Gold Standard,
Protection and Prosperity.
Just Pension Laws,
And To Redeem All
REPUBLICAN PLEDGES
To The People.

FOR PRESIDENT
WILLIAM McKINLEY.

FOR VICE PRESIDENT
THEODORE ROOSEVELT.

In one of the noisiest and most ardent campaigns in the nation's history, supporters wore either "gold bugs" or "silver bugs," sported badges and buttons with a clock face with hands pointing to "16 to 1," joined marching societies, and created women's clubs to support their candidate.

delivered campaign speeches to the party faithful who were brought there by train and carriage. This late-nineteenth century campaign innovation had been successful for Republican presidential candidates Garfield and Harrison. The front porch campaign allowed for maximum control and packaging of the candidate by his party handlers, in this case Mark Hanna, who tightly scripted both the campaign and McKinley's speeches. Campaigning from his porch had additional benefits for McKinley, whose wife, Ida, had long been an invalid. He could remain at home with her while still conveying his message to the voters. The campaign of 1896 focused on two

issues: Should the United States adhere to the gold standard as the basis of its currency? And were high protective tariffs good or bad for American manufacturing and trade? McKinley supported the gold standard and had helped author the protective tariffs. In general, the gold standard favored urban bankers and wealthy creditors. McKinley ran against William Jennings Bryan, a noted orator and supporter of the silver standard, which favored farmers, laborers, miners, and rural and western interests who owed debt. Bryan, a Democrat from Nebraska, favored the unlimited coinage of silver at a ratio of 16 to 1 (sixteen ounces of silver to one ounce of gold). The campaign slogan "16 to 1" referred to the silver faction's demand that the government increase the money supply. This simplistic economic policy was supposed to produce inflation that would ease the burden of debt.

Q: What was the background of William and Ida McKinley?

A: McKinley was a lawyer, former congressman, and governor of Ohio. Ida Saxton was a lively, intelligent, competent, and attractive young woman, the daughter of a wealthy banker and businessman in Canton, Ohio. After graduation from school and a grand tour of Europe, Ida worked as a teller in her father's bank, a very unusual position for a young woman of her era. In her early twenties, Ida began to suffer intermittent bouts of severe headaches, perhaps a symptom of her later health problems. She met McKinley, a Civil War veteran and rising lawyer, in Canton. After a short but intense courtship, the couple married on January 25, 1871. By all accounts the marriage was a happy one. They had two daughters, Katherine, called Katie, born in 1871, and a second daughter, Ida, born in 1873.

Q: What tragedies marred the happiness of William and Ida?

A: In early 1873, Ida's mother, to whom she was very close, died. Baby Ida, who was sickly from birth, died in August of the same year. The deaths of her mother and infant daughter dealt Ida blows from which she never fully recovered, physically or emotionally. When the McKinley's elder daughter, Katie, died of typhoid fever in June 1875, Ida's nerves and psyche were shattered. She began to suffer from seizures, events that permanently altered the dynamic of the McKinleys' marriage. Ida became increasingly anxious and irritable, dependent upon her husband, and jealous of other women. For his part, McKinley's devotion to his wife, and his apparently selfless and untiring efforts to accommodate her demands and anxieties, were well known. His steadfast devotion was even touted during his campaign as evidence of his decency and compassionate character.

Ida and William with McKinley's mother, Nancy. The McKinleys devotion to each other was legendary in Washington circles. Jennie Hobart, wife of Vice President Garret A. Hobart, noted, "The relationship between them was one of those rare and beautiful things that live only in tradition."

The graves of the McKinleys' daughters, Katie and Ida, in Canton, Ohio. The first lady never fully recovered from the shock of losing both her daughters within two years of each other.

> "I have never been in doubt since I was old enough to think intelligently that I would someday be made president."
>
> —WILLIAM MCKINLEY

Ida McKinley insisted on fulfilling her role as first lady despite her ill health and sudden seizures. One White House "regular," Countess Cassini, wrote of the awkward moments guests often faced. "Mrs. McKinley, looking fragile and drawn . . . suddenly, making no sound, stiffens in her chair and begins to quiver violently. Calmly, the President throws his pocket handkerchief over her face, rises, lifts her gently in his arms and carries her from the room without a word."

Foreign policy dominated the McKinley administration. McKinley led the country into the Spanish American War, bringing the former Spanish colonies in the Pacific, Guam and the Philippines, and in the Caribbean, Cuba and Puerto Rico, under American control.

Q: Who served as first lady?

A: Despite her known invalidism and continuing illness, which was whispered to be epilepsy, Ida insisted on serving as first lady. She waged a hard-fought battle to maintain a social presence and strove to fulfill her public role as fully as possible. Yet, as one biographer of first ladies has noted, with Ida, "the line between real illness and personality was a fine one."

In the White House, the McKinleys entertained elegantly. Public receptions were held at noon three times a week. The first lady received guests while seated next to the president and often appeared in magnificent gowns despite being sedated and propped up by pillows. Jennie Hobart, the tactful and empathetic wife of the vice president, frequently assisted Ida. Responsibility for formal state dinners fell to the staff, and the McKinleys hired a French chef to provide twelve-course repasts. Ida attended state dinners at which the customary protocol of seating arrangements, by which the president and first lady sat across from each other on opposite sides of the table, was altered by McKinley so that he could remain at her side to assist her in case of a seizure. Otherwise, strict protocol was observed.

Although the first lady's illness was a continuing source of anxiety to the president and even caused the cancellation of the 1901 White House social season, her debilitating ailment was, by unspoken consent, never mentioned in the press. When Ida suffered an attack in public, McKinley calmly placed a handkerchief or a napkin over his wife's face as her body visibly stiffened, and kept it in place until the seizure had passed. Once it ended, those present were expected to carry on the conversation as if nothing had happened.

Q: What tragic event marked the end of the McKinley presidency?

A: In September 1901, the president, along with the first lady, who was enjoying a period of relative good health, attended the Pan-American Exposition in Buffalo, New York. On September 6, McKinley appeared, surrounded by his entourage, at a public reception in the Temple of Music. A large crowd had assembled to shake hands with the popular president, who greeted each person with a smile and a few words. Leon Czolgosz, a Detroit-born anarchist of Polish descent, waited near the front of the line with his right hand wrapped in a handkerchief. Assuming that the man had an injury, McKinley extended his left hand to Czolgosz. Onlookers reported that they then heard two loud pops before the president clutched his chest and slumped forward. Czolgosz had fired two shots into the president. As his aides rushed to support him, McKinley's first thoughts were for Ida. As he collapsed,

he warned them, "My wife, be careful . . . how you tell her." Although the initial reports were optimistic that he would recover, gangrene had formed along the path of the bullet. He died in Buffalo on September 14, 1901, surrounded by a small group of family and friends.

The assassination of McKinley was a shock to the nation. Equally shocking was Ida's transformation. As a White House staff member noted, "To the amazement of her physician . . . Mrs. McKinley bore up surprisingly." She acted as her husband's nurse while he lingered, and calmly rode the train from Buffalo to Washington seated beside his coffin. After participating in her husband's funeral ceremonies at the Capitol, she descended the steps with a firm walk. She departed from Washington with the official party for her husband's burial in Canton, Ohio, where she lived with her sister for six years after her husband's death—completely free from seizures.

After Leon Czolgosz fired two shots into him, McKinley was rushed to the hospital and underwent emergency surgery. For just over a week he clung to life as the nation waited for word of a recovery. McKinley was the third U.S. president to be assassinated.

> " Nothing can make me happy again. "
> —IDA MCKINLEY,
> *after her husband's assassination*

The Presidents of the United States

1. George Washington

POLITICAL PARTY None, Federalist
TERM OF OFFICE 1789–97
VICE PRESIDENT John Adams
BORN February 22, 1732
BIRTHPLACE Westmoreland County, Virginia
MARRIED Martha Dandridge Custis
DIED December 14, 1799, age 67

John Adams

2. John Adams

POLITICAL PARTY Federalist
TERM OF OFFICE 1797–1801
VICE PRESIDENT Thomas Jefferson
BORN October 30, 1735
BIRTHPLACE Braintree, Massachusetts
MARRIED Abigail Smith
DIED July 4, 1826, age 90

3. Thomas Jefferson

POLITICAL PARTY Democratic-Republican
TERM OF OFFICE 1801–09
VICE PRESIDENTS Aaron Burr, George Clinton
BORN April 13, 1743
BIRTHPLACE Albemarle County, Virginia
MARRIED Martha Wayles Skelton
DIED July 4, 1826, age 83

4. James Madison

POLITICAL PARTY Democratic-Republican
TERM OF OFFICE 1809–17
VICE PRESIDENTS George Clinton, Elbridge Gerry
BORN March 16, 1751
BIRTHPLACE Port Conway, Virginia
MARRIED Dolley Payne Todd
DIED June 28, 1836, age 85

5. James Monroe

POLITICAL PARTY Democratic-Republican
TERM OF OFFICE 1817–25
VICE PRESIDENT Daniel D. Tompkins
BORN April 28, 1758
BIRTHPLACE Westmoreland County, Virginia
MARRIED Elizabeth Kortright
DIED July 4, 1831, age 73

6. John Quincy Adams

POLITICAL PARTY Democratic-Republican
TERM OF OFFICE 1825–29
VICE PRESIDENT John C. Calhoun
BORN July 11, 1767
BIRTHPLACE Braintree, Massachusetts
MARRIED Louisa Catherine Johnson
DIED February 23, 1848, age 80

7. Andrew Jackson

POLITICAL PARTY Democrat
TERM OF OFFICE 1829–37
VICE PRESIDENTS John C. Calhoun, Martin Van Buren
BORN March 15, 1767
BIRTHPLACE Waxhaw settlement, South Carolina
MARRIED Rachel Donelson
DIED June 8, 1845, age 78

8. Martin Van Buren

POLITICAL PARTY Democrat
TERM OF OFFICE 1837–41
VICE PRESIDENT Richard M. Johnson
BORN December 5, 1782
BIRTHPLACE Columbia, New York
MARRIED Hannah Hoes
DIED July 24, 1862, age 79

Martin Van Buren

9. William Henry Harrison

POLITICAL PARTY Whig
TERM OF OFFICE 1841
VICE PRESIDENT John Tyler
BORN February 9, 1773
BIRTHPLACE Charles City County, Virginia
MARRIED Anna Tuthill Symmes
DIED April 4, 1841, age 68

William Henry Harrison

10. John Tyler
POLITICAL PARTY Whig
TERM OF OFFICE 1841–45
VICE PRESIDENT None
BORN March 29, 1790
BIRTHPLACE Charles City County, Virginia
MARRIED Letitia Christian, Julia Gardiner
DIED January 18, 1862, age 71

James K. Polk

11. James K. Polk
POLITICAL PARTY Democrat
TERM OF OFFICE 1845–49
VICE PRESIDENT George M. Dallas
BORN November 2, 1795
BIRTHPLACE Mecklenburg County, North Carolina
MARRIED Sarah Childress
DIED June 15, 1849, age 53

12. Zachary Taylor
POLITICAL PARTY Whig
TERM OF OFFICE 1849–50
VICE PRESIDENT Millard Fillmore
BORN November 24, 1784
BIRTHPLACE Orange County, Virginia
MARRIED Margaret Mackall Smith
DIED July 9, 1850, age 65

13. Millard Fillmore
POLITICAL PARTY Whig
TERM OF OFFICE 1850–53
VICE PRESIDENT None
BORN January 7, 1800
BIRTHPLACE Cayuga County, New York
MARRIED Abigail Powers, Caroline McIntosh
DIED March 8, 1874, age 74

14. Franklin Pierce
POLITICAL PARTY Democrat
TERM OF OFFICE 1853–57
VICE PRESIDENT William R. King
BORN November 23, 1804
BIRTHPLACE Hillsboro, New Hampshire
MARRIED Jane Means Appleton
DIED October 8, 1869, age 64

15. James Buchanan
POLITICAL PARTY Democrat
TERM OF OFFICE 1857–61
VICE PRESIDENT John C. Breckinridge
BORN April 23, 1791
BIRTHPLACE Cove Gap, Pennsylvania
DIED June 1, 1868, age 77

Abraham Lincoln

16. Abraham Lincoln
POLITICAL PARTY Republican
TERM OF OFFICE 1861–65
VICE PRESIDENTS Hannibal Hamlin, Andrew Johnson
BORN February 12, 1809
BIRTHPLACE Hardin County, Kentucky
MARRIED Mary Todd
DIED April 15, 1865, age 56

17. Andrew Johnson
POLITICAL PARTY National Union
TERM OF OFFICE 1865–69
VICE PRESIDENT None
BORN December 29, 1808
BIRTHPLACE Raleigh, North Carolina
MARRIED Eliza McCardle
DIED July 31, 1875, age 66

18. Ulysses S. Grant
POLITICAL PARTY Republican
TERM OF OFFICE 1869–77
VICE PRESIDENT Schuyler Colfax,

Ulysses S. Grant

Henry Wilson
BORN April 27, 1822
BIRTHPLACE Point Pleasant, Ohio
MARRIED Julia Dent
DIED July 23, 1885, age 63

19. Rutherford B. Hayes
POLITICAL PARTY Republican
TERM OF OFFICE 1877–81
VICE PRESIDENT William A. Wheeler
BORN October 4, 1822
BIRTHPLACE Delaware, Ohio
MARRIED Lucy Ware Webb
DIED January 17, 1893, age 70

20. James A. Garfield
POLITICAL PARTY Republican
TERM OF OFFICE 1881
VICE PRESIDENT Chester Arthur
BORN November 19, 1831
BIRTHPLACE Orange, Ohio
MARRIED Lucretia Rudolph
DIED September 19, 1881, age 49

21. Chester A. Arthur
POLITICAL PARTY Republican
TERM OF OFFICE 1881–85
VICE PRESIDENT none
BORN October 5, 1829
BIRTHPLACE Fairfield, Vermont
MARRIED Ellen Lewis Herndon
DIED November 18, 1886, age 57

22 and 24. Grover Cleveland
POLITICAL PARTY Democrat
TERM OF OFFICE 1885–89, 1893–97
VICE PRESIDENTS Thomas A. Hendricks, Adlai E. Stevenson
BORN March 18, 1837
BIRTHPLACE Caldwell, New Jersey
MARRIED Frances Folsom
DIED June 24, 1908, age 71

Benjamin Harrison

23. Benjamin Harrison
POLITICAL PARTY Republican
TERM OF OFFICE 1889–93
VICE PRESIDENT Levi P. Morton
BORN August 20, 1833
BIRTHPLACE North Bend, Ohio
MARRIED Caroline Lavinia Scott
DIED March 13, 1901, age 67

William McKinley

25. William McKinley
POLITICAL PARTY Republican
TERM OF OFFICE 1897–1901
VICE PRESIDENTS Garret A. Hobart, Theodore Roosevelt
BORN January 29, 1843
BIRTHPLACE Niles, Ohio
MARRIED Ida Saxton
DIED September 14, 1901, age 58

26. Theodore Roosevelt
POLITICAL PARTY Republican
TERM OF OFFICE 1901–09
VICE PRESIDENT Charles Fairbanks
BORN October 27, 1858
BIRTHPLACE New York, New York
MARRIED Alice Lee, Edith Kermit Carow
DIED January 6, 1919, age 60

27. William H. Taft
POLITICAL PARTY Republican
TERM OF OFFICE 1909–13
VICE PRESIDENT James S. Sherman
BORN September 15, 1857
BIRTHPLACE Cincinnati, Ohio
MARRIED Helen Herron
DIED March 8, 1930, age 72

28. Woodrow Wilson
POLITICAL PARTY Democrat
TERM OF OFFICE 1913–21
VICE PRESIDENT Thomas R. Marshall
BORN December 28, 1856
BIRTHPLACE Staunton, Virginia
MARRIED Ellen Louise Axson, Edith Bolling Galt
DIED February 3, 1924, age 67

29. Warren G. Harding
POLITICAL PARTY Republican
TERM OF OFFICE 1921–23
VICE PRESIDENT Calvin Coolidge
BORN November 2, 1865
BIRTHPLACE Corsica, Ohio
MARRIED Florence Kling
DIED August 2, 1923, age 57

30. Calvin Coolidge
POLITICAL PARTY Republican
TERM OF OFFICE 1923–29
VICE PRESIDENT Charles G. Dawes
BORN July 4, 1872
BIRTHPLACE Plymouth, Vermont
MARRIED Grace Anna Goodhue
DIED January 5, 1933, age 60

Calvin Coolidge

31. Herbert Hoover
POLITICAL PARTY Republican
TERM OF OFFICE 1929–33
VICE PRESIDENT Charles Curtis
BORN August 10, 1874
BIRTHPLACE West Branch, Iowa
MARRIED Lou Henry
DIED October 20, 1964, age 90

32. Franklin D. Roosevelt
POLITICAL PARTY Democrat
TERM OF OFFICE 1933–45
VICE PRESIDENTS John N. Garner, Henry A. Wallace, Harry S. Truman
BORN January 30, 1882
BIRTHPLACE Hyde Park, New York
MARRIED Anna Eleanor Roosevelt
DIED April 12, 1945, age 63

Harry S Truman

33. Harry S Truman
POLITICAL PARTY Democrat
TERM OF OFFICE 1945–53
VICE PRESIDENT Alben Barkley
BORN May 8, 1884
BIRTHPLACE Lamar, Missouri
MARRIED Elizabeth Wallace
DIED December 26, 1972, age 88

34. Dwight D. Eisenhower
POLITICAL PARTY Republican
TERM OF OFFICE 1953–61
VICE PRESIDENT Richard Milhous Nixon
BORN October 14, 1890
BIRTHPLACE Denison, Texas
MARRIED Mamie Geneva Doud
DIED March 28, 1969, age 78

35. John F. Kennedy
POLITICAL PARTY Democrat
TERM OF OFFICE 1961–63
VICE PRESIDENT Lyndon B. Johnson
BORN May 29, 1917
BIRTHPLACE Brookline, Massachusetts
MARRIED Jacqueline Lee Bouvier
DIED November 22, 1963, age 46

36. Lyndon B. Johnson
POLITICAL PARTY Democrat
TERM OF OFFICE 1963–69
VICE PRESIDENT Hubert H. Humphrey
BORN August 27, 1908
BIRTHPLACE near Stonewall, Texas
MARRIED Claudia Alta
"Lady Bird" Taylor
DIED January 22, 1973, age 64

37. Richard M. Nixon
POLITICAL PARTY Republican
TERM OF OFFICE 1969–1974
VICE PRESIDENTS Spiro Agnew,
Gerald R. Ford
BORN January 9, 1913
BIRTHPLACE Yorba Linda, California
MARRIED Patricia Ryan
DIED April 22, 1994, age 81

38. Gerald R. Ford
POLITICAL PARTY Republican
TERM OF OFFICE 1974–77
VICE PRESIDENT Nelson A. Rockefeller
BORN July 14, 1913
BIRTHPLACE Omaha, Nebraska
MARRIED Elizabeth Bloomer

39. Jimmy Carter
POLITICAL PARTY Democrat
TERM OF OFFICE 1977–81
VICE PRESIDENT Walter Mondale
BORN October 1, 1924
BIRTHPLACE Plains, Georgia
MARRIED Rosalynn Smith

Ronald Reagan

40. Ronald Reagan
POLITICAL PARTY Republican
TERM OF OFFICE 1981–89
VICE PRESIDENT George H. W. Bush
BORN February 6, 1911
BIRTHPLACE Tampico, Illinois
MARRIED Jane Wyman, Nancy Davis
DIED June 5, 2004, age 93

41. George H. W. Bush
POLITICAL PARTY Republican
TERM OF OFFICE 1989–93
VICE PRESIDENT James Danforth
(Dan) Quayle
BORN June 12, 1924
BIRTHPLACE Milton, Massachusetts
MARRIED Barbara Pierce

William J. Clinton

42. William J. Clinton
POLITICAL PARTY Democrat
TERM OF OFFICE 1993–2001
VICE PRESIDENT Albert Gore Jr.
BORN August 19, 1946
BIRTHPLACE Hope, Arkansas
MARRIED Hillary Rodham

43. George W. Bush
PARTY Republican
TERM OF OFFICE 2001–
VICE PRESIDENT Richard Cheney
BORN July 6, 1946
BIRTHPLACE New Haven, Connecticut
MARRIED Laura Welch

Presidential Wives

Martha Dandridge Custis Washington

Martha Wayles Skelton Jefferson
NEVER SERVED AS FIRST LADY
BORN October 19, 1748
BIRTHPLACE Charles City County, Virginia
MARRIED January 1, 1772
CHILDREN By first marriage: John Skelton (1767–71); by second marriage: Martha (1772–1836), Jane (1774–75), an unnamed son (1777, died in infancy), Maria (1778–1804), Lucy Elizabeth [1] (1780–81), Lucy Elizabeth [2] (1782–85)
DIED September 6, 1782, age 33

Martha Dandridge Custis Washington
YEARS AS FIRST LADY 1789–97
BORN June 2, 1731
BIRTHPLACE New Kent County, Virginia
MARRIED January 6, 1759
CHILDREN By first marriage: Daniel Parke Custis (1751–54), Frances Parke Custis (1753–57), John Parke Custis (1754–81), Martha Parke Custis (1756–73); raised: grandchildren George Washington Parke Custis (1781–1857), Eleanor Parke Custis (1779–1852)
DIED May 22, 1802, age 70

Abigail Smith Adams
YEARS AS FIRST LADY 1797–1801
BORN November 11, 1744
BIRTHPLACE Weymouth, Massachusetts
MARRIED October 25, 1764
CHILDREN Abigail Amelia (1765–1813), John Quincy (1767–1848), Susannah (1768–70), Charles (1770–1800), Thomas Boylston (1772–1832)
DIED October 28, 1818, age 73

Dolley Payne Todd Madison

Dolley Payne Todd Madison
YEARS AS FIRST LADY 1809–17
BORN May 20, 1768
BIRTHPLACE Guilford County, North Carolina
MARRIED September 15, 1794
CHILDREN By first marriage: John Payne Todd (1792–1852), William Isaac Todd, (1793, died in infancy)
DIED July 12, 1849, age 81

Elizabeth Kortright Monroe
YEARS AS FIRST LADY 1817–25
BORN June 30, 1768
BIRTHPLACE New York, New York
MARRIED February 16, 1786
CHILDREN Eliza (1786–1840), James Spence (1799–1801), Maria Hester (1803–50)
DIED September 23, 1830, age 62

Louisa Catherine Johnson Adams
YEARS AS FIRST LADY 1827–29
BORN February 1, 1775
BIRTHPLACE London, England
MARRIED July 26, 1797
CHILDREN George Washington (1801–29), John II (1803–34), Charles Francis (1807–86), Louisa Catherine (1811–12)
DIED May 15, 1852, age 77

Rachel Donelson Jackson
NEVER SERVED AS FIRST LADY
BORN June 15, 1767
BIRTHPLACE Pittsylvania County, Virginia
MARRIED June 8, 1845
CHILDREN Adopted: Andrew Jr. (1808–65), Lyncoya (c. 1811–28)
DIED December 22, 1828, age 61

Hannah Hoes Van Buren
NEVER SERVED AS FIRST LADY
BORN March 8, 1783
BIRTHPLACE Kinderhook, New York
MARRIED February 21, 1807
CHILDREN Abraham (1807–73), John (1810–66), Martin Jr. (1812–55), Winfield Scott (1814, died in infancy), Smith Thompson (1817–76)
DIED February 5, 1819, age 35

Anna Tuthill Symmes Harrison
YEARS AS FIRST LADY 1841
BORN July 25, 1775
BIRTHPLACE Sussex County, New Jersey
MARRIED November 22, 1795
CHILDREN Elizabeth Bassett (1796–1846), John Cleves Symmes (1819–30), Lucy Singleton (1800–26), William Henry

II (1802–38), John Scott (1804–78), Benjamin (1806–40), Mary Symmes (1809–42), Carter Bassett (1811–39), Anna Tuthill (1813–45), James Findlay (1814–17)
DIED February 25, age 88

Letitia Christian Tyler
YEARS AS FIRST LADY 1841–1842
BORN November 12, 1790
BIRTHPLACE New Kent County, Virginia
MARRIED March 29, 1813
CHILDREN Mary (1815–47), Robert (1816–77), John Jr. (1819–96), Letitia Christian (1821–1907), Elizabeth (1820–70), Alice (1827–54), Tazewell (1830–74)
DIED September 10, 1842, age 51

Julia Gardiner Tyler
YEARS AS FIRST LADY 1844–45
BORN May 4, 1820
BIRTHPLACE Gardiner's Island, New York
MARRIED June 26, 1844
CHILDREN David Gardiner (1846–1927), John Alexander (1848–83), Julia (1849–71), Lachlan (1851–1902), Lyon Gardiner (1853–1935), Robert Fitzwalter (1856–1927), Pearl (1860–1947)
DIED July 10, 1889, age 69

Sarah Childress Polk

Sarah Childress Polk
YEARS AS FIRST LADY 1845–49
BORN September 4, 1803
BIRTHPLACE Murfreesboro, Tennessee
MARRIED January 1, 1824
CHILDREN None
DIED August 14, 1891, age 87

Margaret Mackall Smith Taylor
YEARS AS FIRST LADY 1949–50
BORN September 21, 1788
BIRTHPLACE Calvert County, Maryland
MARRIED June 21, 1810
CHILDREN Sarah Knox (1813–35), Anne Margaret Mackall (1811–75), Octavia Pannel (1816–20), Margaret Smith (1819–20), Mary Elizabeth (1824–1909), Richard (1826–79)
DIED August 14, 1852, age 63

Abigail Powers Fillmore
YEARS AS FIRST LADY 1850–53
BORN March 13, 1798
BIRTHPLACE Stillwater, New York
MARRIED February 5, 1826
CHILDREN Millard Powers (1828–89), Mary Abigail (1832–54)
DIED March 30, 1853, age 55

Jane Means Appleton Pierce
YEARS AS FIRST LADY 1853–57
BORN March 12, 1806
BIRTHPLACE Hampton, New Hampshire
MARRIED November 19, 1834
CHILDREN Franklin Jr. (1836, died in infancy), Frank Robert (1839–43), Benjamin (1841–53)
DIED December 2, 1863, age 57

Mary Anne Todd Lincoln
YEARS AS FIRST LADY 1861–65
BORN December 13, 1818
BIRTHPLACE Lexington, Kentucky
MARRIED November 4, 1842
CHILDREN Robert Todd (1843–1926), Edward Baker (1846–50), William Wallace (1850–62), Thomas (1853–71)
DIED July 16, 1882, age 63

Eliza McCardle Johnson
YEARS AS FIRST LADY 1865–69
BORN October 4, 1810
BIRTHPLACE Greeneville, Tennessee
MARRIED May 17, 1827
CHILDREN Martha (1828–1901), Charles (1830–63), Mary (1832–83), Robert (1834–69), Andrew Jr. (1852–79)
DIED January 15, 1876, age 65

Julia Dent Grant
YEARS AS FIRST LADY 1869–77
BORN January 26, 1826
BIRTHPLACE St. Louis County, Missouri
MARRIED August 22, 1848
CHILDREN Frederick Dent (1850–1912), Ulysses S. (1852–1929), Ellen Wrenshall (1855–1922), Jesse Root (1858–1934)
DIED December 14, 1902, age 76

Lucy Ware Webb Hayes

Lucy Ware Webb Hayes
YEARS AS FIRST LADY 1877–81
BORN August 28, 1831
BIRTHPLACE Chillicothe, Ohio
MARRIED December 30, 1852
CHILDREN Birchard Austin (1853–1926), Webb Cook (1856–1934), Rutherford Platt (1858–1927), Joseph Thompson (1861–63), George Crook (1864–66), Fanny (1867–1950), Scott Russell (1871–1923), Manning Force (1873–74)
DIED June 25, 1889, age 57

Lucretia Rudolph Garfield
YEARS AS FIRST LADY 1881
BORN April 19, 1832
BIRTHPLACE Garrettsville, Ohio
MARRIED November 11, 1858
CHILDREN Eliza Arabella (1860–63), Harry Augustus (1863–1942), James Rudolf (1865–1950), Mary (1867–1947), Irvin McDowell (1870–1951), Abram (1872–1958), Edward (1874–76)
DIED March 14, 1918, age 85

Ellen Lewis Herndon Arthur

NEVER SERVED AS FIRST LADY
BORN August 30, 1837
BIRTHPLACE Culpepper County, Virginia
MARRIED October 25, 1859
CHILDREN William Lewis Herndon (1860–63), Chester Alan (1864–1937), Ellen Herndon (1871–1915)
DIED January 12, 1880, age 42

Frances Folsom Cleveland

YEARS AS FIRST LADY 1886–89, 1893–97
BORN July 21, 1864
BIRTHPLACE Buffalo, New York
MARRIED June 2, 1886
CHILDREN Ruth (1891–1904), Esther (1893–1980), Marion (1895–1977), Richard Folsom (1897–1974), Francis Grover (1903–1995)
DIED October 29, 1947, age 83

Caroline Lavinia Scott Harrison

YEARS AS FIRST LADY 1889–92
BORN October 1, 1832
BIRTHPLACE Oxford, Ohio
MARRIED October 20, 1853
CHILDREN Russell Lord (1854–1936), Mary Scott (1858–1930), an unnamed daughter (1861, stillborn)
DIED October 25, 1892, age 60

Ida Saxton McKinley

YEARS AS FIRST LADY 1897–1901
BORN June 8, 1847
BIRTHPLACE Canton, Ohio
MARRIED January 25, 1871
CHILDREN Katherine (1871–75), Ida (1873, died in infancy)
DIED May 26, 1907, age 59

Edith Kermit Carow Roosevelt

YEARS AS FIRST LADY 1901–09
BORN August 6, 1861
BIRTHPLACE Norwich, Connecticut
MARRIED December 2, 1886
CHILDREN Theodore Jr. (1887–1944), Kermit (1889–1943), Ethel Carow (1891–1977), Archibald Bullock (1894–1979), Quentin (1897–1918); stepdaughter: Alice (1884–1980)
DIED September 30, 1948, age 87

Helen Herron Taft

Helen Herron Taft

YEARS AS FIRST LADY 1909–13
BORN June 2, 1861
BIRTHPLACE Cincinnati, Ohio
MARRIED June 19, 1886.
CHILDREN Robert Alphonso (1889–1953), Helen (1891–1987), Charles (1897–1983)
DIED May 22, 1943, age 81

Ellen Louise Axson Wilson

YEARS AS FIRST LADY 1913–14
BORN May 15, 1860
BIRTHPLACE Savannah, Georgia
MARRIED June 24, 1885
CHILDREN Margaret Woodrow (1886–1944), Jessie Woodrow (1887–1933), Eleanor Randolph (1889–1967)
DIED August 6, 1914, age 54

Edith Bolling Galt Wilson

YEARS AS FIRST LADY 1915–21
BORN October 15, 1872
BIRTHPLACE Wytheville, Virginia
MARRIED December 19, 1915
CHILDREN By first marriage: an unnamed son (1903, died in infancy)
DIED December 9, 1961, age 81

Florence Kling Harding

YEARS AS FIRST LADY 1921–23
BORN August 15, 1860
BIRTHPLACE Marion, Ohio
MARRIED July 8, 1891
CHILDREN By first marriage: Marshall Eugene DeWolfe (1880–1915)
DIED November 21, 1924, age 64

Grace Anna Goodhue Coolidge

YEARS AS FIRST LADY 1923–29
BORN January 3, 1879
BIRTHPLACE Burlington, Vermont
MARRIED October 4, 1905
CHILDREN John (1906–2000), Calvin Jr. (1908–24)
DIED July 7, 1957, age 78

Lou Henry Hoover

YEARS AS FIRST LADY 1929–33
BORN March 29, 1874
BIRTHPLACE Waterloo, Iowa
MARRIED February 10, 1899
CHILDREN Herbert Clark Jr. (1903–69)
DIED January 7, 1944, age 69

Anna Eleanor Roosevelt

Anna Eleanor Roosevelt

YEARS AS FIRST LADY 1933–45
BORN October 11, 1884
BIRTHPLACE New York, New York
MARRIED March 17, 1905
CHILDREN Anna Eleanor (1906–75), James (1907–91), Franklin (1909, died in infancy), Elliott (1910–90), Franklin Delano Jr. (1914–88), John Aspinwall (1916–81)
DIED November 7, 1962, age 78

Elizabeth Wallace Truman
YEARS AS FIRST LADY 1945–53
BORN February 13, 1885
BIRTHPLACE Independence, Missouri
MARRIED June 28, 1919
CHILDREN Mary Margaret (b. 1924)
DIED October 18, 1982, age 97

Mamie Geneva Doud Eisenhower
YEARS AS FIRST LADY 1953–61
BORN November 14, 1896
BIRTHPLACE Boone, Iowa
MARRIED July 1, 1916
CHILDREN Doud Dwight (1917–21), John Sheldon Doud (b. 1922)
DIED November 1, 1979, age 82

Lady Bird Taylor Johnson

Lady Bird Taylor Johnson
YEARS AS FIRST LADY 1963–69
BORN December 22, 1912
BIRTHPLACE Karnack, Texas
MARRIED November 17, 1934
CHILDREN Lynda Bird (b. 1944), Luci Baines (b. 1947)

Patricia Ryan Nixon
YEARS AS FIRST LADY 1969–74
BORN March 16, 1912
BIRTHPLACE Ely, Nevada
MARRIED June 21, 1940
CHILDREN Patricia (b. 1946), Julie (b. 1948)
DIED June 22, 1993, age 81

Elizabeth Bloomer Ford
YEARS AS FIRST LADY 1974–77
BORN April 18, 1918
BIRTHPLACE Chicago, Illinois
MARRIED October 15, 1948
CHILDREN Michael Gerald (b. 1950), John Gardner (b. 1952), Steven Meigs (b. 1956), Susan Elizabeth (b. 1957)

Rosalynn Smith Carter
YEARS AS FIRST LADY 1977–81
BORN August 18, 1927
BIRTHPLACE Plains, Georgia
MARRIED July 7, 1946
CHILDREN John William (b. 1947), James Earl (b. 1950), Donnel Jeffrey (b. 1952), Amy Lynn (b. 1967)

Jacqueline Lee Bouvier Kennedy

Jacqueline Lee Bouvier Kennedy
YEARS AS FIRST LADY 1961–63
BORN July 21, 1929
BIRTHPLACE Southampton, New York
MARRIED September 12, 1953
CHILDREN Caroline Bouvier (b. 1957), John F. Jr. (1960–99), Patrick Bouvier (1963, died in infancy)
DIED May 19, 1994, age 64

Nancy Davis Reagan
YEARS AS FIRST LADY 1981–89
BORN July 6, 1921
BIRTHPLACE Queens, New York
MARRIED March 6, 1952
CHILDREN Patricia Ann (b. 1952), Ronald Prescott (b. 1958); stepchildren: Maureen Reagan (1941–2001), Michael Reagan (b. 1945)

Barbara Pierce Bush
YEARS AS FIRST LADY 1989–93
BORN June 8, 1925
BIRTHPLACE New York, New York
MARRIED January 6, 1945
CHILDREN George Walker (b. 1946), Pauline Robinson (1949–53), John Ellis (b. 1953), Neil Mallon (b. 1955), Marvin Pierce (b. 1956), Dorothy (b. 1959)

Hillary Rodham Clinton
YEARS AS FIRST LADY 1993–2001
BORN October 26, 1947
BIRTHPLACE Chicago, Illinois
MARRIED October 11, 1975
CHILDREN Chelsea Victoria Clinton (b. 1980)

Laura Welch Bush
YEARS AS FIRST LADY 2001–
BORN November 4, 1946
BIRTHPLACE Midland, Texas
MARRIED November 5, 1977
CHILDREN Barbara (b. 1981), Jenna (b. 1981)

Rosalynn Smith Carter

White House Milestones

James Hoban's exterior drawing, or "elevation," of the proposed President's House.

1793 Construction of the President's House based on James Hoban's design begins

1800 John and Abigail Adams move into partially completed mansion

1806 James Madison Randolph, grandson of Thomas Jefferson, is born

1812 Lucy Payne Washington Todd, sister of Dolley Madison, marries Thomas Todd in the Blue Room

1814 British troops burn the mansion during War of 1812

1817 The Monroes move into rebuilt President's House

1820 Maria Hester Monroe, daughter of James Monroe, marries Samuel Lawrence Gouverneur in the Blue Room

1821 James Monroe Gouverneur, grandson of James Monroe, is christened

1822 Samuel Lawrence Gouverneur, grandson of James Monroe, is christened

Charred timber found during the Truman renovation of the White House, which is believed to have survived the 1814 burning of the building by the British.

1828 John Adams II, son of John Quincy Adams, marries Mary Catherine Hellen in the Blue Room

1829 Mary Louisa Adams, granddaughter of John Quincy Adams, is christened

1829 Mary Donelson, great-niece of Andrew Jackson, is christened

1832 John Samuel Donelson, great-nephew of Andrew Jackson, is christened

1832 Mary A. Eastin, great-niece of Andrew Jackson, marries Lucius J. Polk in the East Room

1834 Andrew Jackson III, adoptive grandson of Andrew Jackson, is christened

1840 Rebecca Singleton Van Buren, granddaughter of Martin Van Buren, is born

1840 Singleton Van Buren, grandson of Martin Van Buren, is born

1841 The funeral of William Henry Harrison is held

"Sally," the White House doll, made around 1829 for Maria Louise Adams, granddaughter of John Quincy Adams.

Angelica Van Buren gave birth to two children in the White House.

1842 The funeral of Letitia Tyler, wife of John Tyler, is held

1842 Elizabeth Tyler, daughter of John Tyler, marries William Waller in the East Room

1842 Letitia Christian Tyler, granddaughter of John Tyler, is christened

1843 Robert Tyler Jones, grandson of John Tyler, is christened

1850 The funeral of Zachary Taylor is held

1862 The funeral of Willie Lincoln, son of Abraham Lincoln, is held

Rolling eggs on the Monday after Easter was a tradition observed by many Washington families.

1878 First White House Easter Egg Roll was held during Hayes administration

1881 The funeral of James Garfield is held

1882 Chester A. Arthur engages Louis Comfort Tiffany to redecorate the mansion

Willie Lincoln died in the White House, at the age of eleven, while his father was president.

1865 The funeral of Abraham Lincoln is held

1873 The funeral of Fred Dent, father of Julia Grant, is held

1874 Nellie Grant, daughter Ulysses Grant, marries Algernon Sartoris in the East Room

1876 The christening of Julia Grant, granddaughter of Ulysses Grant, is held

1877 Scott and Fanny Hayes, son and daughter of Rutherford Hayes, are christened (as young adults)

1878 Emily Platt, niece of Rutherford Hayes, marries Russell Hastings in the Blue Room

After their brilliant White House wedding Nellie Grant and Algernon Sartoris moved to England, where the marriage eventually ended in divorce.

Frances Folsom became a media darling when she married sitting president Grover Cleveland.

1886 Grover Cleveland marries Frances Folsom in the Blue Room

1889 Marthena Harrison, granddaughter of Benjamin Harrison, is christened

1892 The funeral of John W. Scott, father of Caroline Harrison, is held

1892 The funeral of Caroline Harrison, wife of Benjamin Harrison, is held

1906 Alice Lee Roosevelt, daughter of Theodore Roosevelt, marries Nicholas Longworth in the East Room

1913 Ellen Axson Wilson, first wife of Woodrow Wilson, plants the first Rose Garden

1913 Jessie Woodrow Wilson, daughter of Woodrow Wilson, marries Francis Bowes Sayre in the East Room

1914 The funeral of Ellen Wilson, wife of Woodrow Wilson, is held

Eleanor was the second of the Wilson daughters to marry in the White House.

1914 Eleanor Randolph Wilson, daughter of Woodrow Wilson, marries William Gibbs McAdoo in the Blue Room

1915 Francis B. Sayre, grandson of Woodrow Wilson, is christened

1918 Alice Wilson, niece of Woodrow Wilson, marries Isaac Stuart McElroy Jr., in the Blue Room

1923 The funeral of Warren Harding is held

1924 The funeral of Calvin Coolidge Jr., son of Calvin Coolidge, is held

1937 Elliott Roosevelt Jr., grandson of FDR, is christened

1934 West Wing is completed during FDR administration

1939 John Boettiger Jr., grandson of FDR, is christened

1942 Construction of a new East Wing is completed

The West Wing under construction, 1934.

1945 The funeral of Franklin Delano Roosevelt is held

1948–52 Renovation of the White House

1955 Mary Jean Eisenhower, grand-daughter of Dwight Eisenhower, is christened

Jacqueline Kennedy receives flag from the coffin of her husband John F. Kennedy.

Tricia Nixon and Edward Cox share a dance in the East Room on their wedding day.

1963 The funeral of President John F. Kennedy is held

1966 Luci Johnson, daughter of LBJ, marries Patrick Nugent; wedding reception is held in the White House

1967 Lynda Bird Johnson, daughter of LBJ, marries Charles Robb in the East Room

1971 Tricia Nixon, daughter of Richard Nixon, marries Edward Finch Cox in the Rose Garden

1989 Ashley Walker Bush, granddaughter of George H. W. Bush, is christened in the White House

1989 Charles Walker Bush, grandson of George H. W. Bush, is christened in the White House

1994 Anthony Rodham, brother of Hillary Rodham Clinton, marries Nicole Boxer in the White House

Lyndon Johnson escorts his daughter Lynda Bird down the White House steps.

CHAPTER 7

AN EMERGING WORLD POWER

The dawn of the twentieth century saw the United States emerge as an imperial force following its 1898 victory in the Spanish-American War. To reflect the newly acquired prestige of the nation, Washington officials proposed a plan to update the capital's image that included restoring and remodeling the decaying Executive Mansion. To that end, Theodore Roosevelt initiated sweeping changes that structurally transformed the mansion and changed its official name to the "White House." William Howard Taft maintained the social legacy of his predecessor and First Lady Nellie Taft gave the capital an international flair by accepting the famous cherry blossom trees as a gift from Japan. Taft, however, made his own political decisions, such as choosing a new cabinet. In response, Roosevelt again ran for president in 1912, a move that split the Republican vote, paving the way for Democrat Woodrow Wilson's victory. The Wilson administration firmly established the nation's international leadership through victory for the Allied Powers in World War I and Wilson's advocacy of the League of Nations, despite the United States' refusal to join.

Above: U.S. warships under command of Rear Admiral Sampson bombarding San Juan, Puerto Rico, during the Spanish-American War.

Left: *Share in the Victory,* a poster for World War I war bonds. A long-standing policy of isolationism left the United States reluctant to involve itself in what was popularly perceived as a European war.

Theodore and Edith Roosevelt

Above: In the front left, Edith on the ground in front of Theodore, with his brother Elliott and sister Corinne in 1876. Edith and Theodore had been close friends since their childhood days.

Right: Alice Hathaway Lee. Theodore and Alice lived happily in New York City for three years before Alice's sudden death. Disconsolate over her loss, for the rest of his life, Theodore refused to speak about his first wife.

Q: How did Theodore Roosevelt meet Edith Carow?

A: The Roosevelt and the Carow families were neighbors in New York City, sharing the same social circle and often vacationing together. Edith and Theodore grew up as close friends from their earliest childhood. Edith attended private school taught in the Roosevelt's New York mansion before enrolling in Miss Comstock's School for Girls, while Theodore entered Harvard. As teenagers, the two became attracted to each other, and Edith always claimed that Theodore had asked her to marry him several times in the late 1870s. But in February 1878, they quarreled (the reasons for the spat are unclear) and Theodore returned to Harvard.

Q: Who was Roosevelt's first wife?

A: While at Harvard, Roosevelt met the beautiful, ebullient, athletic Bostonian Alice Hathaway Lee and quickly fell in love. When Alice accepted his marriage proposal, he notified Edith of his engagement before it was formally announced. Although Edith was shocked and devastated by the news, she put on a brave face and managed to attend the wedding on

October 27, 1880. Less than four years later, Alice gave birth to a daughter, Alice Lee Roosevelt. Two days after giving birth to her daughter, Alice died of Bright's disease. Tragically, Theodore's mother, Martha, died of typhoid that same day. Double funeral services were held at New York's Fifth Avenue Presbyterian Church. Roosevelt recounted in his memoirs that with his wife's death he felt as if the light had gone from his life forever. Barely able to function in his grief, he placed baby Alice in the care of his eldest sister, Anna, sold his house, and took off for a two-year escape to the Dakota Badlands.

Alice Lee Roosevelt

Q: Who became Theodore Roosevelt's second wife?

A: Edith Carow had remained close to Theodore's family during the years of his marriage, but had taken care to avoid social occasions were she would run into Theodore and Alice together. After Alice's death, she unexpectedly encountered Theodore, who was on a visit home to New York, at the home of one of his sisters. The two mended their rift and renewed their relationship. By the time he returned to the Dakota Territory, he and

Edith were secretly engaged. The couple married in a private ceremony in Saint George's Church in London on December 2, 1886, and took a tour through Europe for their honeymoon. Upon the couple's return to New York, Edith decided to raise young Alice as her own daughter.

Q: **How did Theodore Roosevelt become president?**

A: Roosevelt had been a New York assemblyman, New York City's police commissioner, and assistant secretary of the Navy. After Congress declared war

COL. ROOSEVELT Tells the story of THE ROUGH RIDERS in Scribner's Magazine. It begins in January and will run for six months, with many illustrations from photographs taken in the field.

JANUARY SCRIBNER'S NOW READY PRICE 25 CENTS

Roosevelt tells the story of the Rough Riders in *Scribner's Magazine*. Roosevelt's self-promotion campaign highlighted his role at the famous Battle of San Juan Hill.

against Spain in 1898, he resigned his post to organize a volunteer cavalry regiment —the famed Rough Riders—whose daring wartime exploits catapulted him to national fame. He returned to become governor of New York. In 1900, Roosevelt was elected as William McKinley's vice president on the Republican ticket. He assumed the presidency upon McKinley's death at the hands of an assassin in 1901. He was sworn in as the new president immediately, taking the oath of office at the home of Ansley Wilcox in Buffalo, New York, on Saturday, September 14, 1901.

With the tragic assassination of William McKinley, Theodore Roosevelt, not quite forty-three, became the youngest president in the nation's history.

Theodore Roosevelt

[He] wants to be the bride at every wedding, the corpse at every funeral and the baby at every christening.

—*Alice Roosevelt Longworth,*
about her father Theodore Roosevelt

Q: How did the Roosevelts renovate the White House?

A: For years the mansion had been structurally unsound and the private living spaces crowded by the intrusion of administrative offices. Competing plans to restore and enlarge the mansion had circulated around the capital since Caroline Harrison's time. During the Roosevelt administration, the American Institute of Architects proposed a plan drawn up by New York's famous architectural firm, McKim, Mead, and White. At the same time, Senator James McMillan of Michigan, powerful chairman of the Senate's Centennial [of the White House] Committee advocated a larger vision to restructure the "monumental core" of the nation's capital for the twentieth century, of which a redesigned White House would be part. The American Institute of Architects and Charles McKim captured not only McMillan's imagination but also his financial backing. The Executive Mansion would be enlarged and restored as part of the "McMillan Plan."

There was agreement that the mansion should retain its traditional exterior, and that the restoration should be done during the summer and fall of 1902. Interior restructuring was kept to a minimum. As Edith had urged, a west wing was added to house presidential offices and staff. McKim insisted on rebuilding the

East Wing on Thomas Jefferson's original foundations. New bleached oak floors unified the interior design, steel beams were introduced among the floor joists, the basement was put on a firmer structural foundation, and the old greenhouses were demolished. Edith worked closely with McKim, and took charge of the interior restoration, selecting upholstery and drapery fabric, new wallpaper, and carpets. Her deft hand can be seen in the final results. The heavy upholstery, overly patterned wallpapers, and musty carpeting were gone. Respectful of the mansion's history and desirous of institutionalizing the first lady's role, Edith hauled the antique furniture from storage, created a gallery of first ladies' portraits, and hired journalist Abby Gunn Baker to research and identify previous presidential china patterns, and to solicit other pieces from descendants of former presidents. Together Edith and Baker organized and displayed the White House china collection. As part of the formalized effort to preserve history, Edith successfully pressed for a law to end the "decayed furnishings" sales of White House furniture and china at public

Above: Edith Roosevelt. An aide once described the first lady as "always the gentle, high-bred hostess; smiling often at what went on about her, yet never critical of the ignorant and tolerant always of the little insincerities of political life."

Right: The president at work in his new office. At Edith's insistence, the White House renovation included a greater separation between the public and private areas of the mansion.

Being in the centre of things is very interesting, yet the same proportions remain. . . . I don't believe I have been forced into the 'first lady of the land' model of my predecessors.
—EDITH ROOSEVELT

auction, as was the custom throughout the nineteenth century. The White House emerged with a strong, sophisticated new image. The entire project cost $467,105.

Q: How did the restored White House reflect Roosevelt's view of the presidency?

A: Roosevelt and his wife entered the White House as the nation entered a new century. By conviction and personality, T. R. believed in a strong chief executive, and in the wake of the victory in the Spanish-American War, decided that the Executive Mansion needed an updated image that reflected the nation's stature as an emerging world power. The Roosevelts deliberately reshaped the White House as the larger-than-life president's stage and used drama and ceremony to embody the "imperial" presidency. The couple initiated a series of dramatic changes that physically restructured the mansion, changed its official name to the "White House," and codified and formalized rules for social style. Their view of the presidency also called for expanded entertaining, such as a series of musicales that were the talk of the nation's capital. Edith hired the first social secretary to a first lady, Isabelle ("Belle") Hagner, to assist with the increased entertaining and state dinners, and to help her shape the first family's image in the press. She realized that her husband's flamboyant personality and her six rambunctious children invited more than usual press coverage. Stating that "one hates to feel that all one's life is public property," and detesting "camera fiends," she injected both decorum and whimsy

into newspaper coverage of the family, screened photographers, oversaw selection of photographs, and chose the journals in which articles would appear and the authors who would write them.

During the Roosevelt administration, the capital was unmistakably the social center of the nation. Shown here, at left, are Theodore and Edith greeting guests at a White House reception.

Edith guarded the privacy of a family that attracted everyone's interest. From left to right: Quentin, Theodore, Theodore Jr., Archie, Alice, Kermit, Edith, and Ethel.

Dubbed "Princess Alice" by the ever-interested press, Alice Roosevelt Longworth, the president's daughter by his first wife, was a high-spirited, outspoken young woman. She loved to deliberately flout convention, often shocking White House guests by bringing her pet snake with her wherever she went.

Q: Who were the Roosevelt children?

A: The Roosevelts entered the White House with six boisterous children and a menagerie of pets. The children were Alice (seventeen), Ted (fourteen), Kermit (twelve), Ethel (ten), Archie (seven), and Quentin (three). Alice drew attention to herself with outrageous behavior (no doubt to gain her parents' attention), and the press recounted her every move. She smoked in public, danced on the roofs of cars, set off firecrackers, shot at telegraph poles from a train, jumped into pools fully clothed, and was photographed betting at the racetrack—all unseemly activities for a young woman of her social class. She loved ragtime music, which was then all the rage, and was an excellent dancer. She brought to the White House her favorite pet, a green snake named "Emily Spinach" (named for her very thin Aunt Emily), which she took with her everywhere—to the consternation of party hostesses and White House guests. The Roosevelt menagerie also included Ted's macaw, Alice's Pekinese that danced on its hind legs, the pony Algonquin, and assorted ducks, dogs, and cats.

"Princess" Alice, as she had been dubbed in the press, refused to attend school at all while in the White House. She was too busy having fun with socialite friends. Ted Jr. and Kermit both attended Groton School in Massachusetts and then Harvard College. Archie and Quentin attended public school in Washington, and then Archie went on to Groton and Quentin to Episcopal High School, a boarding school in Alexandria, Virginia. Ethel attended the National Cathedral School for Girls in Washington.

MISS ALICE ROOSEVELT.
THE CHARMING DAUGHTER OF THE PRESIDENT, WHO HAS BEEN ASKED BY EMPEROR WILLIAM TO CHRISTEN HIS NEW YACHT—HER LATEST PHOTOGRAPH, TAKEN IN HER DEBUTANTE GOWN, AND WEARING THE NECKLACE WHICH WAS THE GIFT OF THE PRESIDENT.

The four boys styled themselves as the "White House Gang," as they ran through the state rooms playing hide-and-seek or appropriated metal trays from the kitchen to slide down the stairs to the State Dining Room. They staged war games on the mansion's lawn, skated in the East Room, shot water pistols at each other and visiting officials, and lobbed spitballs into the faces of presidential and first lady portraits. Archie and Quentin played White House police, complete with old uniforms, rode their pony Algonquin around the grounds of the White House, and on one occasion, when Archie was sick with measles, Quentin pushed and pulled Algonquin into the elevator and rode him up to Archie's room—just the thing to speed his brother's recovery.

On other capers, the boys rode on top of the White House elevators. They took seriously their father's advocacy of the "strenuous life." Although Edith injected restraint into the family's public image, her comment about Kermit summed up her private feelings, "I know he's a naughty boy, but I just love him."

Q: Who married in the White House during the Roosevelt administration?

A: The president sent Alice along with a large official party making a four-month goodwill trip to the Far East. Ohio congressman Nicholas Longworth was among the officials. Aboard ship, Alice engaged in her usual antics, which shocked some passengers but endeared her to Longworth. Before the junket was over, Alice and Longworth were engaged. "Alice in Wonderland," reported one newspaper. The couple married in a White House wedding ceremony on February 17, 1906. The marriage took place in the East Room with some 700 guests in attendance.

Fifteen reporters covered the event while 101 servants, maids, and butlers bustled to bring it off in grand style. The large East Room was awash in Easter lilies in February, while Alice lived up to her name of "princess," wearing an ivory satin gown with an eighteen-foot train. Although there were eight ushers, Alice had no bridal attendants and was escorted and given away by her father. Lavish gifts poured in from around the world and the Cuban government selected a string of pearls that became Alice's signature jewelry.

The marriage was not a happy one, however, but it nonetheless endured because divorce was still unacceptable in this era. Longworth became Speaker of the House, but was a notorious woman-izer. Washington's rumor mill linked Alice with Senator William Borah of Idaho. "Aurora Borah Alice," went one ditty, lampooning the pair. Yet Alice remained irrepressible and outrageous, illuminating the capital's social scene well into old age. Known for her biting wit, she died in 1980 at the age of ninety-six.

Quentin, the Roosevelts' youngest son, mounted on Algonquin. The boys often included the pony in their pranks about the White House.

Although the society debut of Ethel Roosevelt did not receive the same fanfare as her older sister's wedding, it was still a significant White House event.

> "I can run the country, or I can control Alice. I cannot possibly do both."
>
> —THEODORE ROOSEVELT

William Howard and Helen Taft

Q: How did William Howard Taft win the presidency?

A: Taft was Roosevelt's handpicked successor, the man Roosevelt believed was most likely to follow his policies. Taft, who possessed a brilliant legal mind, had been a judge on the Superior Court of Ohio and the Sixth Federal Circuit Court of Appeals, governor of the Philippines, and secretary of war prior to becoming president. He was the only president to serve as Chief Justice of the Supreme Court after his presidency. He and Roosevelt parted ways as Taft entered the presidency because Taft's choices for his cabinet did not always accord with Roosevelt's views.

Puck cartoon of William Howard Taft, wearing crown, seated on shoulder of Theodore Roosevelt. Although Roosevelt's hand-picked successor was expected to carry out his policies, Taft disappointed his predecessor and chose his own path.

Q: Who was Taft's first lady?

A: Helen Herron Taft, known as "Nellie," was born into a prosperous Ohio family on January 2, 1861. The Taft and Herron families lived close to each other in an affluent neighborhood of Cincinnati. Nellie attended Miami University in Oxford, Ohio, made her society debut at nineteen, briefly taught school, but loved the law and politics—interests thought improper for a woman of her day. Bright and curious, Nellie and several friends initiated a salon with invited guests who discussed intellectual, political, and economic issues, providing Nellie with the mental challenge she craved. There she met fellow salon member, William Taft, who was attending Cincinnati Law School. The couple became engaged in 1885 and married on June 19, 1886. They honeymooned in Europe.

Nellie became a partner in Taft's work throughout his career and served as his most valuable advisor. As the more politically ambitious of the two, Nellie steered his career choices at several junctures away from the Supreme Court and toward the presidency. Taft jokingly described her as "the politician in the family," and she warned him that accepting a seat on the Supreme Court would be "the biggest mistake" of his life.

The Tafts riding in a horse-drawn carriage with mounted escort en route to the White House after the inauguration.

> **Presidents come and go, but the Supreme Court goes on forever.**
> —*WILLIAM HOWARD TAFT*,
> *who served as Chief Justice of the Supreme Court after his presidency*

A visit to the Hayes White House as a girl of seventeen fired Nellie's political ambition to be first lady. Her ambition was fulfilled in 1908, when Taft was elected president. The night before the March 4, 1909, inauguration was the occasion of a bitter snowstorm in Washington. Reluctantly, Taft decided to move the swearing-in ceremony from its usual location outside of the Capitol to the Senate Chamber inside. In the crowded chamber, Taft took the presidential oath. Afterward, breaking with precedent, Nellie became the first wife of a president to ride beside her husband from the inaugural ceremonies at the Capitol to the White House, signifying her role as his partner and advisor. In her memoirs she recalled that, "In spite of protests [I] took my place at my husband's side."

On a ship bound for the Philippines, the Tafts play cards on deck with two fellow passengers. The years spent in the Far East had a profound effect on Nellie.

Q: What experience did Nellie Taft have that influenced her role as first lady?

A: When her husband served as governor of the Philippines, Nellie was profoundly influenced by the culture of the Far East. She had been impressed by the beauty and ceremony of the Philippines and sought to create a park as the people's gathering place in the nation's capital similar to the famed Luneta in Manila. With the president's support, she created West Potomac Park along the Tidal Basin and Potomac River, had a bandstand built for the Marine Band to entertain, and announced that the public was invited to listen to music and meet friends every Wednesday and Saturday night in the spring and summer. Anxious that no one would attend, she and the president were overjoyed when a crowd of ten thousand greeted them on the opening evening of April 17, 1909.

Tokyo's Cherry Blossom Festival particularly impressed Nellie. As the first civic project undertaken by a first lady, she resolved to landscape Potomac Drive on Washington's Tidal Basin with ornamental cherry trees. An influential Japanese scientist, Dr. Jokichi Takamine, heard about the project and donated two thousand trees as a gesture of thanks to the United States for its role in ending the Russo-Japanese War in 1905. Unfortunately, all of the trees died of blight. Through the influence of the Japanese ambassador, Mayor Ozaki of Tokyo donated three thousand trees that were planted around the Tidal Basin in 1911. Their blossoming each year brings thousands of tourists to the nation's capital to admire their beauty.

Inspired by the Luneta in Manila, Nellie created West Potomac Park, and lined the drive with the famous cherry trees that were a gift from Japanese officials. Tourists still flock to Washington every spring to witness their stunning bloom.

Q: Who were the Taft children?

A: The Tafts were a family of bright children with Robert A. Taft, the eldest son of nineteen, in his junior year at Yale; Helen, seventeen, who was a student at National Cathedral School and then Bryn Mawr College; and their youngest son, Charley, eleven, who was familiar with the White House from his friendship with Quentin during the Roosevelt days. The Tafts indulged the children while in the White House because, as Taft said, "They are not children to be spoiled by a little luxury now." Taft often enjoyed horseback rides with Helen and Charley. The president declared, "Let them have a good time while they can." Robert later became the famous senator from Ohio, while Helen earned a Ph.D. in history from Yale and became dean of Bryn Mawr. Charley pursued a career in reform politics.

Nellie and William Taft, seated, with their three children, from left to right, Charley, Helen, and Robert, standing behind.

Q: How did Nellie Taft restructure the functioning of the White House?

A: Colonel Archie Butt, the president's assistant, was skilled in protocol and diplomacy and assisted Nellie with all social arrangements. As wife of the governor of the Philippines, Nellie had found that a strong administrative structure freed her from day-to-day household administration. As first lady, she replaced the White House steward and restructured authority by hiring an executive housekeeper, Mrs. Elizabeth Jaffray, in charge of running the mansion. Nellie did not like dinners prepared by outside caterers, so she hired three cooks under the direction of Mrs. Jaffray, as well as a special chef, waiters, and maids for state occasions.

The Tafts entertained political and personal guests at breakfasts, luncheons, and dinners, and Nellie "received" callers three afternoons a week seated in the Red Room. She was famed for her champagne punch.

Other White House staff reported to Mrs. Jaffray, who was not always popular with them. Mrs. Jaffray lost no time in establishing her authority. She took an office and bedroom in the second-floor family quarters and ruled over the house for the next seventeen years through four presidential administrations.

Q: What unfortunate circumstance thwarted Nellie Taft's reign as first lady?

A: Less than three months after moving into the White House, Nellie was felled by a stroke aboard the presidential yacht, *Sylph,* on May 17, 1909, while en route to Mount Vernon. She suffered paralysis in her right arm and leg, and could not speak. In a cruel irony of fate, just as she had reached the fulfillment of her life-long dream to become first lady, she could not carry out her role for nearly two years. Unable to act as hostess, she asked her sisters, Eleanor Moore, Jennie Anderson, and Maria Herron, "to represent me" and then her daughter, Helen, to act in her behalf. Writing that the burdens of the presidency were "heavier to bear because of Mrs. Taft's condition," the president insisted that no woman, even his daughter, be allowed to take the place of his wife as first lady. Her devoted husband personally taught her to speak again. Although it is clear today that the first lady suffered a stroke, it was not acknowledged to the press or public at the time. She had recovered sufficiently by 1911 to resume her official duties.

In 1914, Nellie was the first wife of a president to publish her memoirs, *Recollections of Full Years,* in which she chronicled her life with her husband in politics and as first lady. Although Julia Grant had written her memoirs earlier, she could not find a publisher for them, and they were not published until 1975.

Below left: Nellie's life-long desire to be the first lady had been fulfilled, but a stroke kept her from her official duties for nearly two years. Daughter Helen, shown here with her father, sometimes filled in for Nellie as White House hostess.

Below: William Howard Taft. Taft was known for his brilliant legal mind, and after his term as president, served as Chief Justice of the United States Supreme Court.

> I had always had the satisfaction of knowing almost as much as he about the politics and intricacies of any situation in which he found himself, and my life was filled with interests of a most unusual kind.
>
> —HELEN HERRON TAFT

Woodrow and Ellen Wilson

Q: Who was Woodrow Wilson's first wife?

A: Ellen Axson Wilson was a talented artist who had seriously considered a professional career after her studies at the Art Students League of New York. Born in Savannah, Georgia, on May 15, 1860, Ellen met Wilson, a young Atlanta lawyer, when both were visiting in Rome, Georgia. Their meeting initiated a passionate courtship but Ellen struggled to come to terms with her love for Wilson and the necessity of giving up her plans to pursue an artistic career. She chose marriage and wed Wilson in 1885. The Wilsons' family of three daughters, Margaret, Jessie, and Eleanor ("Nell") followed in quick succession. Despite a busy family life and her complete involvement in her husband's career as president of Princeton and as a rising political star, Ellen maintained her love of art. She frequented the artists' colony in Cornish, New Hampshire, where the Wilsons often summered, and set up an art studio with a skylight on the third floor of the White House, where she painted floral canvasses and landscapes. She sold her artwork and donated the money to Washington charities. Her best-known artistic expression was her design and implementation of the White House Rose Garden, her permanent legacy to the Executive Mansion.

An early photograph of Ellen Wilson. Before her marriage, Ellen studied painting at the Art Students League of New York during the 1880s.

Q: Which of the Wilson daughters married while in the White House?

A: Wilson daughters Jessie and Nell married in the White House. Jessie, the middle daughter, wed Francis Bowes Sayre, a young assistant district attorney in New York City, on November 25, 1913, at a large and glittering East Room ceremony. The bride, her mother, and Belle Hagner, whom Ellen had asked to return as White House social secretary, planned the elaborate wedding. Hagner patterned the event after Alice Roosevelt's brilliant White House wedding. The tall, blonde bride wore white satin with a long train and veil, and a troop of bridesmaids

Side Porch, Griswold House by Ellen Axson Wilson. Ellen spent several summers in Old Lyme with members of the art colony. Often accompanied by her teenaged daughters and her husband, she went to Lyme to resume the study of art that she had begun as a young woman.

> **I am naturally the most unambitious of women and life in the White House has no attractions for me.**
> —*ELLEN AXSON WILSON*

Ellen, second from right, with her three daughters, Jessie, Margaret, and Eleanor. Margaret aspired to a singing career and made several recordings for the San Francisco Exposition in 1915 before she damaged her voice and had to abandon her recording career. She never married and later moved to India, where she joined a commune.

wore pink silk in many different shades. The Marine Band played the wedding march before the couple exchanged vows at a satin-covered altar. The festivities included a wedding cake three feet in diameter that weighed 130 pounds.

Nell, the youngest daughter, married her father's trusted advisor, Secretary of the Treasury William McAdoo, a widower and father who was twenty-six years her senior, on May 7, 1914. The age difference concerned the Wilsons but her mother reported that "[I] know that you are happy." Nell's wedding was more intimate in scale. The bride descended the grand staircase on the president's arm and they walked into the Blue Room where the ceremony was performed at dusk. Her two sisters served as her attendants, carrying tall shepherd's crooks adorned with festoons of roses and lilies of the valley.

Q: How was Ellen Wilson involved in social activism as first lady?

A: Ellen, as did many Progressive Era women, took up social reform. "Alley uplift," as it was called, sought to improve the wretched living conditions in Washington's notorious alley slums. She considered her work "the duty of the southern Christian woman." Concealing her identity to conduct fact-finding tours, she was appalled by the rat-infested alley dwellings that housed poor black laborers, often within the shadow of the Capitol. Ellen advocated the Slum Clearance Act of 1914 to demolish alley dwellings. Although the bill did not provide for alternative housing, Ellen optimistically assumed that it would force the displaced inhabitants into better neighborhoods. Leading social reform journals featured her work noting, "It was laughingly said that no one could move in polite society in Washington who could not talk alleys." But after Nell's wedding, Ellen's health had declined rapidly. She died of Bright's disease, a fatal kidney ailment, on August 6, 1914. Just before her death, she told the president, "I should be happier if I knew the alley bill had passed." Word of the bill's passage reached her just before she died. Wilson was disconsolate over her death; for several days her body remained on a sofa in the bedroom. Finally, he permitted her to be placed in a coffin in the East Room. Her funeral was held in Rome, Georgia, where the couple had met many years before.

Ellen replaced Edith Roosevelt's colonial garden with a rose garden on the site of the present-day rose garden. The West Garden has been known as the Rose Garden ever since.

Woodrow and Edith Wilson

Woodrow Wilson with Edith Bolling Galt, riding in a carriage on the way to his second inauguration. A mix of politics and romance characterized Wilson's second marriage.

Q: Who was Woodrow Wilson's second wife?

A: Edith Bolling Galt, a wealthy Washington widow, became the president's second wife. Born in Wythville, Virginia, on October 15, 1872 to a Virginia family long on ancestry and short on money, Edith claimed to be a seventh-generation descendant of Pocahontas. Edith received little formal education. While visiting her sister in Washington, she met and married Norman Galt, owner of a prosperous jewelry store. A son born to them lived only three days and Galt died in 1908. Helen Bones, Wilson's cousin who lived and worked in the White House, became friends with Edith and invited her to the White House one afternoon for tea, where they "accidentally" ran into Wilson. In March 1915, Edith was invited to dinner at the mansion and continued to socialize with the Wilsons. By May, Wilson, who had been severely depressed after Ellen's death, fell for the lively Edith and quickly proposed marriage. Their romance, coming so soon after Ellen's death, was carried on secretly for months for fear that adverse public reaction would cause Wilson's defeat in the coming election. Despite these concerns, the president and Edith were married in the bride's home on December 18, 1915.

Q: How did the new first lady assist President Wilson?

A: Edith and Wilson were virtually inseparable from the time of their engagement. Wilson immediately took Edith into his confidence in political and international affairs. She wrote him, "I feel I am sharing your work and being taken into a partnership as it were." Wilson taught her the secret codes, and both before and during World War I she regularly encoded and decoded top-secret messages to allies in Europe. She was the first presidential wife to accompany a president on an official mission abroad while in office. Edith joined him at the Paris Peace Conference after World War I, where she was greeted as a "queen" accompanying a head of state. Paris greeted the couple at a tumultuous parade where crowds shouted, "*Vive* Wilson!" At the signing of the Treaty of Versailles, no women were invited to the ceremonies, but Edith observed the historic moment hidden behind draperies.

Q: After the Peace Treaty, what did Wilson propose to deter future wars?

A: As part of the historic peace initiative, Wilson proposed the creation of a League of Nations that would arbitrate international disputes and keep world peace. The initiative faced fierce opposition in the Senate and Wilson decided to take his case to the people through an arduous speaking tour across the country. During the tour, he suffered a physical collapse and his aides rushed him back to

U.S. defeat of the League of Nations. Wilson remained a politically crippled and ailing executive.

When Wilson's presidential term of office ended, he and Edith moved to an elegant home on S Street in Washington, D.C., where Wilson lived as an invalid until his death in February 1924. Edith stayed on in the house, becoming the custodian of his papers and his official legacy. She bequeathed their home to the National Trust for Historic Preservation after her death in 1961.

President Wilson asking Congress to declare war on Germany, April 2, 1917. After the Armistice, Wilson devoted his few remaining years to the futile pursuit of persuading the United States to join the League of Nations, the precursor to the United Nations.

the White House; he suffered a stroke on October 2, 1919. Paralyzed and unable to speak, the president was totally incapacitated. Edith determined that he would not relinquish presidential power and that the public should not be told the extent of his illness. She kept everyone away except his doctors and monitored all communications with the president, meeting congressional and diplomatic delegations, and writing memoranda herself, signing them "Edith Bolling Wilson." "My stewardship," she called it. Others, not so kind, called it "petticoat government." The extent of her actual power is debated among historians, but there is agreement that she was instrumental in shutting out some of his closest advisors, and may have kept information from him that influenced the

Roosevelt's bid to run against Taft in the 1912 election split the Republican Party's vote, enabling the Democrats to elect Woodrow Wilson, former president of Princeton and governor of New Jersey, as president.

" I myself never made a single decision regarding the disposition of public affairs. The only decision that was mine was what was important and what was not, and the very important decision of when to present matters to my husband. "

—*Edith Bolling Wilson*

CHAPTER 8

ISOLATIONISM AND THE DEPRESSION

Still recovering from the horrors of World War I, on a wave of conservative isolationism, United States voters elected Warren G. Harding as president in 1920. Sure that isolation offered protection from further involvement in European conflicts, the nation rejected Wilson's vision for a League of Nations. Harding promised that the country would "return to normalcy"—the United States would mind its own business. Looking inward, Calvin Coolidge declared that "the business of America is business." With prosperity seemingly assured, his pro-business policies produced a false sense of security, encouraging monetary speculation and postwar inflation. The Harding and Coolidge administrations reflected a national pulling back from the responsibilities of international power won by previous administrations, but ignored international economic and political trends that led to economic depression and another world war. Herbert Hoover, who directed food relief in war-torn Europe and served as secretary of commerce after the war, seemed unaware of the magnitude of the potential economic disaster. The stock market crash ushered in a massive failure of businesses and banks, sinking the nation into the Great Depression.

Above: A *Life* magazine cover by John Held Jr. from 1926 epitomizes the carefree attitude of the prosperous "Roaring Twenties."

Left: Thousands of unemployed workers from Pennsylvania marched on Washington in 1932, during the height of the Great Depression.

Warren and Florence Harding

Q: Who was Florence Harding?

A: Florence Kling was born into a wealthy Marion, Ohio, family on August 15, 1860. Her father owned a hardware store but earned his wealth by branching out into real estate, banking, and investments. Florence was educated in public schools and learned a great deal about business and finance from her father, who was known as something of a tyrant. Athletic and musically talented, she attended the Cincinnati Conservatory of Music for a short time. At the age of nineteen, Florence became pregnant by her young boyfriend, Henry DeWolfe, and eloped with him in 1880. It soon became clear after the birth of their son, Marshall, that DeWolfe was a spendthrift and a heavy drinker. After a brief, unhappy marriage, DeWolfe deserted Florence and their son. Florence returned to Marion. Refusing to ask her father for help, she instead rented a room and began giving piano lessons. In the late 1880s, she met Warren Harding, who was five years her junior and the brother of one of her students. Florence relentlessly pursued Harding, by then the owner and editor of the *Marion Star,* and married him on July 8, 1891. Her father vehemently disapproved of the marriage. Harding's newspaper was only moderately successful until Florence joined the business. "I went down there intending to help out for a few days, and I stayed for fourteen years," she recalled. Florence reorganized the paper, took over as comptroller, and created a home delivery service through the use of paperboys, turning it into a financial success and one of Ohio's leading Republican dailies. Yet, she soon refocused her business acumen on her husband's budding political career.

Q: What kind of election campaign did Warren G. Harding run in 1920?

A: Warren G. Harding had served in the Ohio state senate and as lieutenant governor before being elected in 1914 to the U.S. Congress as a Republican senator from Ohio, where he had opposed the United States' entry into the League of Nations. Harding ran another of the successful "front porch" presidential campaigns so popular among Midwestern Republicans, in which Florence played a leading role. Having worked at the newspaper for many years, she was knowledgeable about modern journalism and acutely aware of the power

Florence Kling Harding. Although her husband's many infidelities brought her public humiliation, Florence remained one of his staunchest supporters.

> " I know what's best for the President. I put him in the White house. He does well when he listens to me and poorly when he does not. "
>
> —*FLORENCE HARDING*

candidate, and distributing the images to the press. This campaign became the prototype for modern campaigns of the twentieth century—with celebrity guests, silent movie stars, varied ethnic groups, African Americans (an important voting block for Republicans as the "party of Lincoln"), and the constituency of soon-to-be-enfranchised women voters.

Left: Although historians list him among the worst presidents, Harding was immensely popular during his presidency. The press loved stories and "photo ops" with his dog Laddie Boy, shown here with a framed picture of himself that had been presented to the first lady.

Below: Warren G. Harding. Newspaperman turned politician, President Harding did not monitor the ethics of the cronies he appointed to political positions.

of the press in creating an image. This understanding was vital to her husband's political success. Florence also had a network of newspaper connections; she courted reporters—whom she referred to as "my boys"—and issued carefully crafted statements to them.

Because the campaign was conducted on their front porch—the porch being the place where private and public life meet—Florence had a legitimate reason, as a supportive spouse, to appear active without violating the norms of woman's place "in the home." The front porch campaign camouflaged the extent to which she acted as an unofficial campaign manager. She became the master of what we today call the "photo op," orchestrating which groups visited the front porch, insuring that they were photographed with the

The Boy Scouts of America presented President Harding with this sunwatch in 1921.

Q: What personal scandals marred the Harding marriage?

A: Two of Harding's extramarital affairs became notorious and threatened to derail his presidential aspirations. Home in Ohio, he had conducted a fifteen-year affair with Carrie Phillips, wife of the owner of a department store in Marion. When he decided to run for president, Harding ended the affair, although the pair remained friends. Fearing that scandal might surface during the campaign, Harding's handlers paid Carrie and her husband $20,000 and a monthly stipend to take an extensive trip around the world—which they did—not to return home until after Harding's death. Harding's biographer, Francis Russell, wrote: "Carrie Phillips was clearly the love of his life." Harding's and Carrie's letters to each other are in the Library of Congress, under seal until 2014.

Another well-known affair was with Nan Britton, a young blonde thirty years Harding's junior. Elizabeth Ann, the baby born to Britton in 1919 was rumored to be Harding's daughter. Harding made no public reply to the charge, but quietly sent child support money to Britton each month. Britton later wrote a tell-all book, *The President's Daughter*, detailing trysts with the president near the Oval Office and in White House closets. The public nature of these affairs embarrassed Florence and brought her great pain.

Q: What other scandalous and illegal behavior occurred in the White House?

A: While publicly Florence was known for opening up the White House to the public and visitors again after the war and for reinstituting garden parties, less well known at the time were the other parties given for the Hardings' friends and cronies, known as the "Ohio Gang," upstairs in the family quarters. The Hardings seemed to feel that Prohibition was for *others*. Harding kept a makeshift bar beside his poker table, enjoying his

> " I have no trouble with my enemies. I can take care of my enemies in a fight. But my friends . . . they're the ones who keep me walking the floor at nights! "
>
> —WARREN G. HARDING

private liquor stash. Although the first lady did not drink, the "Duchess," as Harding called his wife, liberally poured alcoholic beverages for others while the president and his friends gambled at poker.

Q: What political scandals plagued the Harding administration?

A: Although Harding was an affable and popular president, he did not monitor the friends he appointed to government positions and cabinet posts. In 1922, Secretary of the Interior Albert Fall secretly leased naval oil reserves stored at Teapot Dome, Wyoming, to oilman Harry Sinclair for an enormous profit. The Hardings' close friend, Charles Forbes, who headed the Veterans Bureau, was suspected of graft in the sale of goods from that agency, prompting a Senate investigation. Both Forbes and Fall resigned in January 1923. Other intimates suspected of corruption, Jess Smith and Charles Cramer, committed suicide. The Harding presidency was collapsing in scandal.

Wan and depressed with worry over the talk of corruption among his friends, Harding organized a tour of the western states and Alaska in an attempt to meet the public and explain his policies. The presidential train, the *Superb*, set out in the summer of 1923 on what was called the "Voyage to Understanding," accompanied by staff and press. The president attracted great crowds as the *Superb* chugged westward, but after becoming ill with what was at the time attributed to ptomaine poisoning, the Hardings boarded the train for San Francisco and rushed to the Palace Hotel. He died there suddenly on August 2, 1923. Florence was alone with him at the time. According to the doctors, the cause of death was a cerebral hemorrhage; modern doctors believe it was a heart attack. Whatever the cause, Florence refused to permit an autopsy, fueling speculation and unfounded rumors that she had poisoned him. Harding died just before the evidence of widespread corruption in his administration was made public. Although Florence had no part in the political scandals of his presidency, she spent months burning most of his official and personal papers before her own death on November 21, 1924. Perhaps fearing further revelations, she deepened the mystery surrounding his death and controlled his image to the end.

In 1923, in an attempt to draw attention from the scandals brewing in his administration, Harding set out on a train tour through the West.

The funeral cortege for the president as it leaves the White House, August 8, 1923.

Calvin and Grace Coolidge

Q: What was unusual about how Calvin Coolidge became president?

A: The vice president and his wife were vacationing at his family home in Plymouth, Vermont, when word reached the Coolidge farmhouse around midnight that president Harding had died unexpectedly. The vice president felt that he should be sworn in immediately. Coolidge's father, John Coolidge, a notary, administered the presidential oath of office to his son by the light of an oil lamp in their sitting room.

Above: Upon word of the sudden death of Warren Harding, Vice President Calvin Coolidge chose to be sworn in as president immediately. His father administered the oath of office to him in the Vermont family home.

Right: Calvin Coolidge was the only president to be born on the Fourth of July. A taciturn New Englander, he was known as "Silent Cal." The tight-lipped president did not allow the press to quote him directly, or even to attribute his remarks to "a White House spokesman."

Q: What was Coolidge's background and temperament?

A: Calvin Coolidge was born in 1872, in Plymouth, Vermont, graduated from Amherst, practiced law, and worked in grassroots Republican Party politics. He served as lieutenant governor and then governor of Massachusetts, where he gained national attention by putting down a labor strike by Boston's police union. His pro-business policies earned him the nomination as vice president on the Harding ticket in 1920. Coolidge was well known as a man of few words, emotionally inexpressive and with a dour personality. His taciturn nature masked both an innate shyness and a wry wit, earning him the nickname "Silent Cal."

Q: How did Calvin Coolidge and Grace Goodhue meet?

A: Grace Goodhue, an only child, was born into a prominent Burlington, Vermont, family on January 3, 1879. She graduated from the University of Vermont where she had been a founding member of the Pi Beta Phi women's fraternity, an interest that foreshadowed her concern and support for professional women's organizations throughout her life. She maintained her lifelong involvement in Pi Phi, becoming eastern regional president in 1915. After graduation, she was trained to teach the deaf and took a post at the Clarke School for the Deaf in Northampton, Massachusetts, for three years. Her experience with the hearing impaired developed her continuing dedication to improve life for the physically challenged. While at the Clarke School, Grace was watering flowers outside her residence and looked up at the window of a nearby house to see a young man shaving himself, dressed only in his underwear and a hat. Laughing, she turned away. It was Calvin Coolidge, who was boarding with the school steward, Robert Weir. Intrigued by the laughing young woman, Coolidge asked Weir to introduce him to Grace. When they met, Coolidge explained to her that he put on his hat while shaving to keep his unruly red hair out of his eyes. Weir commented wryly to Grace about Coolidge that, having taught the deaf to hear, she might cause the mute to speak. Coolidge was a persistent suitor and the couple married in the Coolidge home on October 4, 1905. They had two sons, John, born on September 7,1906, and Calvin Jr., born on April 13, 1908.

Calvin and Grace Coolidge were complete opposites in personality. Grace possessed a warm, vivacious, outgoing personality that genuinely charmed all she met. The president was difficult to know, but Grace had a knack for putting people at ease. When Massachusetts Republicans were considering Coolidge for governor, one important backer observed, "One of his greatest assets is Mrs. Coolidge. She will make friends wherever she goes." Popular Grace's "sunny" personality aided her husband's administration, overcoming his reputation as "Silent Cal." In fact, she was so beloved by the White House staff that they called her "Sunshine."

Q: **What promise did the president extract from the first lady during his term of office?**

A: During his term of office, Coolidge forbade Grace from giving interviews or publicly speaking out on political matters, issuing the edict: "Make no political statements." Although she kept her promise and refused to give interviews or be quoted publicly on any issue, she nonetheless displayed a subtle feminism by inviting numerous women's professional and social reform groups to the White House. She entertained such organizations as the Red Cross, her Pi Beta Phi fraternity, teachers and board members from the Clarke School for the Deaf, and the Visiting Nurses Association, making certain that they were photographed with the first lady. In this manner, Grace provided White House recognition, national visibility, and advancement for women's professional work without publicly saying a word.

Top: Helen Keller reads the lips of the first lady. Grace was a trained teacher of the deaf.

Bottom: Grace Coolidge with her pet raccoon.

" **She is the only woman in official life of whom I have never heard a single disparaging remark in the course of nearly twenty years.** "

—*FRANCES PARKINSON KEYES,*
author, about Grace Coolidge

Q: What major renovation took place during the Coolidge administration?

A: The third floor of the White House, which had housed attic storage and sleeping quarters for servants, was completely reconstructed. For years, engineers had warned that the third floor was in danger of collapsing. Walls on the second floor were severely cracked and debris fell through cracks in the ceiling. Repairs required the removal of the entire roof structure and attic floor, and the ceilings of the second floor as well. Heading this project was Lieutenant Colonel Ulysses Grant III, grandson of former President Grant, who was delighted to improve the structure that had featured so prominently in his family history. Grant secured funding of $375,000 from Congress to rebuild the attic, roof, and second-floor ceilings. The upper wooden parts of the house were replaced with steel framing, and Grant made major modifications to achieve a full third floor. Construction began in March 1927 and work was completed in September of that year. The third floor contained expanded storage and servants' bedrooms and baths. The crowning achievement was the creation of a room specially designed for Grace: the "sky parlor," which is known to us today as the solarium. Built on the roof of the South Portico, this lofty sunroom offered magnificent views of the city of Washington and has remained a favorite retreat of White House families ever since.

During the restoration, the Coolidges rented the grand, four-story, white marble mansion of *Washington Times-Herald* publisher, Eleanor "Cissy" Patterson, at 15 Dupont Circle, one of the most fashionable neighborhoods in the nation's capital. When the restoration was complete, Grace usually held four state dinners, each followed by a musicale in the East Room, during the White House social season. She also hosted five large receptions and several garden parties in late April and early May. In addition, there were state receptions at which about 3,500 guests attended. A seated state dinner, such as those for the cabinet or Supreme Court, served about 100 guests. Grace's warmth and vivacity made these affairs a great success. William Howard Taft, the former president who was now Chief Justice of the Supreme Court recalled, "Mrs. Coolidge . . . was most gracious. Coolidge is Coolidge and he does the pump-handle work [handshaking] without a great deal of enthusiasm." But, as White House chief usher Ike Hoover claimed, Grace was "90 percent of the Coolidge administration."

Grace Coolidge loved the color red in which she posed for this portrait painted by Howard Chandler Christy in 1924. Commissioned by her Pi Beta Phi fraternity, it shows Grace, wearing an elegant silk dress, standing with her collie, Rob Roy, named after the popular cocktail as a wry reference to Prohibition. Despite her husband's thrifty New England nature, his one well-known extravagance was purchasing beautiful clothes for Grace.

Grace Goodhue Coolidge

> **If you don't say anything, you won't be called on to repeat it.**
> —*CALVIN COOLIDGE*

Q: What was one of Grace Coolidge's favorite pastimes?

A: Grace Coolidge was an avid baseball fan who understood the game as well as any man. Attending as many games as possible of the Boston Red Sox while living in Boston when her husband was state governor, she always had her scorecard with her and sometimes sat in the dugout. Dubbed the "First Lady of Baseball," when in the White House, Grace attended Washington Senators' games and had a front-row seat for the 1925 World Series.

Q: What tragedy struck the Coolidge family in the White House?

A: The Coolidge sons, John and Calvin Jr., spent most of the year in an exclusive boarding school, Mercersburg Academy, in nearby Pennsylvania, and came to the White House during the summers. The taciturn president loved to engage in verbal teasing with his sons, and the boys enjoyed playing baseball on the South Lawn and using the tennis courts built during the Roosevelt administration. John had just graduated from Mercersburg Academy in the summer of 1924 and was to enter Amherst that fall. In late June, young Calvin, also home from the academy, played tennis on the White House courts in shoes without socks and rubbed a blister on his toe. He thought little of it, but by the time he told his parents, the blister was infected; he was in pain and feeling weak. By early July, the infection had become blood poisoning. In a final, frantic effort to save his life, he was taken by ambulance to Walter Reed Hospital where it was hoped that surgery might save him. But it was too late. Both parents were with Calvin when he died on July 7, 1924, at the age of sixteen. The following day, his funeral ceremony was held in the East Room; he was buried in Vermont. The president, devastated by his son's death, wrote in his autobiography, "When he went, the power and the glory of the presidency went with him."

The first lady was a committed baseball fan. Here she stands beside her husband while he shakes hands with a Washington player at a 1924 World Series game.

The Coolidges flanked by their sons, Calvin Jr. (on the left) and John (to the right). Calvin Jr. died from blood poisoning from an infected blister that he developed while playing tennis on the White House courts.

Herbert and Lou Hoover

Q: Why were the Hoovers considered a "power couple" in the White House?

A: Herbert and Lou Hoover brought intellectual prowess and humanitarian accomplishment to their roles as president and first lady. Lou Henry was born in Waterloo, Iowa, on March 29, 1874; her husband was born in West Branch, Iowa, on August 10, 1874. The couple met when they were both students at Stanford University in California where Lou became the first woman to graduate

Herbert Hoover with one of his dogs. One of the Hoovers' crowning intellectual achievements was their collaboration on the translation of *De Re Metallica,* an important sixteenth-century mining text, from Latin into English. This five-year endeavor was recognized as a major contribution to the history of science and won them the Mining and Metallurgical Society's Gold Medal in 1914.

with a degree in geology. Hoover took a mining engineer's position with a firm in Australia and cabled Lou a proposal of marriage, which she accepted. They wed on February 10, 1899. She then accompanied him to China, where she became a partner in his work.

Hoover and Lou shared an exciting life together in foreign lands. He made a fortune in the mining industry, which the

couple devoted to humanitarian causes. During World War I, Lou mobilized the Society of American Women in London to provide for the relief of American women and children stranded in London. Hoover also worked on the Commission for Relief in Belgium, and directed food relief in war-torn Europe. Returning home after the Armistice, Hoover became a member of the Supreme Economic Council and head of the American Relief Administration, which organized shipments of food for starving millions in central Europe. He also served as director of the U.S. Food Administration and then as secretary of commerce under Harding and Coolidge.

Q: What women's organization did Lou Hoover enthusiastically support?

A: The athletic first lady, who enjoyed camping, hiking, and the outdoors as a young woman, was a lifelong supporter of the Girl Scouts. She believed in women's equality and thought scouting, with its emphasis on outdoor activities, self-reliance, and community service offered the best training for girls to be active and fit, in body and mind, for their roles as mature women. Lou began her work with Girl Scouts in 1917 as a troop leader in Washington and then as a national commissioner. She became national president in 1922, and devoted her considerable administrative and organizational talents toward expanding membership and providing a strong financial base; this

and promote charitable assistance to the needy as ways to cope with the Great Depression. She addressed the nation's youth by radio, particularly girls, emphasizing physical and intellectual fitness for an independent and productive life. In addresses to Girls Scouts and the 4-H clubs of America, the first lady emphasized the equal sharing of work in the home by men and women, and urged young boys to share the responsibility of making a home harmonious. She frequently spoke of the value of community service and voluntarism, a lifetime commitment she shared with her husband.

Lou Hoover dressed in her uniform as president of the Girl Scouts of America in 1924. As first lady, in 1932, she addressed the nation's Girl Scouts by radio. Lou regularly broadcast radio talks, most of them aimed at the nation's youth, who she encouraged to live responsible, physically active lives.

included sponsoring the group's first national cookie sale. She continued to be active in scouting during her White House years, often giving speeches to troops and inviting them to the White House.

Q: What White House "firsts" can be claimed by Lou Hoover?

A: In 1929, Lou Hoover was the first first lady to broadcast a radio address to the nation from the White House. Her first speech was the dedication of the Daughters of the American Revolution's Constitution Hall in Washington, D.C. She had a recording "laboratory" set up in the mansion to practice her speaking technique. Recognizing the growing power of radio as a popular medium in the 1920s, she used it to encourage self-reliance

She was also the first to abandon two White House social traditions. She felt that the long-engaged-in custom of "calling" on the wives of cabinet members and government officials had become so cumbersome and time-consuming that she abandoned it as an empty ritual. And because the crowds had grown into the thousands seeking entry to the mansion, she ended the annual New Year's Day receptions, a tradition since Washington's time. She also insisted that pregnant women be allowed in reception lines, a radical departure from previous custom.

> " It is very possible to have both a home and a career, for in this modern age we are released from so many of the burdens our grandmothers and great-grandmothers had to bear. "
>
> —*Lou Hoover*

Q: Did the Hoovers' sons live with them in the White House?

A: The Hoovers had two sons, Herbert Jr. and Allan Henry, who traveled the world with their parents while they were growing up. During the presidency, the size of the Hoover family in residence at the White House fluctuated. It reached its largest number in 1930 when their daughter-in-law Margaret, the wife of Herbert Jr., came to live there with their two children, Peggy Ann and Herbert III. Herbert Jr. had become ill with tuberculosis and was recuperating at a sanitarium in the mountains of Asheville, North Carolina. He completed his recovery at Camp Rapidan, in Virginia, which the Hoovers had purchased as a private mountain retreat away from the bustle of Washington. Camp Rapidan was a 164-acre tract of land in the Blue Ridge Mountains of Virginia near the Rapidan

River. Lou designed the cabins, but the camp was as complete a residence as the White House. At this spot, the Hoovers enjoyed camping and entertaining guests. The president worked and fished, the first lady held women's and Girl Scout retreats, and she broadcast speeches from Camp Rapidan as well. The buildings were furnished with beautiful, sturdy, wooden furniture made by the craftsmen at Virginia's Clore's furniture factory. At the end of Hoover's presidency, the family donated the retreat to the government for the use of future presidential families, and it remains in the care of the National Park Service.

Allan made only occasional visits to the White House between college and his travels. After graduating from Stanford, he attended Harvard Business School. He held parties when he returned "home," and at one holiday party he brought an orchestra from New York so that he and his friends could dance. This was the only time that the president permitted dancing at the White House. Allan was known to dislike the mansion, complaining, "If I don't get out of here soon I'll have the willies."

Q: How did the first lady express her historical interest in the White House?

A: It was scholarly Lou Hoover who seriously studied White House furnishings as historical artifacts and approached the subject not as art but as history. She sought to return a sense of history to

The Hoovers take a stroll at their Virginia mountain retreat, Camp Rapidan. There they could find peace and relaxation, away from the stresses of life in the capital.

> I'm the only person of distinction who has ever had a depression named for him.
> —HERBERT HOOVER

The Hoover family poses at the 1931 Washington community Christmas tree lighting. From left to right: son Allan; the first lady; the president; daughter-in-law Margaret and her husband, Herbert Jr.; and Colonel James A. Ulio, aide to the president. The grandchildren are Herbert III, known as Pete, left, and Peggy Ann, holding the president's hand.

Poster for "Czechoslovaks for Hoover's Children's Relief Committee." The Hoovers worked hard to organize food relief and other aid during and after the war, yet the public perceived them as uncomprehending of the desperation engendered by the Depression.

Q: How did the Hoover administration mishandle the Great Depression?

A: With their record of public service, their concern for the well-being of the nation, and their wealth of government experience, it is surprising that the Hoovers were perceived by the public as being somehow responsible for the Great Depression and lacking in empathy toward the severe economic dislocation it caused. Committed philosophically and politically to self-sufficiency and private charity, their well-meaning voluntarism was an insufficient response to severe and systemic economic problems exposed by the Depression. The Hoovers were intensely private people who did not cooperate with the press, refused to "humanize" their public image by having their numerous acts of charity publicized, and entertained lavishly while others stood in bread lines. Despite paying for entertaining out of their private wealth, they seemed out of touch with the reality experienced by the nation.

the home, and searched storage areas and warehouses, and took oral histories from long-term employees. She visited the James Monroe Law Library in Fredericksburg, Virginia, to study the Monroe furnishings purchased in France that Monroe bought back from the government when he left the presidency. At her own expense, the first lady had exact reproductions made of this furniture and set up the "Monroe Drawing Room" on the second floor of the mansion. She hired an assistant, Dare Stark McMullin, to prepare an inventory of the mansion's holdings and create cross-references for an illustrated volume of the furnishings. McMullin completed the book after the Hoovers left Washington but, unfortunately, it was never published. In re-creating this historical room, Lou built on the tradition of prior first ladies' interest in the mansion's history, and anticipated the historical work of later first ladies such as Jacqueline Kennedy and Pat Nixon.

CZECHOSLOVAKS FOR HOOVER'S CHILDREN'S RELIEF COMMITTEE

CHAPTER 9

WORLD WAR II AND PROSPERITY

The administrations of Franklin Delano Roosevelt, Harry S Truman, and Dwight D. Eisenhower grappled with the worst national crises since the Civil War: disastrous economic depression at home, an all-consuming world war abroad, a postwar transition of the economy, and international political and military realignments that brought protection from and confrontation with communist powers in the Cold War.

Roosevelt's innovative economic policies and job-creation programs helped lift the nation out of the Great Depression. His prosecution of the war through total mobilization set the stage for Allied victory, but his untimely death elevated a virtual unknown to the nation's highest office. Truman stepped into the presidency unaware of the atom bomb, yet made the tough decision to use it to save combatants' lives during what could have been a protracted land invasion of Japan. He then guided the transition to a peacetime economy, and helped shape NATO (the North Atlantic Treaty Organization) in the postwar realignment of power. Eisenhower, who led the Allied victory and headed NATO, shaped the policy of "containment" of communist expansion in Europe and Asia. His programs rebuilt the nation's infrastructure and produced peacetime prosperity.

Above: During the major reconstruction of the decaying mansion, the Trumans lived across the street from the White House in Blair House from 1948 to 1952.

Left: Franklin D. Roosevelt. Americans voted in FDR as president four times, making him the only chief executive to serve more than two terms of office.

Franklin and Eleanor Roosevelt

FDR was a vigorous speaker on the campaign trail during the Democrats' unsuccessful bid for the presidency in 1920. In 1921, polio would strike down the rising young leader and delay his return to the political arena for seven years.

Eleanor in her wedding dress, New York City, 1905. Despite a troubled marriage, Franklin and Eleanor's respect for each other never wavered.

Q: What distinguished Franklin and Eleanor Roosevelt?

A: Born in 1882 to James and Sara Delano Roosevelt, Franklin was raised in a lavish estate overlooking the Hudson River in Hyde Park, New York. There he led a sheltered, pampered existence, with his mother, who would remain a strong influence throughout his lifetime, supervising his early education until he was fourteen years old. He then attended the Groton School in Massachusetts and, later, Harvard. Anna Eleanor Roosevelt was his fifth cousin once removed. Eleanor, as she was called, was born in 1884, the child of Anna Hall and Elliott Roosevelt. Her family had wealth and status, but her childhood was nonetheless troubled. Elliott often drank to excess, and Anna struggled with depression. In 1892, her mother contracted diphtheria and soon died. Two years later, Eleanor, at the age of ten, suddenly found herself alone when her father, too, died. She was sent to live with her maternal grandmother. Despite a lifetime of achievements, she would always fear abandonment. Yet, Eleanor and Franklin's shared family background, intellectual acumen, and idealism drew them together, and they married on March 17, 1905. Eleanor's Uncle Theodore, then president of the United States, gave her away at the altar.

In 1910, Franklin entered politics as a New York State senator; three years later, he was appointed the assistant secretary of the Navy. In

1920, he was chosen as the running mate of presidential candidate Governor James M. Cox of Ohio. Although they lost the election, Franklin had established himself as a leader among progressive Democrats. His future looked bright. Tragedy struck, however, in August 1921. One evening at his summer home, Campobello, after a day of vigorous exertion followed by a swim in the icy waters of the Bay of Fundy, Franklin went to bed with a chill. The next morning he awoke with a fever and acute pain in his legs. In a few days, they were paralyzed by polio. He never again stood unaided. The following years saw him wage a fierce battle to regain movement in his legs through the use of heavy leg braces and crutches. In 1928, despite his disability, he reentered the political arena and was elected governor of New York. In 1932, he won the Democratic Party nomination for president. He won that election and was reelected in 1936, 1940, and 1944.

Despite marital problems, Franklin and Eleanor forged a powerful political partnership and led the nation through its worst crises since the Civil War: the Great Depression and World War II.

Q: Who were the Roosevelt children?

A: By the time Franklin and Eleanor arrived in the White House, their five surviving children, Anna, James, Elliott, Franklin Jr., and John, were adults. Their sons attended Groton and then, with the exception of Elliott, went on to Harvard. During World War II, all four joined the armed forces and saw action in the war: James served in the Marines; Elliott in the Army Air Corps; and Franklin Jr. and John in the Navy. James, Franklin Jr., and Elliott all later ran for political office, and James and Elliott served in Congress. Elliott wrote fourteen books, and John was a businessman and investment banker. Between university terms, wartime assignments, divorces, and remarriages, all of them lived for periods of time at the White House.

Anna moved into the White House with her two children, Eleanor ("Sistie") and Curtis ("Buzzie"), in the early 1930s while going through a divorce from stockbroker Curtis Dall. While living in the White House, Anna wrote two best-selling children's books. She then married John

Eleanor with four of her children, Elliott, John, Franklin Jr., and Anna, at Campobello.

Boettiger, a correspondent for the *Chicago Tribune* and moved to Seattle where they worked together on a newspaper that was part of the William Randolph Hearst publishing empire. During the war, she moved back to the White House to help care for her ailing father, to act as one of his many companions, and substitute as White House hostess when Eleanor was away. In 1952, after Boettiger's suicide, she married Dr. James Halsted, a doctor with the Veterans Administration.

Perhaps reflecting the tensions of their parents' marriage, and the usurpation of their mother's role by Franklin's mother, Sara, the Roosevelt children had difficulty sustaining relationships. Among the four sons there were eighteen marriages. Anna married three times. Both Franklin and Eleanor were reluctant to discipline their children. Eleanor later explained that they were "five individualists who were given too many privileges on the one hand and too much criticism on the other."

> **They had the most separate relationship I have ever seen between man and wife. And the most equal.**
> —*WHITE HOUSE USHER J. B. WEST,*
> *on the Roosevelt marriage*

Q: How did Eleanor revolutionize communication with the American public?

A: Eleanor introduced sweeping changes in a first lady's use of the media, deftly exploiting every communication tool then available. Early in the administration, she initiated weekly press conferences exclusively for women reporters; her first conference took place in the Red Room the first Monday after her husband's inauguration. She formed close working relationships with female journalists and gave them not only social news but also information about New Deal policies and her own reform activities. The message was clear—professional women reporters would have "hard news" stories for their papers and editors would be forced to hire more female journalists. Her actions assured additional jobs for women and gained favorable coverage for the Roosevelt administration.

Eleanor was entirely comfortable with the media. She took advantage of the radio by giving frequent radio talks, wrote magazine columns, authored books, and gave speeches to promote her vision of social reform. Her two syndicated newspaper columns, *My Day,* published six times a week from 1936 until 1962, and *If You Ask Me* kept her in constant communication with the public. Eleanor received more letters than any previous first lady. To keep up with the tens of thousands of letters she received each year, yet maintain her busy schedule, Eleanor hired two secretaries to assist her, Malvina ("Tommy") Thompson and Edith Helm. By harnessing the power of various media, Eleanor made herself one of the most influential political forces in twentieth-century America.

Q: How did Eleanor entertain in her role as first lady?

A: Because of her intense social activism, many erroneously assume that Eleanor was unconcerned about White House entertaining. Yet, Eleanor, who had acted as a political hostess for her husband for many years, was acutely aware of the social responsibilities of her role and the goodwill that entertaining engendered. Despite the constraints of the Depression, the Roosevelts entertained on a large scale. In addition to five state dinners and five receptions, Eleanor held events in series—luncheons, teas, and garden parties, often several on the same afternoon. She insisted on music in the East Room following state dinners, and afterward cookies and punch were served in the State Dining Room. Since Prohibition

Above: Eleanor's style of communication was to present herself as a personal friend and advocate. Mothers wrote to ask for food or clothing and unemployed workers appealed to her for jobs. Here she talks with a machinist during her goodwill tour of Great Britain during the war.

Right: FDR was as adept as Eleanor in connecting to the public. In his weekly fireside chat radio addresses, his listeners felt as if he was talking to them personally.

had been repealed, wine was reintroduced at the White House. Eleanor carefully observed her guests' religious or dietary preferences, serving only food that they could eat. For large receptions, the Roosevelts received thousands in the Blue Room until the outbreak of World War II forced the cancellation of all social events.

The first lady was innovative in using her White House entertaining to feature and publicize a broad spectrum of American cultures, often the same groups whose advancement she promoted in other venues: women, African Americans, Appalachian folk singers, labor songsters, and Native Americans.

After being received by the Roosevelts at Union Station in Washington, the British royal couple posed following a twenty-one-gun salute and playing of both nations' national anthems. From left: King George, the president, his secretary General E. M. Watson, the first lady, and Queen Elizabeth.

Q: What special relationship was forged with an important ally before the outbreak of World War II?

A: As Great Britain and the United States faced war with Germany and its allies, both nations realized the strategic importance of American assistance in winning the war in Europe. As Eleanor recalled, Franklin "wanted to make contact with those [he hoped would] be allies against fascism." To cement this strategic friendship, the president and first lady invited the British royal couple, King George VI and Queen Elizabeth, to visit the United States in June 1939. The Roosevelts' most spectacular social event was the state dinner for the first British monarch ever to visit this country. Eleanor purchased a smart new wardrobe for the events, which was featured in national magazine articles. Weeks of preparations and transatlantic cables preceded the dinner so that the royal couple could experience the best in American food and entertainment. Eighty guests were treated to an extraordinary evening of American music where Kate Smith, Marian Anderson, Alan Lomax, the Spiritual Singers, and the Coon Creek Four presented American standards, opera, folk songs, and African American spirituals. The royals stayed overnight in the White House, and then traveled to Roosevelt's home at Hyde Park the next day. The picnic at Hyde Park featured "favorite" American foods such as hot dogs, smoked turkey, Virginia hams, baked beans, and strawberry shortcake.

"It is common sense to take a method and try it. If it fails, admit it frankly and try another. But above all, try something."

—FRANKLIN ROOSEVELT

In one of the only two extant photos of FDR shown in a wheelchair, he holds his beloved Scottish terrier, Fala, on a terrace at Hyde Park, alongside a young visitor.

Q: What special pet delighted the president and first lady?

A: The president derived great pleasure and companionship from a black Scottish terrier named Fala, given to him by his devoted cousin, Margaret Suckley, as a Christmas present in 1940. FDR named the Scottie "Murray of Fala Hill" in honor of an outlaw Roosevelt ancestor whose home was Fala Hill in Scotland. Fala became an inseparable companion to the president, who traveled the world with his famous dog. Fala joined the president in his office, at the dinner table, and when entertaining world-renowned guests. The president humorously invoked Fala in speeches, once declaring that his enemies had criticized his policies, his wife, his family, but now they had even attacked "my little dog, Fala"—and that he would not tolerate. After the president's death, Fala lived with Eleanor at her home, Val-Kill, until he died in 1952.

Q: How did the longest presidential administration in American history end?

A: After twelve years of leading the nation through the Great Depression and World War II, Franklin's health had seriously deteriorated. He suffered exhaustion, frequent headaches, and extreme weight loss. Shortly after his fourth presidential inauguration, he traveled to his presidential retreat in Warm Springs, Georgia, to relax and recuperate. His daughter, Anna, acceded to his request that she invite his dear friend and former lover, Lucy Mercer Rutherford, to join him there. Lucy brought an artist friend, Elizabeth Shoumatoff, to paint Franklin's portrait. While he was sitting for the portrait he suffered a cerebral hemorrhage and died on April 12, 1945. Tens of thousands of mourners lined the route of the train that carried his body back to Washington, where it was taken to the White House East Room. His wish not to lie in state was scrupulously observed and, after a viewing of five hours, the body was taken to Hyde Park for burial in the rose garden.

The funeral procession of FDR, with horse-drawn casket, as it makes its way down Pennsylvania Avenue.

Q: **What path did Eleanor choose for herself after the White House?**

A: Soon after Eleanor moved back to New York, reporters asked her what she planned to do. She told them, "The story is over." But life in her own right was just beginning. President Truman appointed her to the U.S. delegation to the United Nations, where she stunned the delegates with her political and diplomatic finesse in directing the drafting and unanimous passage of the Universal Declaration of Human Rights—one of the landmark documents of the twentieth century. She actively shaped the Democratic Party's postwar liberal agenda, continuing her advocacy for women and African American civil rights. JFK appointed her chair of the President's Commission on the Status of Women in 1961. She died in New York City on November 7, 1962, at the age of seventy-eight.

Eleanor at Val-Kill with Fala two years after her husband's death. Rather than retire from public life, Eleanor truly came into her own in the post–White House years.

"As for accomplishments, I just did what I had to do as things came along."

—*ELEANOR ROOSEVELT*

Harry and Bess Truman

Bess Wallace Truman at the time of her high school graduation. Despite being portrayed by the press as an average housewife, Bess was recognized as a no-nonsense woman with an independent streak who charted her own course.

Q: How did Harry S Truman attain the presidency?

A: Harry S Truman became president upon the sudden death of Franklin D. Roosevelt. Truman had accepted the vice-presidential nomination never thinking that he would actually become the chief executive. The Trumans entered the White House as virtual unknowns in a time of great crisis. The former Missouri senator and vice president knew nothing of the atomic bomb, but decided to use the weapon to shorten the war and save lives. Following the war, he guided the country through economic transition, helped rebuild Europe with the Marshall Plan, and participated in organizing the North Atlantic Treaty Organization (NATO).

Q: Who was Truman's first lady?

A: Bess Wallace Truman, the president's wife, served as his first lady. The Trumans first met when they were children in

a Presbyterian Sunday school class in Independence, Missouri. They became secretly engaged in 1913 because Bess's mother considered Harry "below" the Wallaces in social standing. Shortly before Truman left to enter military service in World War I, Bess wanted to marry immediately, but he insisted that they wait until the war was over. Their nine-year courtship ended in marriage on June 28, 1919. Harry was then thirty-five and Bess was thirty-four.

Harry fondly called Bess "his chief advisor always," and "a full partner" in everything, including his political career. He consulted her before making important decisions, a pattern that dated back to the days when he owned a haberdashery business and continued through

Harry S Truman taking the oath of office on April 12, 1945, the day that Franklin Roosevelt died.

his years in the Senate when she ran his office. Bess had advised Harry not to become vice president because she intensely disliked what she called "this awful public life." She was angry when he accepted the post as Roosevelt's vice president and said accusingly, "What would happen if he should die? You'd be president."

Q: How did Bess Truman play her role as first lady?

A: Because Bess Truman was uncomfortable in the public spotlight, she returned to a traditional interpretation of the first lady's role. She did not hold press conferences or speak out publicly on political issues, as did her predecessor, Eleanor Roosevelt. She turned over to her secretary, Edith Helm, the job of feeding information to the press and responded only to written questions to which she wrote terse, sometimes one-word answers for Helm to pass on. Maintaining that she was not the one elected to office, she stated unequivocally, "I have nothing to say to the public." Keeping her public silence on current issues, she emphasized the most accustomed and noncontroversial aspects of her role—entertaining and greeting organizations representing worthy causes such as the Girl Scouts, the March of Dimes, the Red Cross, crippled children, and wounded war veterans.

Lacking substantive news, the corps of women reporters conjured their own image of Bess. In a postwar America that embraced a "back-to-the-home" ethos for women, the press cast the first lady in that light. Bess Furman, a reporter who had covered first ladies for several decades, announced, "Bess Truman is a real person pursuing a stable and honest life pattern of her own design." They portrayed Bess as a loyal, supportive wife, the president's helpmate. This image was immensely popular in postwar society and gained Bess the title of "a model first lady." As another woman columnist proclaimed, "Bess Wallace Truman is Mrs. America moved into the White House."

Below: Harry and Bess pose together on their wedding day in 1919.

Bottom: Harry and Bess relax in Key West with their daughter, Margaret.

> " I hope someday someone will take time to evaluate the true role of the wife of the President, and to assess the many burdens she has to bear and the contributions she makes. "
>
> —*HARRY TRUMAN*

Q: What gave President Truman "that sinking feeling"?

A: Despite many "renovations," the White House basically remained a wooden structure built upon shifting ground. As additions were made, rooms reconfigured, load-bearing walls removed, and a full third floor added in the Coolidge renovation, the old mansion began to shift under the added weight. Truman was startled to hear the tinkling of chandeliers swaying, and noticed that "the floor sagged like a ship at sea." Returning to the mansion after a trip the president noted in his diary, "Found the White House 'falling down.'"

Below left: Folksy Truman popularized the phrase, "The buck stops here." Although few Americans knew much about their new president, he stepped out of the long shadow of his charismatic predecessor to guide the nation during an eventful period.

Below right: By nature a very private person, Bess preferred the more intimate scale of life at Blair House, where she is shown here in the backyard with Margaret.

One evening the leg of his daughter's grand piano sank into the floor, causing plaster on the ceiling below to fall in. The house was clearly unsafe.

Truman ordered a thorough structural survey, which confirmed his fears—the mansion was structurally unsound. The options were to tear it down completely or gut it and rebuild the entire interior. Many in Congress, the press, and the public wanted to pursue the cheaper option—tear down the White House and build a completely new house. Bess would not hear of that option. She personally lobbied senators, representatives, and Speaker of the House Sam Rayburn to preserve the White House. It was the only issue for which she lobbied as first lady. And she proved successful; the option to save the White House prevailed.

Engineers placed the foundation on a secure stratum of sand and gravel; removed all the interior walls; built a freestanding structural steel frame within the old shell of stone walls and supported it with concrete; and transferred to the new independent interior structural steel frame "the weight of the structure and its contents." Truman was thoroughly involved in the rebuilding process and a fine

arts committee oversaw the interior restructuring and decoration of the rooms.
The prestigious New York department
store B. Altman repainted and refurnished
the mansion with showroom reproductions. Truman was directly involved with
the redecoration, although Bess assisted
with choosing colors and fabrics.

During the reconstruction, the Truman
family moved directly across Pennsylvania
Avenue to Blair House, which in later years
was used to house visiting dignitaries.
Francis Blair, a prominent editor from an
old Maryland family, originally built the
mansion in 1824. Andrew Jackson often
talked politics with Blair and other political
intimates around Blair's kitchen fireplace—
the origin of the term "kitchen cabinet."
The Trumans found this house more to
their liking than the Executive Mansion;
it was smaller, homier, and entailed fewer
official demands. Bess was relieved of the
duty of hosting many of the social functions that she intensely disliked.

**Q: How did the Trumans' daughter,
Margaret, spend the White House years?**

A: Only child Margaret was a college
coed during the first years of her father's
term of office. She attended the capital's
George Washington University, where she
majored in history and political science.
She invited classmates for movies in
the White House and sleepovers in the
Lincoln bedroom, and hosted her college
history seminar in the State Dining
Room every Thursday, saying, "It was the
only place we could get any
privacy." She hosted her
Pi Beta Phi sorority sisters
to a dinner and showing
of *Henry V* in 1945.

The press labeled
Margaret, "A Great Catch
for Anyone," but she wisely
deferred romance while
living in the goldfish bowl
of national publicity.
After she graduated from
GWU in 1946, she moved
to New York City to study
singing and pursue a
concert career. She
undertook a national
concert tour and made
guest appearances on
television and sang on the
radio. Some critics found
her performances lacking.
Washington Post music
critic Paul Hume described
her as "extremely attrac-
tive," but declared, "Miss
Truman cannot sing very
well." Hume's review so
angered Harry that he later
admitted that he "wrote
him a letter saying that if I could get my
hands on him I'd bust him in the jaw."

In 1956, Margaret married *New York
Times* editor Clifton Daniel in a wedding
ceremony in Independence, Missouri.
They had four sons. Margaret transferred
her talents to writing, authoring a book
on her parents, editing their letters, and
writing successful mystery novels.

Top: Margaret tried to
launch a singing career. In
1952 she appeared on the
hit *Jimmy Durante Show*.

Above: Careful to avoid
romance under the glare
of White House publicity,
Margaret married Clifton
Daniel several years after
her father's term of office.

I remember crying myself to sleep on my first night in the place. It all looked so shabby.

—*MARGARET TRUMAN*

Dwight and Mamie Eisenhower

Q: How did the Eisenhowers enter the White House?

A: Dwight Eisenhower was touted as a military hero who had commanded the allied armies in Europe, won World War II, and headed the North Atlantic Treaty Organization (NATO). "Ike," as he was known, was an acclaimed wartime leader and American voters welcomed his executive abilities in a postwar world. His campaign rhetoric in 1952 suggested that, as a man who knew the horrors of war, he valued peace and could "bring the boys" home from the Korean conflict and end that war as well. The public immediately embraced Mamie, a virtual unknown before the campaign, as a woman who epitomized the definition of femininity in the postwar world—one who made her husband and family the center of her life.

Below: An acclaimed military leader, here General Eisenhower speaks with American paratroopers in England.

Bottom: The first lady had a lifelong interest in fashion and developed a flair that was strictly the "Mamie Look"—from her feminine dresses to her trademark bangs.

Q: What did Bess Truman warn reporters and the public to expect from the incoming first lady?

A: When Mamie took the customary White House tour with her predecessor before moving in, the press asked Bess Truman what they could expect from the new first lady. Bess summed it up succinctly: "Expect a lot of pink." The color pink became Mamie's trademark. For the inauguration celebrations, she chose a pastel pink full-skirted gown encrusted with two thousand pink rhinestones, accompanied by pink gloves, pink high heels, and a pink purse covered with pink pearls and beads. The general's wife immediately set up her "command post" in her bedroom, which she redecorated in pink. It was her custom to awaken early, read the newspapers, direct the staff, and answer correspondence from her king-sized bed with pink pincushion headboard and pink sheets and blankets. Completing the room were a monogrammed pink wastebasket and pink slip-covered furniture. She held court in a pink satin breakfast jacket, pink nightgown, pink housecoat, and spike-heeled pink bedroom shoes with feathers. But beneath the pink femininity was concealed what White House usher J. B. West called, "a spine of steel. . . . She knew exactly what she wanted . . . exactly how it should be done. And she could give orders, staccato crisp, detailed, and final, as if it were she who had been a five-star general."

Q: How did Mamie Eisenhower view her role as first lady?

A: Mamie viewed her primary duty as that of a successful White House hostess. She brought many years of social experience as the wife of a career military officer, and relished the role. The Eisenhower administration was renowned for the return of large-scale, formal entertaining to the mansion after years of curtailment by World War II and the White House restoration. In

Ike's leadership role abroad, the couple had moved in top official circles and foreign heads of state streamed to the White House. Formal entertaining was always "white tie and tails," and dinners were served at an E-shaped table with liquor and wine. The E-shaped table accommodated additional guests but also allowed Mamie to sit beside her husband facing their guests, rather than across the table as was customary. For state dinners, the menus and the protocol were equally elaborate. To insure the best cuisine for their international guests, the Eisenhowers employed a French chef, François Rysavy, to prepare state dinners.

Mamie enjoyed after-dinner musical programs. The Eisenhowers invited the occasional "high-brow" performer, but Mamie and Ike preferred the mainstream, popular artists of the day: Fred Waring and the Pennsylvanians, Mitch Miller's Sing-Along group, the Meyer Davis orchestra, and barbershop quartets.

Q: What other forms of entertaining did the first lady introduce?

A: The Eisenhower administration featured "his" and "her" entertaining. For the president, Mamie hosted a series of breakfasts, luncheons, and dinners for all congressional members, and numerous small, "stag" dinners for business and labor leaders, scientists, educators,

editors, and old friends from the military days. Mamie featured "theme" parties (usually for the ladies) for every season and holiday, including Halloween, and decorated the White House in keeping with the theme, whether it was Easter bunnies popping out of eggs or Saint Patrick's Day shamrocks and dyed-green carnations. At Halloween there were witch heads, dessert in pumpkin molds, and orange lights in the chandeliers.

Mamie excelled at the personal touch and welcomed thousands of White House visitors almost daily, greeting each guest in a warm, intimate manner. One biographer described her as a "master of sincere small talk." In addition to the state dinners and receptions, she held teas, luncheons, and receptions for her husband and for numerous women's groups.

Mamie loved to entertain, whether on a grand scale for visiting dignitaries or on a more intimate level, such as this Christmas 1960 celebration with the family. During Ike's military career, at almost every post, he and Mamie were the centers of the social scene and their quarters were known as "Club Eisenhower."

"Of course, being mistress of the White House is a terrific responsibility, and I am truly grateful for my Army wife training."

—MAMIE EISENHOWER

Below: When Eisenhower played golf it was an accepted rule that no one talk business or politics while on the course.

Bottom: Mamie and Ike watch TV during the Republican National Convention. When home, Mamie preferred soap operas and comedies.

Q: How did the Eisenhowers relax?

A: The Eisenhowers were symbols of a newly prosperous nation thoroughly enjoying its leisure time. The president was a golf fanatic and had a putting green installed on the White House lawn so that he could practice. Mamie and Ike spent so many vacations at the golf club in Augusta, Georgia, that one of the cottages there was permanently reserved for them. They also frequented the golf course in Palm Desert, California. Mamie enjoyed watching television soap operas, especially *As the World Turns*, and the sitcom *I Love Lucy*. The couple also enjoyed one of the favorite pastimes of the 1950s: card games. Mamie played canasta or bridge with a group

of friends, army wives she had known for years who were jokingly tagged, "Mamie's Bridge Cabinet." These sessions were held in the solarium. Ike held stag poker nights in the Treaty Room. He also found relaxation and creativity in painting, and set up an art studio for himself in the White House. The Eisenhowers relaxed on weekend getaways at the presidential retreat in Maryland's Catoctin Mountains. "Shangri-La," originally built during the Depression by the Civilian Conservation Corps for FDR, was renovated by the Eisenhowers and renamed, "Camp David," after their grandson, David Eisenhower.

Q: How did Mamie's attitude toward her family reflect the times?

A: A longing for stability, an emphasis on women's femininity and dependence, and a return to "traditional" family values, marked the postwar era. Mamie cultivated a public image that was the embodiment of these popular concepts of womanhood, declaring that she was "perfectly satisfied to be known as a housewife." Mamie's widowed mother, Elivera, who shared a close relationship with Ike, lived with the couple in the White House for much of the first five years of the administration. Mamie cherished her only son, John, and his wife, Barbara, whom John married in 1947. John worked as assistant staff secretary to his father in the White House beginning in 1958. Although they maintained their own residence, their children, David, Anne, Susan, and Mary Jean, frequently spent overnights at the White House, and the youngest, Mary Jean, was christened in the mansion. Mamie was happy with

As his parents, grandparents, and great-grandmother look on fondly, David makes a birthday wish at a party featuring cowboy stars Roy Rogers and Dale Evans.

Q: What special celebration occurred during the Eisenhower presidential years?

A: Ike and Mamie, kept apart by his military service during World War II, happily celebrated their fortieth wedding anniversary in the White House in 1959. They renewed their wedding vows at a ceremony in the East Room. Afterward, at a dinner with friends, Ike toasted his wife, proclaiming that their enjoyment in each other had increased over the years. Together they danced "The Anniversary Waltz." For Mamie, the White House years had brought the marriage closer.

Below left: Christmas pageant program made by the Eisenhower grandchildren.

Below: Eisenhower was stricken with a heart attack while on vacation in 1955. Ike later wrote: "Mamie, above all others, never accepted the assumption that I had incurred a disabling illness. While solicitous . . . for my health and welfare, she . . . retained the conviction that my job as President was not yet finished." Ike announced he would run for a second term.

the arrangement, asserting that, "Every moment I spend with my grandchildren is the best moment of my life." Although she created a playroom for them on the third floor, the hallways were filled with toys, tricycles, electric trains, and dolls. Mamie invited them for movies in the East Wing theater on the weekends, and they enjoyed swimming in the pool. David displayed his extensive baseball card collection on the second floor, and Susan kept her doll collection in the linen room. Ike particularly indulged David and said, "the toys strewn across the path to the office . . . somehow helped to remind me that the country would not go to the dogs nor the world collapse in ruins."

"In the White House, in bad weather, painting was one way to survive away from the desk."

—DWIGHT D. EISENHOWER

CHAPTER 10

CONSOLIDATING WORLD POWER

The turbulent decades of the 1960s through the 1980s were marked by continuing containment of and conflict with communism abroad and the struggle for civil rights and women's rights at home. After his humiliation by communist Cuba over the Bay of Pigs, John F. Kennedy faced down the Russians in the Cuban Missile Crisis, which avoided nuclear war, but began a military buildup intended to contain communism in Vietnam. Meanwhile civil rights became a national issue with the 1963 March on Washington. Lyndon Johnson's Vietnam policy escalated into all-out war and increasingly bitter anti-war demonstrations undercut his success with civil rights and voting rights legislation. Richard Nixon ended the war, but his foreign diplomacy achievement, renewing relations with communist China, was overshadowed by Watergate and his eventual resignation. After a decade of protest and scandal, Gerald Ford sought to heal the bitterly divided nation and restore integrity to the presidency. Although his successor, Jimmy Carter, negotiated a historic peace agreement between Egypt and Israel, the early years of the 1980s would presage an era of global terrorism when Iran took fifty-two Americans hostage.

Above: African Americans peacefully protesting for equal rights, integrated schools, and decent housing during the 1963 March on Washington.

Left: Upon taking office after the assassination of JFK, Lyndon B. Johnson immediately pressed for passage of the Civil Rights Act and began his campaign in the "War on Poverty."

John and Jacqueline Kennedy

Bobby, Eunice, Jean, Ted, and Pat Kennedy, smiling, surround their brother Jack and his new wife, Jacqueline, during the couple's wedding reception at Hammersmith Farm. Over the years, Bobby and Jacqueline became particularly close.

Q: Who was John Kennedy?

A: John Fitzgerald ("Jack") Kennedy was born in Brookline, Massachusetts on May 29, 1917, the second of nine children. Politics was in the bloodlines on both sides of his family. Jack's paternal grandfather, Patrick, rose from saloon-keeper to powerful ward boss to state senator. His maternal grandfather, John Francis "Honey Fitz" Fitzgerald, became Boston's first Irish Catholic mayor. Jack's mother, Rose, was Honey Fitz's eldest and favorite child and assumed the roles of his companion, confidante, and hostess. Rose's marriage to Joseph Patrick Kennedy united two powerful Irish Catholic clans. Joseph built his fortune on Wall Street and in Hollywood's budding film industry, but his real money was made in running liquor during

Prohibition. He raised his nine offspring with his family ethic of vigorous competition and winning, while Rose gave them food for their intellect and an unwavering faith. Before his untimely death in World War II, both parents thought that their first son, Joseph, his father's namesake, would be a natural leader and politician who would someday run for president. The family mantle then fell to Jack, the second son, to fulfill his father's dream of sending a son to the White House.

After his 1940 graduation from Harvard University, Jack enlisted in the navy. In 1943, his PT 109 patrol boat was attacked by a Japanese destroyer, killing two of his men. Jack managed to save himself and several others, and was later awarded the Navy and Marine Corps Medal for leadership and courage.

John F. Kennedy. His grandfathers on both sides had scrapped their way into Boston politics and to the top of Irish society in Boston. By the mid-twentieth century the Kennedys and the Fitzgeralds wielded enough political clout to see a grandson become the nation's first Roman Catholic president.

Q: Who was Jacqueline Kennedy?

A: Jacqueline Lee Bouvier was born on July 28, 1929, in Southampton, New York, the first of two daughters born to the elite, wealthy Janet Norton

Lee and John ("Black Jack") Vernou Bouvier III. Caroline Lee ("Lee") was born four years later. The Bouvier sisters shared an intense intimacy and rivalry throughout their lives.

Jacqueline's father, an extraordinarily handsome man, was a magnet for scores of women throughout his life, and his sexual attractiveness was matched only by his self-indulgence. His myriad affairs led Janet to divorce him in 1940. In 1942, her mother married twice-divorced stockbroker, Hugh D. Auchincloss II, heir to a Standard Oil fortune. Jackie and Lee resided with them at two elaborate estates, Merrywood in McLean, Virginia, and Hammersmith Farm in Newport, Rhode Island, where they had unlimited access to privileged society. Janet's second marriage produced two half siblings, Janet and James. Jacqueline's combined families provided her a powerful social network that she employed successfully throughout her life.

After graduation from college, Jacqueline took a full time job as "Inquiring Reporter" at the *Washington Times Herald,* a position secured with the help of her stepfather. Through mutual friends, in 1951, Jacqueline met Jack Kennedy, then a Massachusetts congressman about to run for the U.S. Senate, and they began a courtship. The merger of two wealthy and socially prominent families took place when the couple wed at Saint Mary's Catholic Church in

A smiling Jacqueline prepares to toss her bridal bouquet. Her father, who was too drunk to show up at her wedding, strongly influenced her feelings about sex and love, instilling in her his own conviction that "all men are rats."

Newport, Rhode Island, September 12, 1953, followed by a reception at the bride's father's estate at Hammersmith Farm. Jacqueline insisted, over her mother's hesitation if not opposition, that her father be invited to the wedding and give her away in marriage. At the last moment, her father got drunk and failed to show up for the ceremony, and her stepfather walked her down the aisle. Maintaining an iron composure through what must have been a painful, embarrassing, and excruciating disappointment, Jacqueline first displayed the iron will and composure that she would demonstrate throughout her marriage and at her husband's funeral.

Jacqueline deeply loved her husband. His first love, however, was politics. His womanizing brought tension and pain to the relationship, but Jacqueline appeared to have accepted this behavior as a part of the marriage. She "tuned out" all but his most blatant infidelities, which continued until his death.

> " I think 'Hail to the Chief' has a nice ring to it. "
> —*JOHN F. KENNEDY*

Q: How was the Kennedy presidency a "revolution in style"?

A: The 1960 election ushered in a revolution in presidential style not seen since Theodore Roosevelt. Kennedy was the youngest president ever elected and the first president born in the twentieth century. With their two young children, Jack and Jacqueline represented the ideal American family. They brought youth, intelligence, culture, and sophistication to the White House. Each possessed an elegance of mind and manner; she, especially, understood the connection between pomp and power, ceremony and compelling historical drama. Like the title of their campaign song, the Kennedys brought "High Hopes" to the presidency and the American people.

During her tour before the family entered the mansion, Jacqueline was disappointed to find little of American history or culture reflected in its rooms. As a student of art and history, she began to plan a White House restoration that would embody the nation's past. Toward this goal, she formed a Fine Arts Committee to guide her with David Findley, chairman of the National Fine Arts Committee, and the distinguished expert on Americana, Henry Francis DuPont, creator of the famed Winterthur Museum, as leading members. She also recruited noted lawyer Clark Clifford to set up the White House Historical Association as a nonprofit organization to raise funds, to continue preservation, and to publish a White House guidebook, the sale of which would provide continuing income for the project. Jacqueline formed special committees of subject matter experts to advise on museums, paintings, furnishings, art and antiques, and on materials to acquire for the White House, while distinguished historian Arthur Schlesinger provided consultation on history. She personally searched

Above: The Kennedys presented an image of youthful vigor and style. Jacqueline became a fashion icon and her simple elegance, including the trademark "pillbox" hat, was widely imitated.

Right: Jacqueline, shown with Charles Collingwood, during her televised tour of the White House.

> " It would be sacrilege merely to redecorate . . . It must be restored . . . It is a question of scholarship. "
>
> —*Jacqueline Kennedy,*
> *on the White House restoration*

storage within the mansion and in White House warehouses, identifying historic pieces. She sought congressional aid to help draw up legislation to protect the treasures being donated and give the mansion and its contents museum status under the National Park Service. "Jackie's bill" passed; she then set up guidelines for gift acceptance. To authenticate and maintain the historic furnishings, she hired the first White House curator, Lorraine Pearce, whose first *White House Guidebook* she personally edited.

To make the family's living quarters more comfortable, Jacqueline had a private kitchen and dining room installed. Known as the President's Dining Room, it was the space where the family dined alone or with friends. Outdoors, she oversaw the redesign of the Rose Garden. This magnificent setting was a beautiful backdrop for daytime ceremonies and speeches. After the restoration was completed, the first lady accepted the suggestion of CBS television to lead a tour of the restored White House on national television. Jacqueline's tour with CBS anchorman Charles Collingwood aired on February 14, 1962.

Q: What did Jacqueline wish to accomplish by her entertaining?

A: In her role as the nation's hostess, the first lady staged a stunning array of cultural events not simply for the Kennedys and their guests, but to demonstrate that American culture was equal to any in the world. Jacqueline's presentation of the Pablo Casals concert at the White House, the gathering of Nobel Prize winners at a state dinner, hosting the American Ballet Theater, the National Symphony Orchestra, the American Music Festival, and others reinforced her belief in the need for a national cultural center and a cabinet post for the Arts, which evidence suggests Kennedy had intended to create. Jacqueline, despite her grief following his death, continued to lobby Lyndon Johnson for the creation of the cultural center, which she described as "the cause closest to my heart." LBJ honored her wishes, pushing the funding efforts and pressing for passage of a joint congressional resolution renaming it the John F. Kennedy Center for the Performing Arts. Jacqueline also lobbied for the cabinet post. Her efforts paid off when LBJ signed legislation creating the National Endowments for the Arts and Humanities, which embodied many aspects of the cabinet role she had envisioned and provided funding for American arts and culture.

The nation's fascination with Jacqueline did not cease even after Jack's death, her subsequent remarriage to shipping tycoon Aristotle Onassis, and her own death in 1994. Shown here in 2001 is her daughter, Caroline Kennedy Schlossberg, at the opening of a special exhibition of Jacqueline's original clothing and accessories worn at state events at home and abroad at the John F. Kennedy Library in Boston.

Q: What recreational activities did the Kennedy family enjoy?

A: The president's chronic lower back problems prompted him to monitor his sports activities carefully. He kept a daily exercise routine, working with light weights. An expert swimmer, he swam twice daily in the White House pool and golfed regularly. He most enjoyed the ocean, and sailed his yacht, the *Victura*, off the coast of Hyannis Port, Massachusetts, where the Kennedy family owned a compound of homes. He did not, however, engage in his family's famous touch football games, which were considered potentially dangerous to his back.

Jacqueline also loved physical activity. She, too, included in her daily routine a half hour of morning exercise. She walked, rode her favorite horse, Sardar, a gift from Pakistani leader Ayub Khan, at the rented family retreat at Glen Ora in the Virginia hunt country. She also swam regularly and water skied.

Right: Jack hand-in-hand with his son, John Jr., outside the White House. John Jr. was born shortly before his father took office and spent his first three years under the glare of photographers' flashbulbs.

Below: The Kennedys pose with their children on the porch of their home in Hyannis Port. Jacqueline summed up her attitude toward motherhood by saying, "If you bungle raising your children, I don't think whatever else you do well matters very much."

Q: What activities did the Kennedy children enjoy in the White House?

A: The Kennedys were devoted to their children, Caroline and John Jr. (a third child, Patrick, was born on August 7, 1963, and died two days later), and time with them was paramount to both. Jacqueline set up a kindergarten in the White House solarium to continue Caroline's play group from their years in Georgetown. She filled the integrated class with children of administration officials. The group of seven girls and four boys had two instructors, Elizabeth Boyd and Alice Grimes.

The parents paid for all school furniture, supplies, and the teachers' salaries. The class featured reading from classic children's books, printing lessons, art time, calisthenics, snacks, nap time, and French lessons four days a week, taught by Jacqueline Hirsh. The students put on performances for their parents, and were always accorded a special view of arriving foreign guests, American astronauts, and other distinguished White House visitors. The kindergarten had their class photograph taken on the White House lawn.

When their parents were away, Caroline and John were brought up under the watchful and loving care of their English nanny, Maud Shaw, who became like one of the family. The Secret Service agents who guarded them on the "Diaper Detail" also became friends and extended

family. In the wintertime, Jacqueline liked to hitch Caroline's pony, Macaroni, to a sleigh and take the children for rides on the snow-covered White House lawn, or to give Caroline riding lessons on the pony. She frequently took the children, accompanied by Maud Shaw, for long weekends at Glen Ora, where she could play and read to them alone on her famous "Thursday to Tuesday" weekends. John was fascinated by helicopters and loved to watch them take off and land, listening intently as they flew in overhead shouting, "Chopper! Chopper!" in anticipation of the arrival of his father. He was sometimes allowed to enter the "chopper" to explore for himself.

The first lady had a playground built for the children on the White House's South Lawn with a swing set, a children's playhouse, a treehouse, a trampoline, a sliding board, a seesaw, and monkey bars.

Q: What were the circumstances of John F. Kennedy's tragic death?

A: The president's growing appreciation of Jacqueline's singular contributions to his administration, and his recognition of her popularity, prompted him to seek her help with campaigning. She accompanied him on a precampaign foray to Dallas, Texas. On November 22, 1963, as their motorcade drove through Dealey Plaza, shots rang out and the president slumped forward. Rushed to Parkland Memorial Hospital, he was pronounced dead in the emergency room. Official investigative commissions would fix the blame on a lone assassin, Lee Harvey Oswald, although conspiracy theories thrive to this day.

Having structured the image of his presidency through her White House restoration and brilliant entertaining, Jacqueline now shaped the pageantry of his globally televised funeral, imbuing his tragic death with dignity in carefully orchestrated ceremonies. She further shaped his legacy in an interview with author Theodore White, fixing the Kennedy administration in the American collective memory as "Camelot." Her own time in the White House, after which no presidential spouse could be successful without a significant national project, marked a watershed in redefining the first lady's role.

The photograph that touched the heart of an already-grieving nation: Three-year-old John Jr. salutes his father's casket.

Caroline and John Jr. shown with their Uncle Ted. Both of the Kennedy children grew into intelligent, thoughtful adults, but John Jr.'s untimely death in 1999 left Caroline the sole survivor of her immediate family.

" I am the man who accompanied Jacqueline Kennedy to Paris, and I have enjoyed it. "
—JOHN F. KENNEDY

Lyndon and Lady Bird Johnson

Flanked by his wife and the newly widowed Jacqueline Kennedy, Lyndon Johnson is sworn in as president by Judge Sarah Hughes aboard *Air Force One* on November 22, 1963.

Q: Who were the Johnsons?

A: Although she had been christened Claudia Alta Taylor, the future first lady was dubbed "Lady Bird" as a small child—and the name stuck. After the death of her mother when she was only five, she was raised by her father and aunt in a country mansion outside Karnack, Texas. She attended the University of Texas and received a degree in arts and journalism. Lyndon Baines Johnson was born into rural poverty in 1908, not far from Johnson City, which his family had helped settle. He worked his way through Southwest Texas State Teachers College, and then began his political career in 1931, serving as secretary to Congressman Richard Kleberg. While visiting Austin in his official capacity, he met Lady Bird Taylor. He promptly asked her for a date; she quickly accepted. After returning to Washington, Lyndon began a long-distance courtship. When he returned to Texas seven weeks later, he proposed to her and she accepted. They were married in November 1934. In 1937, he ran for his first elected office, as the U.S. congressman from Texas, an office he held until 1948 when he was then elected to the Senate. In 1955, he was elected Senate majority leader, the youngest man to hold this position in either political party. He was elected vice president in 1960 as John F. Kennedy's running mate and became president himself after Kennedy's tragic assassination. Following on his work in the Senate, Johnson initiated a package of domestic programs known as the "Great Society," that embodied visions of the American Dream for all segments of the nation. The program included civil rights, economic opportunity, job creation and training, enhanced educational opportunities through the Head Start program, voting rights legislation, and historic and environmental protection—what Lady Bird termed "a just and compassionate society."

Newlyweds Lady Bird and Lyndon pose in front of the capitol. Theirs was a whirlwind courtship— they were married just two short months after meeting in Austin, Texas.

> " Sometimes Lyndon simply takes your breath away. "
> —LADY BIRD JOHNSON

Q: How did the first lady entertain?

A: Lady Bird continued the Kennedy tradition of brilliant entertaining, and introduced innovative settings: state dinners were presented in the Rose Garden, buffet suppers were held on the South Lawn. Lady Bird chose to use Rene Verdon, the Kennedys' French chef, until his departure, and then hired Henry Haller to maintain the standard of haute cuisine. The Johnsons also introduced world leaders to their Texas ranch, presenting the best of food and culture in a "down-home" setting. A barbecue on the banks of the Pedernales River and a tour of the ranch, guided by the president, were mandatory. The Johnsons were also the first to hold a "cookout" at the White House. Lady Bird initiated monthly "women doers" lunches to honor and publicize women's achievements.

Q: What family members lived in the Johnson White House?

A: The Johnsons' two daughters, Lynda Bird and Luci Baines, were teenagers when the family entered the mansion. Lynda was a student at the University of Texas, but transferred to George Washington University. Luci was a student at National Cathedral School who aspired to a career in nursing. Living through their teenage years while under the glare of national publicity was not easy for them, and dating provided them with challenges few young women ever face. How could prospective boyfriends relax and have fun when they were accompanied by Secret Service agents? Both girls found sanctuary in the White House solarium, which they equipped with soda machines and used as their private hangout. Here Luci, nicknamed "Watusi Luci" because of her enthusiastic dancing, could let herself go. The solarium was also the site of her surprise graduation party with friends from the National Cathedral School. Knowing she wanted to go into nursing, they sneaked in a "cadaver," while she was upstairs. The "cadaver" was a friend who suddenly "came to life" when Luci entered. Luci also fell in love during her White House years, with Patrick Nugent, a student at Marquette University. She had visited the campus for a fun weekend disguised in a blonde wig and using a fake name, "Amy Nunn," to escape the ever-vigilant press.

The first lady and president share a quiet moment at the LBJ Ranch along the banks of the Pedernales River with their dog Yuki. The Johnsons often invited state guests to the ranch to experience "authentic" American culture.

The Johnson family shortly before they moved into the White House. From left to right: Lynda, Luci, Lyndon, and Lady Bird. Luci recalled that on her first night in the mansion, she and a friend wanted to build a cozy fire in her bedroom fireplace but forgot to open the damper. The room filled with billowing smoke, but the staff rushed to the rescue. She lamented, "I spent my first week in the White House getting rid of the smoke on my newly painted walls."

Q: What White House weddings took place during the Johnson administration?

A: Both presidential daughters married during their father's presidency. Luci, who converted to Roman Catholicism, married Patrick Nugent in a religious ceremony at the Shrine of the Immaculate Conception in Washington, D.C., on August 6, 1966. Her gown, by Priscilla of Boston, featured a flowing nine-foot-long Watteau court train that fell from between her shoulders, and was made of English net over white taffeta. She had ten bridesmaids, all of whom wore matching pink gowns, twelve ushers, a matron of honor, a flower girl, and a ring bearer. Her East Room reception featured a thirteen-tier, eight-foot tall, three-hundred-pound wedding cake. Luci tossed her bouquet to Lynda, who caught it, foretelling her own White House wedding.

Lynda's romance with Hollywood actor George Hamilton, begun in 1966, was widely covered by the press, but it was right in the Executive Mansion that she found her real love: young Marine officer Charles Robb, who had been assigned to duty there. Lynda and Chuck courted in the solarium, avoiding publicity. They married on December 9, 1967, in an East Room ceremony. Luci served as her matron of honor. The fifteen-minute Episcopal ceremony was performed by the Reverend Gerald McAllister of San Antonio. Lynda's wedding gown, designed by Geoffrey Beene, was a regal, long-sleeved, high collared, white silk satin. Its front panel was outlined in embroidered silk flowers with seed pearls. Following the ceremony, their five hundred guests feasted on wedding cake while the Marine Band played.

Q: What pets did the Johnsons bring to the White House?

A: The president had two registered beagles, Him and Her, during the White House years that were often photographed with him. In 1964, the president caused a

Below left: Lyndon escorts his daughter Luci to her wedding to Patrick Nugent. The couple had four children: Patrick Lyndon, Nicole, Rebekah, and Claudia. She is now remarried to Ian Turpin, a Canadian financier.

Below right: Lynda and Chuck Robb walking down the aisle. They have three daughters, Lucinda, Catherine, and Jennifer, and live in Virginia where Chuck became governor and then U.S. senator. Lynda served for many years as chair of Reading is Fundamental and is active in many charitable and civic causes.

public relations "incident" when he picked up Him by the ears while greeting a group on the White House lawn. Him later sired a litter of puppies; Luci kept two of them, Kim and Freckles. Yuki, another dog widely photographed with the president, was a charming mixed breed Luci found at a gas station in Texas on Thanksgiving Day 1966, while on her way to the LBJ ranch. Luci named him Yuki from *yukimas,* meaning "snow" in Japanese. At first Yuki lived with Luci but, while visiting the White House, Yuki became LBJ's faithful companion. On his birthday, Luci gave her father the dog as a present.

Q: How did LBJ's presidency end?

A: As involvement in the Vietnam War escalated without victory, American participation became increasingly unpopular at home. Antiwar protests were common, with demonstrations too often escalating into violent confrontations. Protesters carrying signs that read, "HEY, HEY, LBJ, HOW MANY KIDS HAVE YOU KILLED TODAY?" were bitter reminders that confronted the Johnsons daily, in front of the White House and wherever they traveled. Eartha Kitt, an African American singer and actress embarrassed Lady Bird at the first lady's "women doers" lunch on January 18, 1968. Kitt told the first lady that young men did not want to fight in the war and would do anything to avoid it. Lady Bird

responded graciously, but the protests had directly entered the White House. Concerned about her husband's health, she encouraged LBJ not to run again, stating that, "It will kill him." LBJ had his own doubts about running for reelection, remarking, "I do not believe I can unite this country." In a televised speech on March 31, 1968, he announced, "I shall not seek, and I will not accept, the nomination of my party for another term as your President."

After his term of office ended, the Johnsons retired to their beloved LBJ ranch, where they could relax and make plans for his presidential library. His considerable legacy in domestic policy—civil rights, education, historic preservation, and the environment—have been overshadowed by the impact of the Vietnam War. His presidency awaits a future generation to reassess its historical legacy.

The Johnsons were a family of dog-lovers and owned several during the White House years, including the often-photographed beagles, Him and Her, shown here relaxing in a spot of sun at the White House.

With a nation deeply split on the issue of American involvement in Vietnam, demonstrators were an everyday sight outside the White House gates. When entertainer Eartha Kitt was invited to one of the first lady's "women doers" events, she brought the protest inside when she defended the many young men who did not want to fight the war.

Only two things are necessary to keep one's wife happy. One is to let her think she is having her own way, and the other is to let her have it.

—*LYNDON JOHNSON*

Richard and Pat Nixon

Q: Why did Richard Nixon relish his political victory in the 1968 election?

A: Nixon developed presidential ambitions early in his political career and shaped his political development toward that goal. He served in the House of Representatives and in the Senate, becoming famous for his anti-Communist activities. In 1960, he seemed to have reached his political goal with his presidential nomination to run against John F. Kennedy. Nixon lost in one of the closest elections in American history with Kennedy's margin of victory less that one fifth of 1 percent of the total vote. Nixon subsequently lost his bid for governor of California in 1962, seemingly ending his political career. But Nixon engineered a carefully orchestrated comeback. Billing himself as the "New Nixon," his political resurrection was complete in 1968 with his presidential victory. He reveled in the role he had sought so long and for which he had waged a lifelong battle.

In his post-presidential years Richard Nixon sought to rehabilitate his disgraced public image. He became a sort of "elder statesman," with whom both Democratic and Republican successors consulted for advice on foreign policy.

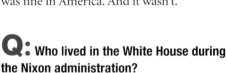

Q: What events overshadowed the Nixon presidency?

A: Although Nixon campaigned on a platform to get the nation out of Vietnam, "Johnson's War" quickly became his as well. The Nixons were dogged by antiwar protesters and his doctrine of "Vietnamization"—gradual withdrawal of United States troops and the training of Vietnamese nationals to take over their own defense—did not prove successful. In October 1969, an enormous national protest brought hundreds of thousands of antiwar activists to Washington as did the "May Day" demonstration in 1970. Both events saw protesters surround the White House. Julie Nixon Eisenhower reflected that her parents were sitting "on top of the powder keg in this time of unprecedented domestic violence in this country, trying to go on as if everything was fine in America. And it wasn't."

Q: Who lived in the White House during the Nixon administration?

A: The Nixons' daughters, Tricia and Julie, now young adults, and Julie's husband, David Eisenhower, lived in the White House. Mamie Eisenhower, grandmother of David, was considered a member of the family and was a frequent house guest. Julie and David, who were both attending college, lived on the third floor of the mansion. The 1970 graduation ceremonies of Julie from Smith College and David from Amherst took

" I'll have to have a room of my own. Nobody could sleep with Dick. He wakes up during the night, switches on the lights, speaks into his tape recorder. " *—Pat Nixon*

David Eisenhower, wife Julie, President Nixon, Pat Nixon, and daughter Tricia pose for a White House photo in 1969.

place amid increasingly violent campus protests, and the president feared that his presence at the ceremonies would provoke riots. The first lady arranged for a commencement party for the graduates at Camp David instead. David continued his education at the George Washington University Law School and Julie acted as an aide to her mother while beginning her writing career for the *Saturday Evening Post*. Tricia was the more reclusive of the Nixon daughters, but enjoyed tutoring inner-city children. She also played a ceremonial role for the president, accompanying him on campaign stops and on trips around the world.

Q: What White House project did Pat Nixon undertake as first lady?

A: The first lady, building on Jacqueline Kennedy's White House restoration, hired Clement Conger, former curator at the State Department, to help her locate additional antique furnishings and works of art and to renovate the state rooms of the mansion. Pat and Conger were successful in adding more than five hundred pieces of eighteenth- and early-nineteenth-century American furniture and authentic works of art to the White House collections. Among the most important acquisitions were portraits of James Madison and Louisa Catherine Adams. Pat brought back to the White House more authentic period furniture and art than any other first lady. Although most of the nation is aware of Jacqueline Kennedy's restoration of the historic mansion, virtually no publicity was given to Pat's preservation work. Nixon's top staff in the west wing, particularly H. R. Haldeman, chose not to publicize her successful acquisition of historic pieces and the general public went unaware of her contributions. Reporter Helen Thomas commented, "She was so much more sophisticated than the Palace Guard I wondered why her husband did not listen to her more often."

Pat Nixon did not enjoy a positive profile with the press—primarily due to the antagonism of her husband's chief advisors and their often dismissive attitude toward her. Pat was nonetheless a popular first lady, although her projects on "volunteerism," were not considered "hard news" and went under-reported.

Q: What weddings took place during the Nixon administration?

A: Julie, the Nixons' younger daughter, married David Eisenhower, grandson of the former president, in a Christmastide ceremony shortly before her father's inauguration. It was an historic union between two prominent first families. Seeking to keep the ceremony as private as possible, the couple was married by Dr. Norman Vincent Peale at the historic Marble Collegiate Church in New York City on December 22, 1968. The bride wore a Priscilla of Boston gown of silk peau d'ange with a high lace collar and pearl-embroidered yoke. The waistline was molded and the skirt flared with a deeply pearled and lace flounced hemline that flowed into a cathedral train. The couple's wedding reception, held in the Grand Ballroom of the Plaza Hotel, was attended by five hundred guests. After a menu of hot and cold buffet dishes, the guests were treated to a six-tiered wedding cake, and danced to the Bill Harrington orchestra.

Although Tricia tended to stay out of the limelight during her father's term of office, her 1971 wedding to Edward Cox was a media event. Here, a beaming Nixon escorts his daughter to the Rose Garden ceremony.

Tricia Nixon married her longtime beau, Edward Finch Cox, in a sumptuous White House wedding. The couple met at a high school dance in 1963 and became engaged in November 1970. On June 12, 1971, the bride was escorted down the stairs of the South Portico to the Rose Garden by her father. She wore a Priscilla of Boston gown of layered silk organdy and Alençon lace with embroidered lilies of the valley over a silk crepe underslip. The sleeveless shaped bodice had an open neckline and the skirt was of a flared trumpet style. Julie served as her matron of honor, two young cousins served as flower girls, and the groom's sister, Maize, was a bridesmaid. After the ceremony, the reception was held in the White House.

Q: How did Pat Nixon "open up" the White House?

A: Pat strongly believed that the White House belonged to "all the people," and wanted to make the mansion and its history easily accessible. She arranged the first White House tours for the visually and hearing impaired in the summer of 1969. At Christmas 1970, she inaugurated candlelight tours in the evening, making a visit to the White House possible for those who could not take daytime tours. She worked with engineers to develop a system of lighting that made the house glow a soft white to showcase its fine architectural details. She also opened the White House gardens to visitors in 1973 and directed that the White House guidebooks be translated into several foreign languages. It is one of the ironies of history that, while the president was noted for cover-

ing up activities in the White House, the first lady undertook projects to make the White House open to all.

Q: What series of events brought down the Nixon presidency?

A: A series of events known collectively as "Watergate" caused Nixon to resign the office of the presidency, the only chief executive in American history to do so. Nixon installed a secret taping system in the White House ostensibly to record conversations with his top aides and other officials for the historical record. A botched break-in at Washington's Watergate Hotel office complex to gain information concerning upcoming 1972 election strategy from the Democratic National Committee headquartered there, led investigators to operatives tied to the White House. When the congressional committee looking into the burglary learned that there were tapes of conversations in the mansion, investigators demanded that they be turned over as evidence. Although Nixon stonewalled for as long as possible, the tapes were finally provided to investigators, detailing the outlines of a presidential cover-up and providing evidence to support charges of obstruction of justice. The congressional committee began to draw up charges of impeachment against the president. Faced with almost certain conviction if he were impeached, Nixon decided to resign the presidency. Rather than being remembered in the public mind for his ending of the Vietnam War, the historic breakthrough in diplomatic relations with Communist China, or an impressive array of domestic programs, Nixon's political legacy has been dimmed by his involvement in the Watergate scandal.

Above left: The Nixons at Tricia's wedding. Pat's greatest successes were in the field of personal diplomacy abroad, where she was considered the president's goodwill ambassador. Her diplomatic missions, as well as her thoughtful historic preservation of the White House, demand a modern reassessment.

Above right: Protesters demanding the impeachment of the president. His wife and daughters, despite the evidence against him, offered Nixon unwavering love and loyalty throughout the Watergate scandal and his eventual resignation.

" I hate being a celebrity—and I use that word hesitantly . . . I am stared at when I walk on campus, eyes and heads turn. Sometimes, when I am speaking, I feel as if people were taking mental notes. And sometimes I feel so disgusted later when I have put on a show. "

—*JULIE NIXON EISENHOWER,*
while in college

Gerald and Betty Ford

Q: What was unique about Gerald Ford's presidency?

A: Gerald Ford is the only person in the history of the American presidency to serve as both vice president and president without having been elected to either office. Because of the circumstances of Nixon's resignation, there were no inaugural ceremonies welcoming the Ford administration.

During the Nixon administration, Vice President Spiro Agnew was charged with income tax evasion and taking monetary kickbacks from contractors while governor of Maryland. Agnew pleaded "no contest" to the charges and resigned his office in October 1973. Nixon then appointed Gerald Ford as vice president and he took office in December. When Nixon also chose to resign in view of pending criminal charges stemming from the Watergate scandal, Ford became president. Nixon's resignation was effective at noon on August 9, 1974 and at 12:03 p.m. Ford was sworn in by Chief Justice Warren Burger in the East Room of the White House. Ford then appointed Nelson Rockefeller, former governor of New York, to the again-vacant office of vice president. Ford believed that his most important job as president was

to heal the nation after the divisiveness of Watergate, and to restore integrity to the White House. Declaring, "our long national nightmare is over," he used his presidential authority to grant Richard Nixon a full pardon. He thought that

Left: Gerald R. Ford, the only man with the dubious distinction of never having been elected to either the vice presidency or the presidency, faced the reality of his new role, stating, "I have not sought this enormous responsibility, but I will not shirk it."

Right: Betty Ford, appearing traditionally elegant in this photograph taken in the Treaty Room, was a forthright advocate of women's issues—both radical and conventional. She strongly supported the ERA, but also spoke out for the right of women to choose domesticity as well as the work world. "We have to take that 'just' out of 'just a house-wife' . . . downgrading this work has been part of the pattern in our society that has undervalued women's talents in all areas."

an extended criminal trial of the former president would further inflame and divide the nation. Many were furious with Ford's decision, and some political pundits presume that the pardon cost Ford his 1976 bid for reelection.

Q: How did Betty Ford interpret her role as first lady?

A: Betty had long been a congressional wife, but was suddenly catapulted into her new role as first lady. She remarked,

"I felt like I'd been thrown into a river without knowing how to swim." She valued candor as her strongest asset and presented herself honestly without "spin" or "crafting" of her image.

In September 1974, soon after entering the White House, she was diagnosed with malignant breast cancer. At the time, breast cancer was a topic discussed only in hushed whispers, but Betty chose to make her illness public to call attention to breast cancer, remove the stigma attached to the disease, and encourage women to have breast cancer examinations. She reflected that by talking about her ordeal she had "saved a lot of lives." In 1975, Betty was interviewed by Morley Safer on the popular television news program *60 Minutes*. She candidly discussed her support of the Equal Rights Amendment (ERA) and legalized abortion, acknowledged that marijuana use had become as routine as drinking beer, and said she would not be surprised if her daughter was having an affair. The public response to her comments was astonishing. The White House was deluged with letters of outrage, some calling her "a disgrace to the White House." The president jokingly told her, "You just lost me twenty million votes." When the negative reaction was made public, Betty received thousands of letters of praise from supporters who found her candor refreshing. In response to those who said she degraded the role of first lady she stated, "being ladylike does not require silence."

Q: How did the first lady entertain while she was in the White House?

A: Betty's use of Americana in formal entertaining was her salute to the nation's Bicentennial. Every detail of the Fords' state occasions was chosen with the honored guests' tastes and interests in mind. Henry Haller continued as White House chef, and dinners were served on small, round tables as the first lady mixed china patterns from previous administrations to stress American history. She turned the mansion into a showcase for all things American using Steuben glass, antique weathervanes, historic silver pieces, and Native American reed baskets as centerpieces, while old wooden spools from New England textile mills became candle holders.

The first lady and her daughter, Susan, work on homemade Christmas decorations in the White House solarium. As the first lady for the nation's 200th anniversary, Betty's taste in decorating ran to traditional American themes and images.

Not my power, but the power of the position, a power which could be used to help.
—*Betty Ford*

Q: Who were the Ford children?

A: The Fords had four children, three sons, Michael, John ("Jack"), and Steven, and one daughter, Susan. The oldest son, Michael, married Gayle Brumbaugh in 1974, shortly before his father became president. He and Gayle lived in Boston while he attended Gordon Conwell Theological Seminary as a graduate student studying for the clergy. Jack was attending Utah State University and, after completing his degree, moved into the White House in 1975, and helped manage Ford's 1976 presidential campaign. Steve lived in the White House before moving west to work as a ranch hand in Montana. He briefly attended Utah State University and then enrolled in a school for rodeo riders in Wyoming. Later, he studied animal science at California Polytechnic University. He also worked as an actor, and today is in demand as a motivational speaker. Susan lived in the White House for the entire presidency and completed high school at Holton Arms Academy in Bethesda, Maryland. In 2005, she succeeded her mother as chairman of the Betty Ford Center for substance addiction.

Q: What activities did the Fords enjoy in the White House?

A: The Ford family enjoyed the third-floor solarium. Susan said, "It was like a family room. We used it a lot for playing cards, listening to music, and watching TV. I took several dates up there just to hang out." Donors provided funds to build an outdoor pool for the White House and the president routinely took advantage of it. Betty recalled that, "Jerry used the new pool all year round. . . . if he had a chance, he'd take a swim." Ford also enjoyed playing tennis and golf. Putting

Below left: The Ford Family in the Oval Office prior to the president's swearing-in on August 9, 1974. From left to right: Jack, Steve, the first lady, the president, Susan, Gayle, and Mike.

Below right: When she moved into the White House, "first daughter" Susan received a letter from a former first daughter, Alice Roosevelt Longworth, urging her to "Have a helluva time!"

" All my children have spoken for themselves since they first learned to speak, and not always with my advance approval, and I expect that to continue in the future. "

—GERALD FORD

The president tries out the new White House swimming pool during the summer of 1975. Ford was an enthusiastic athlete, and was delighted when generous donors provided funding to build an outdoor pool.

the pool to his own use, Jack took scuba diving lessons while in the White House. For her eighteenth birthday, Susan held a festive barbecue on the South Lawn and hosted her classmates at Holton Arms to an elegant East Room prom. She found herself criticized for wearing jeans in the White House and complained that reporters questioned her about her private life after her mother's appearance on *60 Minutes.* The tall and blonde Susan was a beautiful stand-in for her mother at a state dinner while Betty was recuperating from cancer, recalling, "I was not prepared to be the unofficial first lady. . . . I was scared to death that I might do something wrong." Susan apprenticed as a photographer under White House photographer David Kennerly and later studied photography at the University of Kansas.

Q: What special concerns did Betty Ford champion as first lady?

A: Betty became a first lady for women's issues, bringing the women's movement of the 1970s into the mainstream of American life. She staunchly supported women's health issues and the ERA. She personally lobbied legislators and congressional members in key states across the country to pass the amendment, making public appearances and personal phone calls. Her advocacy of the ERA brought a deluge of mail to the White House, both for and against her position. The National Woman's Party, who had been the militant wing of the suffrage movement, presented Betty with their first Alice Paul Award, named after its founder who had first drafted the amendment.

Betty encouraged the president to sign legislation that led to the International Women's Year Conference, which was held in Houston, Texas, in 1977. Prior to the national conference, state conferences were held in all fifty states to discuss issues of concern to women. The national conference adopted a plan of action to improve women's access to health care, economic advancement, political power, and equality. First ladies Betty Ford, Lady Bird Johnson, and Rosalynn Carter attended, demonstrating their support.

After leaving the White House, Betty Ford's ongoing public role as an advocate and speaker in the areas of breast cancer and substance abuse enabled many women to cope realistically with these personal problems.

Jimmy and Rosalynn Carter

Although Rosalynn Carter is better known for her work on mental health reform and women's issues, the first lady did not ignore the arts. The Carters set up a trust fund to continue White House historical acquisitions, and Rosalynn extended the legacy of cultural artists at the White House by arranging for PBS to telecast these important events to the public.

Q: How did the Carters build their successful working partnership?

A: Jimmy Carter and Rosalynn Smith met in Plains, Georgia in 1945. Ruth Carter, Jimmy's sister, was Rosalynn's best friend and introduced the two. At eighteen, Rosalynn married the Naval Academy graduate, whom she idolized, in the Plains Methodist Church on July 7, 1946. Carter's naval career took him to submarine school and he was chosen for the nuclear submarine program. After his father died of cancer in 1953, Carter left the Navy to run the family's peanut farm and warehouse business. Rosalynn hated the move back to Plains, but soon took over keeping the accounts and learning the business. She became a full partner in the Carters' peanut enterprises claiming, "I knew more about the books and more about the business . . . than Jimmy did." She became an integral part of the decision-making process, a pattern for their lifelong relationship. Rosalynn was a partner in Carter's campaigns for the Georgia governorship and for the presidency. During his administration, she was fully briefed on policies and often served as Carter's personal representative.

One historian described her as "surrogate, confidante, and joint policymaker." Carter himself said they "were full partners in every sense of the word."

Q: What social causes did Rosalynn Carter pursue as first lady?

A: Rosalynn entered the White House with an impressive agenda of reforms: mental health care, passage of the ERA, and care for the elderly. She stated that her chief concern was to "develop a strategy for helping the mentally ill," and she lobbied strongly to create the

The president and first lady dance at a White House congressional ball in 1978. The Carters enjoyed a close marriage between equals. Jimmy frankly credited her as a "full partner" who often acted as his personal representative.

President's Commission on Mental Health. Carter did so within a month of his inauguration. Prohibited by law from heading the commission, she directed its agenda as honorary chair and testified before the Senate in support of the commission in 1979. The commission's work resulted in the enactment of the Mental Health Systems Act, passed in September 1980. It emphasized community health care centers, the inclusion of mental health in insurance programs, and increased research and prevention.

Q: **What key role did the first lady play at the Camp David summit?**

A: Pursuit of peace in the Middle East was high on the agenda of international problems addressed by the Carter administration. Carter invited President Anwar Sadat of Egypt and Prime Minister Menachem Begin of Israel—and their wives—to a summit at Camp David in September 1978. Including the wives in the invitation, Carter believed, would help defuse the tense atmosphere of negotiations.

Rosalynn was fully involved in the preparations and understood the high stakes. At the last minute, she arranged for the signing of the Camp David Accords between Egypt and Israel on the White House lawn. Her diary of the two-week summit, totaling two-hundred pages, is the best record of the personal interactions at that historic meeting.

The Begins, Carters, and Sadats share a triumphant moment. The Carters deliberately chose to invite the leaders' wives to the Camp David summit in order to lessen the tensions of the talks. From left to right: Aliza Begin, Carter, Jihan Sadat, Begin, Rosalynn, and Sadat.

> " **A first lady is in a position to know the needs of the country and do something about them. It would be a shame not to take full advantage of that power.** "
>
> —ROSALYNN CARTER

Amy proudly displays her dollhouse to photographers. Inside, her cat Misty Malarky Ying Yang finds a cozy spot. Amy went on to pursue a master's in art history at Tulane University and illustrated some of her father's children's books. Today, she is the mother of a son, Hugo, from her 1996 marriage to James Wentzel.

Jimmy and Rosalynn kiss while surrounded by family, including Amy and Lillian, at the 1976 Democratic National Convention in New York City. Jimmy's outspoken and earthy mother became a media favorite.

Q: Who lived with the Carters in the White House?

A: The Carter clan included a large live-in family with a daughter, two sons, daughters-in-law, grandchildren, and lengthy visits from Miss Lillian, the president's mother. John William ("Jack") and his wife, Judy, did not choose to live in the White House because Jack had established a law practice with his father-in-law in Calhoun, Georgia, but the couple visited frequently with their children, Jason and Sarah, who celebrated her first birthday in the White House solarium. James Earl III ("Chip") and his wife, Caron, lived in the mansion while he worked for the Democratic National Committee and as an aide to the president. Four weeks after the inauguration, the couple's son, James Earl IV ("Digger") was born in Bethesda Naval Hospital. They remained at the White House until their separation in November 1978. Donnel Jeffrey ("Jeff") and his wife, Annette, lived in the White House

while he attended George Washington University. Chip, Jeff, and their wives lived on the third floor where there was a nursery for the grandchildren. After his father's term of office ended, Jeff and Annette remained in the Washington area where he had a computer software business. Their first child was born in 1984.

Miss Lillian, a former nurse who joined the Peace Corps at age sixty-eight and served in India, maintained her home in Plains, Georgia, but visited frequently. When in residence, she stayed in the Queen's Bedroom, "Where I belong!" she quipped. She was the first mother of a president to serve as her son's official representative abroad, attending the state funerals of Pope Paul VI, Marshall Tito of Yugoslavia, and Golda Meir of Israel.

"I have often wanted to drown my troubles, but I can't get my wife to go swimming."

—*Jimmy Carter*

Q: What activities did Amy Carter enjoy while living in the White House?

A: Amy, who was nine when her parents entered the mansion, grew up in the glare of White House publicity despite her parents' best efforts to guard her privacy. Demonstrating their support for public education, the Carters enrolled her in the 108-year-old public Thaddeus Stevens Elementary School in Washington's inner city. She later attended Sidwell Friends School in the nation's capital. Amy engaged in the activities of a young girl, playing in her tree house on the South Lawn, skating on the mansion's driveways, and practicing her diving technique in the White House pool. She invited her friends for sleepovers in the Lincoln bedroom, hoping to see if his ghost would appear. Her love of reading led her to bring a novel to the inaugural ball to avoid boredom, and she read books at the table during state dinners. She slept in a bedroom near her parents' room on the second floor, and did her homework on Eleanor Roosevelt's desk. She took violin lessons, practicing under her mother's watchful eye, and played chess in the third-floor game room. At the White House congressional Christmas party in 1977, she played violin with her music class, and read her poetry at Reading is Fun Day.

Q: What relaxation did the Carters enjoy in the White House?

A: Both Jimmy and Rosalynn engaged in regular exercise programs and they enjoyed jogging and fishing together and taking walks along Washington's Chesapeake and Ohio Canal. The president enjoyed tennis and playing softball with his staff. Carter favored casual dress, relaxing in T shirts and cardigans. Like President Grant before him, he installed a billiards room on the third floor of the White House. He loved classical music and had it piped into his office study, and installed the first video tape machine in the mansion.

After Jimmy's defeat by Ronald Reagan, the Carters returned home to Plains, Rosalynn declaring that she was "bitter enough for both of us." Yet they used their visibility and prestige as former president and first lady to build social programs of international significance.

CHAPTER 11

CHALLENGES OF A NEW AGE

The period from the Ronald Reagan administration through that of George W. Bush was dominated by the weakening of Cold War superpower rivals, the ever-increasing threat of international terrorism, and economic globalization. Reagan restricted the role of government in the economy, reduced taxes, and challenged the domination of the Soviet Union. George H. W. Bush was president during the U.S.S.R.'s collapse and continued the conservative policies of his predecessor. The invasion of Kuwait by Iraq was met with force by the United States and a coalition of nations to prevent Iraq's expansion in the Middle East and protect allied oil interests. William J. Clinton reduced the nation's budget deficit, spearheaded peacekeeping missions to oppose "ethnic cleansing" in the former Yugoslavia (Bosnia, Serbia, and Croatia), and passed the North American Free Trade Agreement. His administration was marred by scandal and impeachment, although he was acquitted. George W. Bush was challenged by terrorist attacks on the World Trade Center in New York and the Pentagon in Washington on September 11, 2001. The response to terrorism led to the bombing of Afghanistan and a "war on terror" in Iraq that polarized the nation.

Above: Ronald Reagan and Mikhail Gorbachev in Geneva, Switzerland, 1985. After the decades-long Cold War, the United States witnessed the collapse of its archrival, the Soviet Union, in 1991.

Left: The twin beams of light represent the fallen twin towers at the September 11th memorial in downtown Manhattan. The terrorist attack presented unprecedented challenges to the American people and to their president.

Ronald and Nancy Reagan

Q: What were the backgrounds of Ronald and Nancy Reagan?

A: Ronald Reagan and Nancy Davis, both former Hollywood film actors,

married on March 4, 1952. Reagan, who was divorced from film star Jane Wyman, and Nancy, who experienced insecurity and loneliness in her early childhood, were deeply committed to each other. Nancy announced repeatedly that her "life began when I met my husband." His well-being and ambitions became her career. Reagan's background in movies and television provided him with an engaging speaking style that contributed to his political success. The intimacy of the Reagans' marriage enabled Nancy to become his closest advisor. Reagan ran successfully for governor of California, where Nancy's Hollywood background proved useful

Newlyweds Ronald and Nancy Reagan cutting their wedding cake at the home of fellow actor William Holden in Toluca Lake, California.

in entertaining and image-making as first lady of California. Their shared film background, expensive tastes, and elegant style shaped his political career and brought Hollywood to the White House, where their interdependent marriage had a profound effect on his presidency.

Q: What was the irony in Reagan's running as a "family values" candidate?

A: As their son, Ron, remarked, "Our family was famously fractious, and it stayed fractious." The family's deep personal resentments, estrangements, and political divisions were played out in the public spotlight of politics.

The Reagans had four children, Maureen and Michael, from Reagan's first marriage to Jane Wyman, and two children of their own, Patti and Ronald Jr. All of the Reagan children felt that they had been ignored while growing up.

The 1981 inaugural family photo was one of the last times the Reagans were photographed together during his term of office. In the center are the president and first lady, standing third from left is Michael, and Ron at far right. Maureen sits second from left and Patti is seated second from right.

Michael, the adopted son, brooded about his status as an outsider. In 1984, a row occurred between Michael and Nancy when the Secret Service wrongly accused Michael of stealing small items (charges were never filed). The Reagans believed the charge and limited their contact with Michael and his family. Nancy termed the situation an "estrangement." Maureen sought approval and a vocation to share with her father as a political operative for the Republican National Committee and through unsuccessful bids for public office. Patti, who shunned the White House and broke with her parents over personal and political differences, changed her surname to Davis (her mother's family name) to distance herself from them. She wrote a novel that proved a thinly veiled, scathing attack on them and spoke out against her father's conservative political policies. Ron grew up in the glare of the political spotlight, and weathered public speculation over his sexual orientation during his time as a dancer with the Joffrey Ballet.

All four children attended Reagan's inauguration in 1981, but photographs taken then were the last pictures of the family together during his entire term of office. Only Maureen visited frequently. She had come to terms with her father and stepmother and stayed in the White House for lengthy periods. Ron,

Patti shares a moment with her father at Nancy's birthday party at Rancho del Cielo, the Reagan's California home, in 1983. Although for many years her relationship with her parents was strained, during the former president's long battle with Alzheimer's disease, she reconciled with them.

who married Doria Palmieri, a clinical psychologist, observed, "In our house, there were Nancy and Ronnie—and then there were the rest of us."

Reagan's lengthy battle with Alzheimer's disease served to heal the fractured family. Patti wrote a book, *The Long Goodbye*, about her family's battle with the disease. Michael, Ron, and Patti paid glowing tributes to their father in a poignant funeral as the sun set literally and figuratively on Reagan's life.

Michael now hosts a syndicated radio talk show on conservative politics. Ron is currently a news and political commentator for television's MSNBC. Maureen died of cancer in 2001 at the age of 60. Patti lectures on families and forgiveness.

> He had written my mother once that he wanted her to be the first thing he saw every morning and the last thing he ever saw. And that's how it turned out.
>
> —RON REAGAN,
> *about his father*

Q: Why was Nancy Reagan's initial public image so negative?

A: In the early years of Reagan's administration, the public noticed only Nancy's conspicuous consumption: a costly redecoration of the White House family quarters, the purchase of an elegant new service of state china, and the flaunting of extravagant clothing. Although these items were purchased with private funds from wealthy friends or provided by American designers, the Reagans' sumptuous lifestyle contrasted sharply with the economic recession and the administration's dismantling of the social service programs set in place during the Great Society years. The president's advisers were concerned that Nancy's low rating in public opinion polls would negatively impact his presidency. Her appearance at Washington's annual Gridiron Club dinner in 1982, however, turned her reputation around. Dressed in exaggeratedly outrageous clothing and singing a parody of herself to the tune of "Second-Hand Rose," Nancy demonstrated a self-deprecating humor that satirized her reputation as a woman with expensive tastes. She later reflected, "It isn't often that one is lucky enough to enjoy a second beginning, but during that five-minute period . . . I was able to make a fresh start with the Washington Press Corps."

Nancy in her "Second-Hand Rose" disguise for the Gridiron Club. The first lady's good-natured self-parody of her reportedly extravagant tastes charmed members of the press, who were willing to give her a second chance after their initial hostility toward her.

Q: What cause did the first lady adopt?

A: Nancy's community service centered on hospitals and health issues. Her most sustained and popular cause as first lady was her program on drug and substance abuse—a serious public health problem in the nation. By 1982, her campaign to promote drug education and prevention attained national significance. In a 1984 trip to an Oakland, California elementary school, when she asked the students how to respond to drug pushers, they chanted, "Just Say No!" This line became the name of her cause. The first lady made numerous television appearances promoting her "Just Say No" program, including a cameo appearance on the popular sitcom *Diff'rent Strokes* with Gary Coleman and on *Good Morning America*. In 1985, she hosted a two-day international drug abuse summit with eighteen first ladies from around the world. Her emphasis on

"How can a president not be an actor?"
—RONALD REAGAN

personal responsibility and private-sector programs, rather than on governmental policies, appealed to Reagan's conservative constituency and also addressed their fears about the disintegration of the American family. Her work against drug addiction proved the most potent factor in the transformation of her public image.

Q: What threat to the president occurred early in the administration?

A: In March 1981, John Hinckley, a mentally disturbed young man, attempted to assassinate President Reagan in Washington, D.C., with a .22 caliber handgun. Reagan's condition was far more critical than the public was led to believe, and his recovery was an arduous one. He underwent major surgery to remove the bullet but developed postoperative infection and fever. Nancy zealously guarded her husband's recovery, limiting his working hours and carefully crafting his postoperative public image.

Q: What other health issues threatened the Reagans in the White House years?

A: In 1985, Reagan was diagnosed with malignant polyps and underwent major surgery for colon cancer. During his convalescence, Nancy limited his schedule and again orchestrated his public image. In October 1987, Nancy faced her own health crisis when a malignant tumor was discovered in her breast. She opted to undergo a modified radical mastectomy. The first lady argued that the best method for treating breast cancer was a decision each woman must make individually.

Yet the furor over the cancer surgeries demonstrated the degree to which the first family had become a focal point of public interest and press coverage.

Q: In what unusual way did the first lady influence the president's scheduling of political events?

A: With their acting backgrounds, Ronald and Nancy found nothing bizarre in consulting an astrologer. Film stars regularly consulted with psychiatrists and astrologers as part of the Hollywood lifestyle. After the assassination attempt, Nancy, who had relied on astrologers for years, sought advice from astrologer Joan Quigley to determine the most opportune dates for success in the scheduling of political events and international negotiations. When this became public knowledge, it ignited a firestorm of negative publicity not only about "consulting the stars," but also about the extent of influence wielded by the first lady over the scheduling of nationally significant events.

Nancy speaking at a "Just Say No" rally in Los Angeles. Her willingness to tackle a tough cause such as drug-abuse prevention and to use whatever means were available to promote it, including guest television appearances, helped her shape a positive public image.

The Reagans celebrated their thirty-third wedding anniversary in the Oval Office in 1985. Nancy won profound respect from admirers and critics alike for her loving care of the president during his final years, when he suffered from Alzheimer's disease, or, as he called it, "the long goodbye."

George and Barbara Bush

Q: What political background did George and Barbara Bush have when they entered the White House?

A: George and Barbara Bush entered the White House as seasoned political veterans. They had spent virtually their entire adult lives together. After meeting as teenagers at a country club dance in Greenwich, Connecticut, over the Christmas break in 1941, the couple was married on January 6, 1945. The son of a U. S. senator from Connecticut, George was a graduate of Yale University and a Navy pilot who distinguished himself in World War II, who then sought his fortune in the Texas oil and gas industry. He proved to be a successful businessman before winning a seat in Congress in 1966. He was defeated for the Senate in 1970, but was appointed to a variety of important governmental posts in the Republican administrations of Nixon and Ford, including ambassador to the United Nations, chairman of the Republican National Committee, U.S. envoy to China, and director of the Central Intelligence Agency. By the time of his nomination as vice president to run with Ronald Reagan, the Bushes had extensive political, diplomatic, international, and Republican Party experience. Barbara's wit, ease with people, self-deprecating humor, and speaking ability made her an excellent political partner when Bush assumed the presidency.

Above: Barbara and George on their honeymoon. Between 1945 and 1999, the Bush family moved twenty-nine times as George served in a variety of government jobs. During his many absences, Barbara became the solid core of the close-knit family.

Right: The family in Houston, Texas, 1959. Seated from left to right: Neil, George H. with Doro on his lap, Barbara with Marvin on her lap; standing are George W. and Jeb. The Bushes' elder daughter, Robin, had died of leukemia in 1953.

Q: Who made up the Bush family?

A: George and Barbara raised a close-knit family of five children: George Walker, John Ellis ("Jeb"), Neil Mallon, Marvin Pierce, and Dorothy ("Doro"). They also had a daughter, Pauline Robinson ("Robin"), who died as a child from acute leukemia. The ordeal of Robin's illness and death devastated both George and Barbara, but also made them value the support of close family ties.

The Bush children were grown by the time the senior Bushes entered the White House, but they made it clear that, unlike the Reagans, the Bush children and grandchildren would be frequent visitors to the mansion. The president and first lady were devoted to their twelve grandchildren, who were highly visible in the 1988 and 1992 presidential campaigns. Jeb's son George P., the oldest grandchild, even addressed the Republican

National Convention in 1992. Barbara told campaign audiences in both races not only about her husband but also about her grandchildren. They were featured in television commercials, posters, and a biographical film for the convention. The grandchildren were a decided asset in a campaign with a theme of "family values." The Bushes transformed the Executive Mansion into a family home, overflowing with children, grandchildren, and dogs. Although none of the Bush grandchildren resided in the mansion, two of them were born during the Bush presidency: Neil's daughter Ashley and Marvin's son, Charles Walker, both born in 1989, were christened at the White House in small family ceremonies. Two of the Bush sons followed their father and grandfather into political life—Jeb was elected governor of Florida and George W. became the forty-third U.S. president, making Barbara

the second woman in American history, after Abigail Adams, to be the wife of one president and the mother of another.

Q: **What pets did George and Barbara bring to the White House?**

A: While Bush was vice president, the family had a cocker spaniel named C. Fred. During the presidency, the Bushes owned a springer spaniel named Millie that became a national celebrity. Millie gave birth to a litter of puppies in the White House, one of whom, Ranger, became an inseparable companion to the president. "One of the ways I really relaxed when I was President was walking with my dog. It didn't matter rain or shine, he was at my side or sleeping on our bed," Bush recalled. At Camp David, he even kept a dog biscuit dispenser shaped like a gumball machine for the dogs.

President Bush with sons George W. and Jeb boating off Kennebunkport. The two eldest Bush sons followed their father into politics. Jeb was voted governor of Florida in 1999; George W. was elected president of the United States in 2000.

Barbara and her dogs Ranger and Millie don matching gray sweat suits for a White House exercise session. The press and the public took an immediate liking to the first lady, perhaps because she appeared, as she herself phrased it, to be like "everyone's grandmother."

" I married the first man I ever kissed. When I tell this to my children, they just about throw up. "

—*Barbara Bush*

The Bushes valued time spent with their large family. Here they enjoy an early-morning visit from a few of their grandchildren on a family vacation in Kennebunkport. From left to right: the president, Barbara, Jenna, and the first lady. Grandson Pierce leans on the bed.

Q: What types of relaxation did the president and first lady enjoy?

A: The athletic and active president enjoyed playing tennis, golf, jogging, and swimming. The first lady often swam in the White House outdoor pool. Both delighted in having their grandchildren visit for movies in the White House theater and birthday parties in the mansion. George and Barbara loved getting away to Kennebunkport, Maine, the Bush family vacation retreat, where the president liked fishing from his speedboat, *Fidelity.* They were the sixth generation of the Bush family to relax at this family retreat.

Q: What important project did Barbara Bush undertake as first lady?

A: Barbara viewed the role of first lady as a grand platform from which to promote the cause of literacy. A reading problem experienced by one of her children prompted her lifelong interest in this campaign. She stated, "Everything I worry about would be better if more people could read, write, and comprehend—drugs, teenage runaways, the environment, crime, school dropouts." As first lady, she brought national visibility to this growing problem

in American life. During the White House years, she visited many schools, reading to children and emphasizing the importance of reading ability. She endorsed a family approach to literacy skills and founded the Barbara Bush Foundation for Family Literacy, a private, Washington-based entity to support literacy programs. Barbara enlisted the help of her dog Millie to promote the program. *Millie's Book,* published in 1990, was "dictated" to the first lady by her dog, and examined life in the White House from a dog's point of view. All royalties—amounting to approximately $1 million—were donated to the Foundation for Family Literacy. Barbara continues to lead an active campaign for literacy and to speak nationally for this cause. Her family approach to literacy skills lent credibility to concerns about family and children championed by the Bush administration.

The first lady reads to children in the White House library. As a committed advocate for literacy she founded the Barbara Bush Foundation for Family Literacy.

" To us, family means putting your arms around each other and being there. "

—*Barbara Bush*

Q: What famous commencement address endeared Barbara to the media and the public?

A: Barbara was invited to deliver the commencement address to graduates of Wellesley College on June 1, 1990. After her acceptance was announced, 150 students at the all-women school presented a petition to the college president protesting her selection as the speaker, stating that she was not a professional woman of the sort the college sought to educate and that she had not achieved anything in her own right but had merely married a man who became president. Despite a furor of media coverage, the first lady remained cool and delivered her speech. With a wry and down-to-earth sense of humor, she told the students that they might learn something from being a wife and mother, and dedicating a life to public service. She concluded with her now-famous line, "Who knows? Somewhere out in this audience may even be someone who will one day follow in my footsteps and preside over the White House as the president's spouse. And I wish him well." Students and press alike enthusiastically cheered her.

Q: Which of the Bush children married during the White House years?

A: The Bushes' daughter, Doro, a working mother of two children who was divorced from her first husband, William LeBlond, and living in her own home,

remarried during the Bush administration. She wed Robert Koch, a Democrat, in a very private ceremony at Camp David on June 26, 1992. The Bushes hosted a rehearsal dinner for her and her children, Sam and Ellie, and the next day her father escorted her down the aisle. Her brother, George W., gave a reading in the contemporary chapel at Camp David. The groom, a former aide to the Democratic House majority leader, resigned from his position before becoming a member of the Republican Bush clan. Doro Bush's marriage is the only wedding of a president's child to be held at this rustic presidential retreat in the Maryland mountains.

Barbara poses with "first dog" Millie on the Truman Balcony of the White House for the cover of *Millie's Book*. The first lady donated the profit earned from the best-seller to her literacy foundation.

George H. W. Bush. With a father who was a senator, a cousin who is a U.S. ambassador, a son who is the governor of Florida, and another son who was governor of Texas before following in his footsteps to the American presidency, his family's political "dynasty" has been compared to that of John Adams and the Kennedy family.

Bill and Hillary Clinton

Q: What 1992 presidential campaign remark caused a political furor?

A: Bill Clinton had stated that if the public elected him in 1992 they would get "two for the price of one." Many interpreted the remark to mean that if he was elected, the first lady, Hillary Rodham Clinton, would help to shape national policy. This hint at a "copresidency" was one that many in the public were unwilling to accept. The first lady is not elected by the people, and to suggest that she might be setting policy implied power without public consent. Although candidate Clinton most likely only meant to suggest that his wife was as intelligent, politically savvy, and well-informed on policy as he, the remark cast Hillary as a politically and socially polarizing figure even before the couple entered the White House. Hillary, herself, became a campaign issue and a symbol for changes in the role of contemporary women that conservatives fought adamantly against.

Q: What major policy initiative did Hillary Clinton undertake?

A: The first lady's background as a lawyer with a personal commitment to families and health led the Clintons to tap her knowledge of social policy to head the administration's major policy initiative: reform of the nation's healthcare system. In January 1993, the president named her to head the President's Task Force on National Health Care Reform. This appointment signaled that Hillary would play a major policy role in the administration—confirming conservatives' fears voiced during the campaign. In testifying before a congressional committee in September 1993, she demonstrated an impressive knowledge of healthcare policy, a command of the legislative facts, and a zeal to provide health care for all Americans. Opponents charged that the health plan had been formulated in secret, would be a step toward socialism, was too complicated to implement, and would limit free choice of doctors. Despite addressing supportive crowds with posters and chants of "Give 'em health, Hillary!" Congress failed to pass the healthcare reform initiative. Nonetheless, Hillary is credited with calling the nation's attention

Bill and Hillary share a dance at an inaugural ball in 1993. Critics of the couple expressed the concern that Bill might allow his ambitious wife to set policy. After the failure of the healthcare policy and the impeachment scandal, Hillary undertook two initiatives that emphasized positive historical concerns and an optimistic agenda for the new millennium.

to the exorbitant costs of health care, the lack of health coverage for millions of Americans, and pioneering in this arena of national social policy.

Q: What approach did the Clintons take to raising their daughter?

A: The Clintons wanted to bring up Chelsea in as normal an environment as possible and to shield her from the glare of the public spotlight, while including her in as many public activities as possible. Hillary sought the advice of Jacqueline Kennedy on bringing up a child in the White House. Jacqueline's advice was concise: "You've got to protect Chelsea at all costs. Surround her with friends and family, but don't spoil her. . . . Keep the press away from her if you can." The Clintons closely followed this advice in guiding their daughter.

Chelsea was the first child of a president to stand with her parents while her father took the oath of office, and was permitted to bring several close friends with her to the inaugural balls to keep her company. While in the White House she attended Sidwell Friends, a private high school in Washington, D.C., and studied at the Washington School of Ballet. While she was in high school, the Clintons tried to schedule trips during school vacation periods so that she could accompany them, and avoided going to Camp David so that she could spend weekends with friends in Washington. She celebrated her birthdays with her parents in the White House, and performed the "Nutcracker Suite" with her ballet class. Despite being able to duck into a bagel and sandwich shop near school, she found that her Secret Service detail, intentionally or not, served as a monitoring device to keep her on the right path.

Her parents accompanied her when she entered Stanford University in California, helping her move into the dorm and get settled. Chelsea decided to retain her Secret Service detail while in college, but the "hands off" press coverage policy during her adolescent years ended when she became a university student. After graduation from Stanford, she spent two years at Oxford. To her enormous credit, Chelsea avoided adverse publicity or scandal that would have reflected badly on her or her parents.

Bill takes the oath of office as his wife and daughter look on. Chelsea was the first child of a president to stand with her father during his inauguration.

Proud parents Bill and Hillary pose with Chelsea at her graduation from Sidwell Friends School. Although the Clintons did their best to shield their only child from the worst aspects of White House life, Bill knew that "Kids go through hell if their folks are in politics. They get all of the burdens and none of the benefits."

Probably my worst quality is that I get very passionate about what I think is right.
—*Hillary Clinton*

Q: What pets did the Clintons have in the White House?

A: The Clintons began their administration with one cat, Socks, who outlasted not only the president's allergy to him, but also the arrival of presidential dog, Buddy, in 1997. These two pets softened and humanized the administration's public image and were the recipients of more than 300,000 letters and emails from children. Hillary published a children's book of these letters called, *Dear Socks, Dear Buddy: Kids' Letters to the First Pets.* The first lady wanted children to know that their questions were heard and answered. Like Barbara Bush, Hillary donated the proceeds to a favorite cause: the National Park Service Foundation to fund endangered national historic sites.

Below left: The president kisses his dog, Buddy, shortly after arriving at the Martha's Vineyard Airport in Massachusetts for a vacation in 1999.

Below right: The first lady holds "first cat" Socks during their visit to Washington Children's Hospital. The intellectual Clintons' open affection with their pets helped soften their images.

Q: What scandal caused the president to face impeachment?

A: During the investigation of sexual harassment charges brought against the president by Paula Jones, an Arkansas state employee while Clinton was governor, an allegation surfaced that he had a sexual affair with a twenty-one-year-old White House intern, Monica Lewinsky, in late 1995. Lewinsky was transferred to a job in the Pentagon where she related details of the affair to Linda Tripp, a government employee, who taped conversations with Lewinsky detailing the affair. Tripp took her tapes to Special Counsel Kenneth Starr, then investigating the Clintons' financial dealings in the Whitewater land affair, who expanded his case to include the unsavory sexual allegations against the president. In a series of events and with a cast of characters worthy of a pulp fiction novel, the Clinton scandal played itself out in the national media from 1997 through 1999. Clinton adamantly denied the affair, telling the nation, "I did not have sexual relations with that woman, Miss Lewinsky." When Clinton's denial proved false, and after interminable legal maneuvering by both sides, the Paula Jones sexual harassment case was dismissed by a judge, but the House Judiciary Committee

"A lot of presidential memoirs, they say, are dull and self-serving. I hope mine is interesting and self-serving."

—BILL CLINTON

brought impeachment charges against the president for committing perjury and providing false testimony in his grand jury appearance and obstruction of justice. Tried by the Senate, on January 7, 1999, the president was acquitted by a vote of 55 to 45. Although the Clinton presidency survived, his administration and reputation were severely tainted by the scandal. He was only the second president in history to face impeachment.

Q: What were the first lady's projects during the latter part of the administration?

A: In 1998, Hillary moved into the arena of historic preservation when she was named honorary chair of the Millennium Committee to "Save America's Treasures," a public-private partnership between the White House Millennium Council and the National Trust for Historic Preservation. In July, 1998, she began a four-day tour of historic sites in need of preservation, beginning at the Smithsonian Institution's National Museum of American History. Standing in front of the Star-Spangled Banner with Ralph Lauren, they announced a $10 million contribution made by Polo Ralph Lauren for the conservation of the nation's most famous symbol. Hillary toured eleven national historic sites, many of them central to the advancement of women, including the Harriet Tubman House and Seneca Falls, New York, site of the first women's rights convention. The White House Millennium Evenings, held to "honor the past and imagine the future," explored the finest American expressions of intellectual ideas, arts, culture, and science that "have defined

An official portrait of President William J. Clinton. Although his term of office was marred by scandal and partisan controversy, he ended his presidential career with a 65-percent approval rating, the highest end-of-term approval rating of any president in the post-Eisenhower era. Bill remains a popular figure, enjoying a career as public speaker and author.

After the couple moved to Chappaqua, Hillary went on to become the junior U.S. senator from New York. The Clinton marriage has survived attacks regarding their personal finances and investments, the so-called "Whitewater" scandal, the charges of insider trading tips for monetary profit, and more than one sex scandal.

our people and our country." To carry out this vision, the Clintons called upon outstanding poets, jazz musicians, artists, geneticists, scientists, and historians ever assembled in the White House. The Millennium Evenings, sponsored by the National Endowment for the Humanities, followed Pulitzer prize–winning historian Bernard Bailyn's theme, "The Living Past: Commitments for the Future," as a fitting way to usher in the new millennium.

George W. and Laura Bush

Q: What were the backgrounds of George W. and Laura Bush?

A: Laura Welch grew up in the west Texas oil town of Midland, where she learned to love books and reading from her mother. Jenna Welch recalled that she read books to Laura "even before she could open her eyes" and, as she was growing up, often took her to the library. George W. Bush was raised in  a political family with a distinguished tradition of public service. He followed in his father's footsteps first to Yale University, then into the oil business, became an owner of a baseball franchise, and, finally, entered politics. After graduating from high school in Midland, Laura attended Southern Methodist University, earned an education degree, and taught elementary school in Dallas and Houston. Pursuing her love of books, Laura earned a masters

Above left: Official White House photograph of President George W. Bush.

Above right: Official White House photograph of First Lady Laura Welch Bush.

Below: George W. with his mother, Barbara; father, George H.; and paternal grandparents, Dorothy and Prescott, in 1949. George W., known in the press as "Dubyah," followed his father and grandfather into a successful political career.

degree in library science at the University of Texas at Austin, and became a librarian in the Houston Public Library. Later, she moved back to Austin to become a librarian at an elementary school. Laura's friends Joey and Jan O'Neill felt certain  that she and their friend George W. Bush would make a great couple, and threw a backyard barbecue to introduce George and Laura. Laura reminisced, "I think our friends wanted to fix us up because we were literally the last two people left who hadn't married of all our friends." They liked each other immediately; he said that for him it was love at first sight. Within six weeks they were engaged, and their whirlwind courtship led to marriage on November 5, 1977. "We were very happy to find each other," Laura recalled.

Q: What career path did Bush follow to become a candidate for the presidency?

A: George W. began his career by running an oil company, but then went on to become the managing partner of the Texas Rangers baseball team. Yet, he was unable to get politics out of his blood. He ran a successful campaign for governor of Texas and was elected in November 1994. Meanwhile, his father had become vice president and then president of the United States. The Bush family was becoming a political dynasty.

Although Laura did not initially like politics, when her husband decided that it would be his career, she transformed herself into an effective public speaker. Her self-assured composure kept her husband focused and, like many political wives before her, she became the center of his emotional support system and a sounding board for his ideas.

Bush became an effective two-term governor of Texas. The continuing influence of his father's prominent and powerful friends in the Republican Party and conservative circles helped make the younger Bush a sought-after candidate for the 2000 presidential race.

Q: What was highly unusual about the 2000 presidential election?

A: In the closest presidential election in United States history, the winner of the presidency was in doubt as the legality of ballots in the state of Florida was contested by both the Republican and the Democratic parties. Legal skirmishes and recounts of ballots punctuated by debates over faulty balloting machines, "hanging chads" (parts of ballots that had been only partially punched through), and accusations of voting fraud delayed the outcome for weeks. The United States Supreme Court ultimately validated the election in a 5 to 4 vote. George W. Bush was declared the winner.

The *Orlando Sentinel* put out four election editions on November 8, 2000. The presidential race between Republican Bush and Democrat Al Gore was the closest election in United States history, decided by only 537 votes in the swing state of Florida. It would be a month before the results were finally certified, and took numerous court challenges and recounts to decide Florida's 25 electoral votes.

" **I'm not the one who was elected. I would never do anything to undermine my husband's point of view.** "

—LAURA BUSH

Q: What project did Laura Bush adopt when she became first lady?

A: As the new first lady, Laura brought to the White House her lifelong passion for books and experience with the innova-tive Texas education programs. One of her first projects was the White House summit on early education held in 2001 at Georgetown University in Washington. Her Ready to Read, Ready to Learn initiative was one of the first lady's educational programs that highlighted the president's educa-tional goals. She went on to host the first National Book Festival, a nationwide version of her Texas program, sponsored by the Library of Congress in September 2001. Children and their parents met more than fifty famous authors and illus-trators and took part in free readings at the Library of Congress. This innovation was part of the first lady's commitment to "work tirelessly to make sure that every child gains the basic skills to be successful in school and in life." Laura has contin-ued to advocate literacy and education programs but, since the war on terrorism began, has taken a more outspoken stance for protecting human rights for women in Afghanistan and Iraq. She has become a forceful advocate for women's full edu-cational and citizenship rights worldwide. In her husband's second term, she has taken on "edgier" social issues in a special effort to emphasize education for boys to counter the rise in street gangs, drugs, and

The first lady reads to a first-grade class in Des Moines, Iowa. As was her mother-in-law, the former teacher and librarian is strongly committed to educational and literacy programs.

violence. "Gangs offer boys a kind of family—support, acceptance and self-respect. I want to spotlight promising programs that keep boys from being involved in gangs, that give them the nurturing we know they need."

Q: Who are the Bush daughters?

A: George and Laura Bush became the parents of fraternal twin girls in 1981. Each was named after a grandmother, Jenna for Laura's mother, and Barbara for George's. The girls grew up in the Texas governor's mansion and attended college, Barbara being the fourth generation of the Bush family to graduate from Yale, while Jenna graduated from her mother's alma mater, the University of Texas at Austin. Neither daughter lived in the White House and both young women have sought to avoid its glaring spotlight, preferring to visit their parents at Camp David and at the ranch in Crawford, Texas. Each pursued the usual pranks of college coeds, giving their Secret Service details the slip, with Barbara partying in the trendy New York social scene and Jenna enjoying nightclub life in Austin. In 2002, Jenna was arrested twice for underage drinking and using a fake ID at an Austin club. She was sentenced to community service. Her mother felt that she was doing "what every teenager does," but grandmother Barbara was character-istically more outspoken, telling *Tonight Show* host, Jay Leno, "It was stupid. They are smart girls—they knew they shouldn't have done that." After graduation, Barbara and Jenna traveled extensively in Europe with friends, describing it as a "blast." They helped campaign for their father's

reelection in 2004, targeting young adult audiences. Both young women have expressed an interest in pursuing careers working with children.

tenderloin and smoked catfish. Laura explained, "It gives us the chance to have very normal, much more intimate conversations with them."

Laura's ecologically planned ranch house was inspired by the environmental advocacy of fellow Texan and former first lady, Lady Bird Johnson. Its beauty blends with the natural environment and reflects the balance of active involvement with quiet relaxation that characterizes the life that Laura Bush has shaped for herself and her family. This family retreat will continue to serve as the couple's home after the White House years.

Twin sisters Jenna, left, and Barbara deliver opening remarks at a "W Stands for Women" women's issues panel in Henderson, Nevada, as part of a campaign effort in support of their father's bid for a second term.

Q: How have the Bushes changed "official" entertaining?

A: In order to relax from their hectic life in Washington, the Bushes spend time at their sixteen-hundred-acre Prairie Chapel ranch in Crawford, Texas. The Bushes all but abandoned formal state dinners, hosting only four in the first presidential term. Changing the style of official entertaining, they prefer to receive foreign dignitaries and conduct diplomatic negotiations at Prairie Chapel. The president, wearing jeans and cowboy boots, often driving a pickup truck, greets state visitors Texas-style, providing traditional southwestern entertainment with a Texas swing band and country-and-western songs and mesquite-smoked beef

Bush walks along a gravel road with his dog Spot at his 1,600-acre ranch in Crawford, Texas. Even after he was elected, Bush chose to spend much of his time there, sometimes entertaining state visitors, but also to spend time alone in order to keep him centered on "exactly what's important in life."

"**People ask me if I ever see my father and I say yes, because he puts in the effort. He calls all the time to tell us he's proud of us.**"

—*JENNA BUSH*

Further Reading

BOOKS

Allgor, Catherine. *A Perfect Union: Dolley Madison and the Creation of the American Nation.* New York: Henry Holt, 2006.

Angelo, Bonnie. *First Families: The Impact of the White House on Their Lives.* New York: HarperCollins, 2005.

Anthony, Carl Sferrazza. *America's First Families: An Inside View of 200 Years of Private Life in the White House.* New York: Touchstone, 2000.

———. *As We Remember Her: Jacqueline Kennedy Onassis in the Words of Her Family and Friends .* New York: HarperCollins, 1997.

———. *First Ladies: The Sage of the Presidents' Wives and Their Power.* Vols. 1 and 2. New York: William Morrow and Co., 1990 and 1991.

Baker, Jean. *Mary Todd Lincoln.* New York: W. W. Norton, 1987.

Beasley, Maureen. *Eleanor Roosevelt and the Media.* Urbana: University of Illinois Press, 1987.

———. *The White House Press Conferences of Eleanor Roosevelt.* New York: Garland Publishing, 1983.

Black, Allida M. *Casting Her Own Shadow: Eleanor Roosevelt and the Shaping of Postwar Liberalism.* New York: Columbia University Press, 1996.

Black, Allida M., ed. *Courage in a Dangerous World: The Political Writings of Eleanor Roosevelt.* New York: Columbia University Press, 1999.

Bush, Barbara. *A Memoir.* New York: Macmillan, 1994.

Caroli, Betty Boyd. *First Ladies.* New York: Oxford University Press, 1987.

Carter, Rosalynn. *First Lady from Plains.* New York: Ballantine, 1984.

Center for Folklife Programs and Cultural Studies, Smithsonian Institution. *Workers at the White House.* Washington, D.C.: The Smithsonian Institution in Cooperation with the White House Historical Association and the National Archives for the 200th Anniversary of the White House, 1992.

Clinton, Hillary Rodham. *It Takes a Village and Other Lessons Children Teach Us.* New York: Simon & Schuster, 1996.

———. *An Invitation to the White House: At Home with History.* New York: Simon & Schuster, 2000.

Cook, Blanche Wiesen. *Eleanor Roosevelt: Vol. 1, 1884–1933* and *Eleanor Roosevelt: Vol. 2, 1933–1938.* New York: Viking Penguin, 1992 and 1999.

Eisenhower, Julie Nixon. *Pat Nixon: The Untold Story.* New York: Simon & Schuster, 1986.

Ford, Betty. *The Times of My Life.* New York: Ballantine, 1979.

Furman, Bess. *White House Profile.* Indianapolis: Bobbs-Merrill, 1951.

Geer, Emily Apt. *First Lady: The Life of Lucy Webb.* Fremont, OH: Rutherford B. Hayes Presidential Center, 1995.

Goodwin, Doris Kearns. *No Ordinary Time: Franklin and Eleanor Roosevelt: The Home Front in World War II.* New York: Simon & Schuster, 1994.

Gould, Lewis, ed. *American First Ladies: Their Lives and Their Legacy.* New York and London: Garland Publishing, 1996.

———. *Lady Bird Johnson and the Environment.* Lawrence: University of Kansas Press, 1988.

Gutin, Myra. *The President's Partner: The First Lady in the Twentieth Century.* Westport, CT: Greenwood Press, 1989.

Heckler-Feltz, Cheryl. *Heart and Soul of the Nation: How the Spirituality of Our First Ladies Changed America.* New York: Doubleday, 1997.

Heyman, C. David. *A Woman Named Jackie: An Intimate Biography of Jacqueline Onassis.* New York: Birch Lane Press, 1994.

Hoff-Wilson, Joan, and Marjorie Lightman, eds. *Without Precedent: The Life and Career of Eleanor Roosevelt.* Bloomington: Indiana University Press, 1984.

Hoover, Irwin H. *Forty-two Years in the White House.* Boston: Houghton Mifflin, 1934.

Jeffries, Ona Griffin. *In and Out of the White House: From Washington to the Eisenhowers.* New York: Wilfred Funk, 1960.

Johnson, Lady Bird. *A White House Diary.* New York: Holt, Rinehart and Winston, 1970.

———. *The First Ladies Cook Book: Favorite Recipes of All the Presidents of the United States.* Chicago: Parents' Magazine Press, 1965.

Klapthor, Margaret Brown. *Official White House China: 1789 to the Present.* 2nd edition. New York: The Barra Foundation, 1999.

Klein, Edward. *Just Jackie: Her Private Years.* New York: Ballantine, 1998.

Lash, Joseph P. *Eleanor and Franklin.* New York: W. W. Norton and Co., 1971.

Mayo, Edith P. *The Smithsonian Book of the First Ladies: Their Lives, Times, and Issues.* New York: Henry Holt, 1996.

Mayo, Edith P. and Denise Meringolo. *First Ladies: Political Role and Public Image.* Washington, D.C.: Smithsonian Institution, 1995.

Means, Marianne. *The Woman in the White House.* New York: Random House, 1963.

Monkman, Betty C. *The White House: Its Historic Furnishings and First Families.* Washington, D.C.: White House Historical Association, 2000.

Morris, Sylvia Jukes. *Edith Kermit Roosevelt: Portrait of a First Lady.* New York: Coward, McCann and Geoghegan, 1980

Osborne, Claire G. *The Unique Voice of Hillary Rodham Clinton: A Portrait in Her Own Words.* New York: Avon, 1997.

Parks, Lillian Rogers. *My Thirty Years Backstairs at the White House.* New York: Fleet Publishing, 1961.

Radcliffe, Donnie. *Simply Barbara Bush.* New York: Warner, 1989.

———. *Hillary Rodham Clinton: A First Lady for Our Time.* New York: Warner, 1994.

Randall, Ruth P. *Mary Lincoln: Biography of a Marriage.* Boston: Little Brown and Co., 1953.

Reagan, Nancy. *My Turn: The Memoirs of Nancy Reagan.* New York: Random House, 1989.

Roosevelt, Eleanor. *The Autobiography of Eleanor Roosevelt.* New York: Harper, 1961.

Russell, Jan Jarboe. *Lady Bird: A Biography of Mrs. Johnson.* New York: Scribner, 1999.

Sanders, Frances Wright. *Ellen Axson Wilson: First Lady Between Two Worlds.* Chapel Hill: University of North Carolina Press, 1985.

Seale, William. *The President's House: A History.* Vols. 1 and 2. Washington, D.C.: The White House Historical Association and the National Geographic Society, 1986.

Seale, William, ed. *The White House: Actors and Observers.* Boston: Northeastern University Press, 2002.

Smith, Margaret Bayard. *The First Forty Years of Washington Society.* New York: Charles Scribner's Sons, 1906.

Smith, Marie. *Entertaining in the White House.* Washington, D.C.: Acropolis Books, 1967.

Smith, Nancy and Mary Ryan, eds. *Modern First Ladies: Their Documentary Legacy.* Washington, D.C.: National Archives and Records Administration, 1989.

Taft, Helen. *Reflections of Full Years.* New York: Dodd, Mead and Co., 1914.

Truman, Margaret. *Bess W. Truman.* New York: Macmillan, 1986.

———. *First Ladies: An Intimate Portrait of White House Wives.* New York: Random House, 1995.

Warner, Judith. *Hillary Clinton: The Inside Story.* New York: Signet, 1993.

Wilson, Edith Bolling. *My Memoir.* Indianapolis: Bobbs-Merrill, 1938.

Weidenfeld, Sheila Robb. *First Lady's Lady: With the Fords at the White House.* New York: Putnam, 1979.

West, J. B. *Upstairs at the White House: My Life with the First Ladies.* New York: Coward, McCann, and Geoghegan, 1973.

Withey, Lynn. *Dearest Friend: A Life of Abigail Adams.* New York: Macmillan, 1981.

BOOKS FOR YOUNG PEOPLE

Brown, Jean. *Martha Washington: America's First First Lady.* New York: Aladdin Paperbacks, 1986.

Ferris, Jeri. *Remember the Ladies: A Story about Abigail Adams.* Minneapolis: Lerner Publishing Group, 2000.

Jacobson, Doranne. *Presidents and First Ladies of the United States.* New York: Smithmark Publishers, 1995.

Kramer, Sydelle A. *The Look-It-Up Book of First Ladies.* New York: Random House, 2000.

Pasten, Amy, in Association with the Smithsonian Institution. *First Ladies.* London: Dorling Kindersley, 2001.

Mayo, Edith P. *The Smithsonian Book of First Ladies.* New York: Henry Holt, 1996.

Pflueger, Lynda. *Dolley Madison: Courageous First Lady.* Berkeley Heights, NJ: Enslow Publishing, 1999.

Santow, Dan. *Elizabeth Bloomer Ford.* New York: Children's Press, 2000.

Wagoner, Jean Brown. *Abigail Adams: Girl of Colonial Days.* New York: Aladdin Paperbacks, 1992.

Weil, Ann. *Eleanor Roosevelt: Fighter for Social Justice.* New York: Aladdin Paperbacks, 1989.

Wilkie, Katherine E. *Mary Todd Lincoln: Girl of the Bluegrass.* New York: Aladdin Paperbacks, 1992.

WEB SITES

The White House: www.whitehouse.gov/history/life. Official biographies of the presidents and first ladies.

White House Historical Association: www.whitehousehistory.org. A nonprofit agency that conserves and interprets the White House; presidential portraits, first lady information.

First Ladies National Historic Site (formerly the First Ladies Library): www.firstladies.org. Located in Canton, Ohio, maintains an extensive bibliography for all first ladies.

Presidential Libraries: nara.gov/nara/president/address.html. Run by the National Archives, this site maintains a link to each of the existing presidential libraries.

American Memory: lcweb2.loc.gov/ammem/odmdhtml/preshome.html. The Library of Congress, created this site to facilitate access to its presidential and first lady collections.

Portraits of presidents and first ladies: www.worldbook.com/fun/presidents/html/portraits.html. General information, portraits, and biographical information.

At the Smithsonian

Right: *Ronald Reagan* by Henry C. Casselli Jr. The National Portrait Gallery holds an extensive collection of portraits of the presidents and their families.

Below: The National Museum of American History is home to a wide variety of artifacts associated with presidential families, such as this Teddy bear, circa 1903. Inspired by Theodore Roosevelt, the toy became an American cultural icon. The Ideal Toy Company presented one of the original stuffed bears to Roosevelt's son Kermit, who donated it to the Smithsonian.

The Smithsonian Institution houses one of the nation's largest and most in-depth collections of objects and research materials on the White House, American presidents and first ladies, presidential campaigns and inaugurals, and White House history. Most of this material is contained in the holdings of the Division of Politics and Reform in the National Museum of American History, Behring Center.

Within these extensive holdings are collections of first ladies' gowns (many of which are not inaugural balls gowns), other articles of wearing apparel, jewelry, fans, and clothing accessories. The research materials include photographic collections, objects and records on inaugurations, White House invitations and menus, and materials related to funerals in the White House that reflect national mourning customs and rituals. Extensive research files yield background information on first ladies and first families that are supplemented by collections of biographies, books, pamphlets, and articles that contextualize the White House and first ladies at various historical periods. Taken together, the collection places first ladies both in the context of the American presidency and the history of women, and demonstrates their importance in expanding public roles for women.

The presidential collections include articles of clothing, objects that reflect presidential pastimes and recreation, various aspects of the role of the president, and popular culture materials that detail the impact of the presidents in American life. A large library of presidential biographies and interpretive books on the history of the presidency supplement the object collections.

One of the largest campaign collections in the nation chronicles candidates' efforts to gain the presidency. The holdings include buttons, badges, tokens, ribbons, posters, smoking devices, bumper stickers, canes, bandannas, banners, stationery, newspapers, games, and gimmicks produced for campaign purposes that recount the history of presidential campaigning and the changing nature of the technology used to bring the candidates' messages to the people. The collection includes nineteenth-century examples of campaign memorabilia, as well as selections of modern media campaign advertising from radio to the Internet. Inaugural activities are represented by invitations, schedules of events, records of inaugural balls, parades and celebratory activities, menus, banners, posters, prints, and photographic records. An extensive card index housed in the division lists inaugural activities and events from Washington to the present.

The Smithsonian's National Portrait Gallery houses portraits, prints, photographic materials, and other likenesses of the presidents and first ladies.

The collections at the Smithsonian represent excellent resources for rich details on dress, social customs, ceremonial rituals, changing campaign techniques, mourning customs, the changing role of women, family life in the White House, and the material culture used to craft the imagery of the White House and the American presidency.

Above: Democrats took advantage of Frances Folsom Cleveland's popularity and used her image on scores of campaign items, such as this poster, part of the Smithsonian's holdings.

Left: One of the stunning pieces in the First Ladies Collection is this two-piece silk taffeta gown worn by Mary Todd Lincoln for a sitting with Mathew Brady in 1861.

Index

Acknowledgments & Picture Credits

ACKNOWLEDGMENTS

The author wishes to acknowledge with deep appreciation of love and support "above and beyond the call" the following in this special book about families: Bert Cohen, who inspired my love of history and my appreciation of the presence of the past; Martin and Edith S. Petersilia, James and Cecil Spaulding, Cecil Dussinger, Jeanne Swanson, Martin J. A. Petersilia, Carol Anne Spencer, Patricia Petersilia, my wonderful family; my Smithsonian "family" and friends in Politics and Reform and SITES, especially Lisa Kathleen Graddy and Larry Hyman, without whom the First Ladies would never have traveled the nation; researchers and friends extraordinaire Denise Meringolo, Dixie Reynolds, and Allison Yoder; Nathalie Dupree, Pippa Jenkins, Lucia Rose for love all along the way; Joan Faye Meacham for unwavering love and support and the use of her home and computer; John Josef for love and encouragement over many years; Ron Rodgers for computer and technical support; Lisa Purcell for the best editing ever; and to the dearly loved First Ladies of My Life: Melanie Mayo Rodgers, Monica Mayo Condon, and Alexandra, Shannon, and Jordan.

The author and publisher also offer thanks to those closely involved in the creation of this volume: James G. Barber and the staffs of the National Museum of American History, Behring Center, and the National Portrait Gallery; Ellen Nanney, Senior Brand Manager and Katie Mann, with Smithsonian Business Ventures; Collins Reference executive editor Donna Sanzone, editor Lisa Hacken, and editorial assistant Stephanie Meyers; Hydra Publishing president Sean Moore, publishing director Karen Prince, senior editor Lisa Purcell, art director Edwin Kuo, designers Rachel Maloney, Greg Lum, Mariel Morris, Gus Yoo, La Tricia Watford, Erika Lubowicki, Brian MacMullen, editorial director Aaron Murray, editors Marcel Brousseau, Suzanne Lander, Gail Greiner, Ward Calhoun, Emily Beekman, and Kristin Maffei, copy editors Glenn Novak and Eileen Chetti, picture researcher Ben DeWalt, production manager Sarah Reilly, production director Wayne Ellis, and indexer Jessie Shiers; Harmony Haskins of the White House Historical Society; Joan Mathys of MJM Picture and Film Research.

PICTURE CREDITS

The following abbreviations are used: NMAH/SI—National Museum of American History, Behring Center, Smithsonian Institution; NPG/SI—National Portrait Gallery, Smithsonian Institution; LoC—Library of Congress; NA—National Archives; AP—Associated Press; WHHA—White House Historical Association (White House Collection); NPS—National Park Service; DDEL—Dwight D. Eisenhower Library; GRFL—Gerald R. Ford Presidential Library and Museum; RRL—Courtesy Ronald Reagan Library; GBPL—George Bush Presidential Library

(t=top; b=bottom; l=left; r=right; c=center)

The White House: Home and Symbol
IIII JFK Library and Museum/Cecil Stoughton IIIr LoC IV LoC IV–Vbackground AP Vt LoC Vbl Division of Politics and Reform, NMAH/SI [83-10446] Vbr NA VI LoC 1 Mary Terribery/ShutterStock 2tl LoC 2br LBJ Library photo by Yoichi R. Okamoto 3 LoC

Chapter 1: The Founders and Their Families
4 LoC 5background AP 5r LoC 6l LoC 6b LoC 7t LoC 7b NPG/SI 8tl LoC 8bl LoC 9t LoC 9b Division of Politics and Reform, NMAH/SI [2000-6311] 10 NPG/SI 11t WHHA b ©

2006 Jupiterimages Corporation 12 WHHA 13l The Colonial Williamsburg Foundation 13r public domain 14 LoC 15l LoC 15r WHHA 16l © 2006 Jupiterimages Corporation 16r Monticello/Thomas Jefferson Foundation, Inc. 17 LoC 18l LoC 18r LoC 19 LoC 20l Division of Politics and Reform, NMAH/SI 20r LoC 21 WHHA

Chapter 2: Consolidating Nationhood
22 LoC 23 LoC 24t NPG/SI 24b © 2006 Jupiterimages Corporation 25 Courtesy of Ash Lawn-Highland, home of James and Elizabeth Monroe, Charlottesville, VA 26 WHHA 27t WHHA 27b Division of Politics and Reform, NMAH/SI [72-2191] 28l LoC 28r LoC 29 Smithsonian American Art Museum 30 LoC 31bl Smithsonian American Art Museum 31tr LoC 31cr LoC 32tl NPG/SI 32br LoC 33 LoC 34 LoC 35l © 2006 Jupiterimages Corporation 35r WHHA

Chapter 3: Manifest Destiny: Expanding Westward
36 LoC 37 LoC 38 LoC 39t © 2006 Jupiterimages Corporation 39b LoC 40 WHHA 41 WHHA 42 LoC 43t LoC 43b LoC 44tl LoC 44bl LoC 44cr © 2006 Jupiterimages Corporation 45 LoC 46l WHHA 46r LoC 47 Division of Politics and Reform, NMAH/SI [2000-7780] 48t LoC 48b © 2006 Jupiterimages Corporation 49 WHHA 50c WHHA 50bl LoC 51 LoC

Chapter 4: Sectionalism and Slavery
52 U.S. Senate Collection 53 LoC 54tl NPG/SI 54br Division of Politics and Reform, NMAH/SI 55tl LoC 55br Division of Politics and Reform, NMAH/SI [77-13939] 56tl NPG/SI 56br LoC 57 NPG/SI 58bl Buffalo and Erie County Historical Society 58c NPG/SI 59bl LoC 59tr LoC 60 VAFO 60tl NPG/SI 60br LoC 61tl New Hampshire Historical Society 61br LoC 62tl NPG/SI 62tr LoC 63tl LoC 63tr Wheatlands, Home of James Buchanan 64 LoC 65tl LoC 65tr Division of Politics and Reform, NMAH/SI [2000-7585] 65br SAAM

Chapter 5: Civil War and Reconstruction
66 LoC 67 LoC 68tl LoC 68br LoC 69t Division of Politics and Reform, NMAH/SI [2000-6322] 69b LoC 70 Behind the Scenes, by Elizabeth Keckley, New York: G.W. Carleton, 1868 71t LoC 71b LoC 72tl © 2006 Jupiterimages Corporation 72br LoC 73t NPG/SI 73b Division of Politics and Reform, NMAH/SI [95-5528] 74l LoC 74r Division of Politics and Reform, NMAH/SI [89-8229] 75t LoC 75b LoC 76tr NPS, Andrew Johnson National Historic Site, Greenville, TN 76bl NPS, Andrew Johnson National Historic Site, Greenville, TN 76br NPS, Andrew Johnson National Historic Site, Greenville, TN 77t NPS, Andrew Johnson National Historic Site, Greenville, TN 77b LoC 78t LoC 78b LoC 79 LoC 80t LoC 80b LoC 81t LoC 81b LoC 82tr Rutherford B. Hayes Presidential Center 82bl NPG/SI 83l LoC 83r Rutherford B. Hayes Presidential Center 84 Rutherford B. Hayes Presidential Center 85tl Rutherford B. Hayes Presidential Center 85bl LoC 85br WHHA

Chapter 6: The Gilded Age
86 WHHA 87 LoC 88l LoC 88c LoC 88br LoC 89 LoC 90tl LoC 90br LoC 91l LoC 91r © 2006 Jupiterimages Corporation 92bl NPG/SI 92br LoC 93 LoC 94l LoC 94r NPG/SI 95 NPG/SI 96 LoC 97t LoC 97b LoC 98l LoC 98r LoC 99t LoC 99b NPG/SI 100tl LoC 100br LoC 101 LoC 102 LoC 103t LoC 103b LoC 104t LoC 104b NPG/SI 105b LoC

Ready Reference
Background AP 106l LoC 106tr LoC 106br LoC 107l LoC 107c LoC 107r NPG/SI 108l LoC 108t LoC 108r LoC 109tl LoC 109c RRL 109r William J. Clinton Presidential Library 110l LoC 110r LoC 111l LoC 111r © 2006 Jupiterimages Corporation 112t LoC 112r LoC 113l LoC 113t LoC 113r LoC

114tl Maryland Historical Society 114tr Division of Politics and Reform, NMAH/SI [2000-7091] 114bl Division of Politics and Reform, NMAH/SI [2000-6831] 114br LoC 115l © 2006 Jupiterimages Corporation 115tr LoC 115br LoC 116tl LoC 116bl LoC 116r LoC 117tl LoC 117tr LoC 117br LoC

Chapter 7: An Emerging World Power
118 Courtesy of the National Museum of the U.S. Army, Army Art Collection 119 LoC 120l Theodore Roosevelt Collection, Harvard College Library 120r LoC 121l LoC 121tr LoC 122tl WHHA 122br LoC 123t LoC 123b LoC 124 LoC 125tl LoC 125br LoC 126l LoC 126r LoC 127tr LoC 127br LoC 128l LoC 128r WHHA 129l LoC 129r LoC 130t LoC 130b Florence Griswold Museum; Given by Dorothy Dunn Griswold in memory of her husband, George Turnure Griswold 131tl LoC 131br Victorian Traditions/ShutterStock 132 LoC 133t LoC 133b NPG/SI

Chapter 8: Isolationism and the Depression
134 AP 135 LoC 136 WHHA 137tl LoC 137br LoC 138 Division of Politics and Reform, NMAH/SI [2000-6347] 139t LoC 139b LoC 140l LoC 140r LoC 141t LoC 141b LoC 142 WHHA 143tl LoC 143br LoC 144 LoC 145 LoC 146 AP 147t AP 147br LoC

Chapter 9: World War II and Prosperity
148 NPG/SI 149 LoC 150l FDR Presidential Library and Museum 150r LoC 151 FDR Presidential Library and Museum 152l LoC 152r Scott Rothstein/Shutterstock 153 AP 154 FDR Presidential Library and Museum 155t LoC 155b FDR Presidential Library and Museum 156tr Harry S. Truman Library 156b Abbie Rowe, National Park Service, courtesy Harry S. Truman Library 157t Harry S. Truman Library 157b Harry S. Truman Library 158tl NPG/SI 158br Harry S. Truman Library 159t Harry S. Truman Library 159b Harry Barth, courtesy Harry S. Truman Library 160t LoC 160b DDEL 161 DDEL 162t DDEL 162b LoC 163tl DDEL 163br NPG/SI

Chapter 10: Consolidating World Power
164 NPG/SI 165 LoC 166bl NPG/SI 166tr LoC 167 LoC 168l AP 168r AP 169 AP 170l AP 170r AP 171t AP 171b AP 172t LBJ Photo Library/Cecil Stoughton 172b LBJ Library 173t LBJ Library photo by Yoichi R. Okamoto 173b LBJ Library photo by Yoichi R. Okamoto 174l LBJ Library photo by Yoichi R. Okamoto 174r LBJ Library photo by Yoichi R. Okamoto 175t LBJ Library photo by Yoichi R. Okamoto 175b LBJ Library photo by Kevin Smith 176 NPG/SI 177t AP 177b Richard Nixon Library and Birthplace 178 LoC 179l Richard Nixon Library and Birthplace 179r LoC 180l NPG/SI 180r GRFL 181 GRFL 182l GRFL 182r GRFL 183t GRFL 183b LoC 184bl LoC 184tr LoC 185 Courtesy, Jimmy Carter Library 186t Courtesy, Jimmy Carter Library 186b LoC 187 NPG/SI

Chapter 11: Challenges of a New Age
188 Jennifer Griner/Shutterstock 189 LoC 190t RRL 190b RRL 191 RRL 192 RRL 193t RRL 193b RRL 194t GBPL 194b GBPL 195t GBPL 195b GBPL 196t GBPL 196b GBPL 197t GBPL 197b NPG/SI 198 LoC 199tr LoC 199c AP 200l AP 200r AP 201t NPG/SI 201b LoC 202tl White House 202tr LoC 202b GBPL 203 AP 204 AP 205t AP 205b AP

At the Smithsonian
210l Political History, Division of Social History, NMAH/SI [93-7206] 210r NPG/SI 211b Political History, Division of Social History, NMAH/SI [92-3644.05] 211r Political History, Division of Social History, NMAH/SI [2003-5871]